BREAKTHROUGH
LEADERSHIP

In memory of civil rights leader, and congressman, John Lewis. RIP.

Friday, July 17, 2020

On the day that *Breakthrough Leadership* goes to press, we honor the passing of one of the great leaders of this century. As recipient of the Congressional Medal of Honor, John Lewis inspired these powerful words from President Barack Obama who bestowed the nation's highest civilian honor:

> *Generations from now, when parents teach their children what is meant by courage, the story of John Lewis will come to mind—an American who knew that change could not wait for some other person or some other time; whose life is a lesson in the fierce urgency of now.*

Mr. Lewis, an American icon of civil rights, viewed our current struggles for equity and racial justice in hopeful terms as he shared with *CBS This Morning*: "People now understand what the struggle was all about. It's another step down a very, very long road toward freedom, justice for all humankind."

On Twitter in 2018, Mr. Lewis encouraged others to follow his persistent and active engagement in the struggle:

> *Do not get lost in a sea of despair. Be hopeful, be optimistic. Our struggle is not the struggle of a day, a week, a month, or a year, it is the struggle of a lifetime. Never, ever be afraid to make some noise and get in good trouble, necessary trouble.*

John Lewis's courageous life sacrifices and dedication will not be forgotten. May we collectively advance this work and his vision for the betterment of our children and humankind. We honor the life of John Lewis and mourn his passing.

BREAKTHROUGH
LEADERSHIP

Six Principles Guiding Schools Where
INEQUITY Is Not an Option

Alan M. Blankstein
Marcus J. Newsome
with Lauren B. Mahan

Foreword by Pedro A. Noguera

FOR INFORMATION:

Corwin

A SAGE Company

2455 Teller Road

Thousand Oaks, California 91320

(800) 233-9936

www.corwin.com

SAGE Publications Ltd.

1 Oliver's Yard

55 City Road

London EC1Y 1SP

United Kingdom

SAGE Publications India Pvt. Ltd.

B 1/I 1 Mohan Cooperative Industrial Area

Mathura Road, New Delhi 110 044

India

SAGE Publications Asia-Pacific Pte. Ltd.

18 Cross Street #10-10/11/12

China Square Central

Singapore 048423

Publisher and Program Director: Dan Alpert

Senior Content Development Editor: Lucas Schleicher

Production Editor: Amy Schroller

Copy Editor: Melinda Masson

Typesetter: C&M Digitals (P) Ltd.

Proofreader: Dennis Webb

Indexer: Molly Hall

Cover Designer: Rose Storey

Marketing Manager: Maura Sullivan

Printed in the United States of America

ISBN 978-1-0718-2441-2

This book is printed on acid-free paper.

SUSTAINABLE FORESTRY INITIATIVE

Certified Chain of Custody
Promoting Sustainable Forestry
www.sfiprogram.org
SFI-01268

20 21 22 23 24 10 9 8 7 6 5 4 3 2 1

DISCLAIMER: This book may direct you to access third-party content via web links, QR codes, or other scannable technologies, which are provided for your reference by the author(s). Corwin makes no guarantee that such third-party content will be available for your use and encourages you to review the terms and conditions of such third-party content. Corwin takes no responsibility and assumes no liability for your use of any third-party content, nor does Corwin approve, sponsor, endorse, verify, or certify such third-party content.

Contents

Visit the companion website at
resources.corwin.com/BreakthroughLeadership
for downloadable resources.

Foreword

Pedro A. Noguera, PhD
Dean, Rossier School of Education
University of Southern California

Inequality in wealth and income is increasing throughout the world, and as it does, our ability to address many of our most pressing problems—poverty, global migration, and climate change—worsens and solutions remain beyond our reach.

As inequality grows, so do resentment and frustration. More and more Americans realize that their children may not have access to the same kinds of opportunities that were once available to them: stable jobs with good health benefits, a home that they own, or paying for a college education without becoming saddled with years of debt. The so-called American Dream has become a faint and distant memory, and as it fades, desperation increases.

Additionally, at the time of this book's publication, we find ourselves grappling with two crises: a pandemic that has infected a greater percentage of the United States population than in any other nation on earth, and a social movement for racial justice that has swept the country even more quickly than the pandemic, aimed at undoing years of deeply embedded structural racism that is manifest in every aspect of life.

For many years, research has shown that education can serve as a resource for addressing many of the problems facing modern societies. This includes economic and social inequality, as well as racism, bigotry, and ignorance. However, more often than not, individuals and communities that need education to improve their lives are the least likely to receive the kind of education that makes progress possible. That is, rather than advancing equality and opportunity, too often education has been implicated in the reproduction of inequality.

The critical variable that determines whether or not our schools can respond adequately to the numerous challenges that they and their children face is leadership. Particularly given our lack of leadership at the national level, educational leaders must step forward to provide the vision and strategies needed to promote equity in educational opportunities and outcomes.

This book is about the work of such leaders. In big cities, small towns, and rural areas, a small number of principals and superintendents are showing that progress can be made when leaders have the resourcefulness and courage to address equity challenges directly.

For the last several years, the United States has embraced educational reforms that rely on standardized testing and competition to promote accountability, while ignoring the need to provide impoverished and underdeveloped communities with adequate resources to pay educators fair salaries and improve conditions in schools. Despite the lofty promises made by reformers, we now have clear evidence that the reforms we have pursued have not led to educational improvement on a large scale.

There is an alternative, and it is described in vivid detail in this book. When educational leaders adopt an equity-centered approach, they work to ensure that conditions conducive to good teaching and learning are in place.

While it would be most helpful if an equity-based approach to education reform were embraced by policymakers, we cannot afford to wait. As you will see in the pages ahead, there are educational leaders who are making significant progress at the school and district level by committing to strategically develop the professional capacity of teachers and the institutional capacity of schools to respond to student needs. Capacity building is a process that over time makes it possible for the skills of teachers to be in alignment with the needs of students. This mismatch in skills and resources is at the base of many of the challenges facing schools. With a commitment to capacity building and a clear understanding of how to carry it out in particular schools, educational leaders are moving forward in creating an environment where all children can learn at high levels.

From poverty to crime, from environmental degradation to economic underdevelopment, we have clear and compelling evidence that as societies make advances in education, many of these problems can be addressed. Educational leaders who succeed in advancing equity and serving the needs of all their students are finding ways to pursue excellence and equity by creating conditions in schools that address the academic and nonacademic needs of children (health, nutrition, safety, etc.). The educational leaders profiled in this book have a clear sense of how to systematically build the capacity of teachers and schools to meet the needs of the students they serve. I urge other leaders to learn from them so that, rather than being the exception, great schools that serve all children well will be the norm.

REFERENCE

Ryssdal, K. (2012, June 6). Economist Joseph Stiglitz on income inequality in the U.S. In *Marketplace*. Minnesota Public Radio. https://www.marketplace .org/2012/06/06/economist-joseph-stiglitz-income-inequality-us/

Acknowledgments

From Alan

This book was born out of a sense of urgency. My co-author, Marcus Newsome, and I set about describing a challenging district formerly bereft of resources and plagued by more than a decade of corresponding results: failure to ever meet full accreditation. The crises that were tackled here in many ways became the norm for our nation and the world as COVID-19 and, soon after, civil unrest dominated the world landscape.

Bringing together the stories and lessons of courageous and breakthrough leadership became a group effort. This began with Marcus Newsome, followed by the extraordinary dedication of the Corwin team beginning with Monica Eckman and Dan Alpert whose moral courage and vision propelled this book forward in rapid response to the pressing needs to address immediate crisis while also redressing inequities in our educational communities and beyond. Lauren Mahan, Lucas Schleicher, Maura Sullivan, and Elena Nikitina likewise modeled a "whatever it takes" attitude and actions needed to get this work quickly into the hands of educators grappling with crisis never before experienced. Amy Schroller led our work through the production process with attentiveness and dedication.

Leadership begins at the top, and the SAGE organization has been endowed with "old school" classic leaders, the likes of which one rarely sees these days. Sara Miller McCune, David McCune, and Blaise Simqu are of a moral fiber and steadfastness in their beliefs and actions that is unparalleled in educational publishing if not in any corporate setting. Without their support and that of Michael Soules, president of Corwin Press, publishing such works as this book would be nearly impossible in today's landscape.

The rest of the "village" that made this book possible included many frontline practitioners and thought leaders who are blazing a trail for equity out of the rubble of the crisis that COVID-19 has dealt school communities. Their courageous leadership, perseverance, and adaptability are laudable, and their willingness to share their time and expertise was vital to this work.

We are also grateful to the following individuals who contributed their expertise to this endeavor: Margo Gottlieb, Dwayne Williams.

This book is dedicated to the "home" team that provided tremendous support, patience, love, and plenty of challenges too—all informing and allowing for this work to go forward:

My wife, Hourieh, who has been both loving soul mate and steadfast and patient partner throughout some ups and many downs in this period;

Ava Blankstein, my youngest little girl of eight years old whose compassion, wisdom, courage, and joy are a blessing and inspiration;

Sarah Blankstein, whose prodigal return to our home has been a blessing, enlightenment, and inspiration for this work, and whose own resilience and light shines brighter each day; and

Nancy Shin, who has been my trusted and unwavering friend, associate, and ally for thirty years influencing future generations in many ways, including as proud and beloved "nana" to Ava and Sarah.

From Marcus

The Lord God is the author and finisher of my faith, and the one to whom I am thankful for giving my life and work purpose and meaning. My grandmother, Tempie Holloman, who was a sharecropper, matriarch, and compass for our family, taught me to love everyone, never to speak negatively about others, and to serve humanity with charity, generosity, benevolence, empathy, civility, and humility. I acknowledge my mother and father, Essie and Henian Newsome, for their unconditional love, encouragement, and sacrifice, taking their four children from a home on a dirt road in rural North Carolina to opportunities to see the world. My siblings Dr. Edward Newsome Jr., Dr. Douglas Newsome, and Shelia (Newsome) Boyd and their families are constant cheerleaders. My college sweetheart and wife, Patsy, has been a rock of support, encouragement, and inspiration, and loving mother to our three beautiful children, Lynnell (husband TJ), Marcus Jr., and Phillip (wife Amanda).

I have been motivated and uplifted by countless dedicated educators and colleagues with whom I've worked in school districts in the District of Columbia, Prince George's County, Newport News City, Chesterfield County, and Petersburg City. I am indebted to principals Ellsworth Mitchell and Dr. Ralph Neil, who served as role models early in my teaching career, and Veolia Jackson, who pushed me out of my comfort zone to pursue leadership experiences, and Dr. Jerome Clarke and Dr. Iris Metts, who were superintendent role models. My friend and mentor Dr. Billy Cannaday, former state superintendent, has been an amazing role model. I am also grateful to the Virginia Association of School Superintendents for their ongoing support.

I am moved by my co-author, Alan Blankstein, for his friendship and belief in me, and Lauren Mahan, who has been an amazing contributor to this book. Finally, I thank the Corwin publishing team, and especially Dan Alpert, who is an incredible editor and person.

Publisher's Acknowledgments

Corwin gratefully acknowledges the contributions of the following reviewers:

Rosa Atkins
Superintendent
Charlottesville City Schools
Charlottesville, VA

Cyndee Blount
Principal
Acquinton Elementary School
King William, VA

Luvelle Brown
Superintendent
Ithaca City School District
Ithaca, NY

Michael Casserly
Strategic Advisor
Council of the Great City Schools

Dallas Dance
Chief Executive Officer
The DDance Group Inc.

Dan Domenech
Executive Director
American Association of School
   Administrators

Susan Enfield
Superintendent
Highline Public Schools
Highline, WA

Michael Fullan
Professor Emeritus, University of
   Toronto
Author, *Coherence* and *Nuance*
Toronto, ON, Canada

Monica George-Fields
President and Chief Executive
   Officer
REACH
New York, NY

Avis Glaze
Founder and Chief Executive
   Officer
Edu-Quest International Inc.

Amy Griffin
Superintendent
Cumberland County Public Schools
Cumberland, VA

Zaretta Hammond
Author, *Culturally Responsive Teaching and The Brain: Promoting Authentic Engagement and Rigor Among Culturally and Linguistically Diverse Students*

Maria Alcon Heraux
KIPP Foundation

William Hite
Superintendent
The School District of Philadelphia
Philadelphia, PA

Matt Hurt
Director
Comprehensive Instructional Program, Virginia

Scott Jeffries
Superintendent
Wythe County Public Schools
Wytheville, VA

Dena Keeling
Chief Equity Officer
Orange County Schools, North Carolina

John Malloy
Toronto District School Board
Toronto, ON, Canada

Jay McTighe
Jay McTighe and Associates

Eric Moore
Senior Accountability Research and Equity Officer
Minneapolis Public Schools
Minneapolis, MN

Pedro Noguera
Dean
University of Southern California
Rossier School of Education
Los Angeles, CA

David Osher
Vice President and Institute Fellow
American Institutes for Research
Washington, DC

Katrise Perera
Superintendent
Gresham-Barlow School District
Gresham, OR

Paul Reville
Francis Keppel Professor of Practice of Educational Policy and Administration
Harvard University
Graduate School of Education
Cambridge, MA

James Schwartz
Lead Leadership Coach
Network for College Success
The University of Chicago
School of Social Service Administration
Chicago, IL

Nancy Shin
Executive Director (retired)
HOPE Foundation

Dennis Shirley
Professor of Education
Lynch School of Education
Boston College
Boston, MA

Aaron Spence
Superintendent
Virginia Beach City Public Schools
Virginia Beach, VA

Susan Szachowicz
Senior Fellow for the Successful
    Practices Network and Retired
    Principal of Brockton
High School

Benny Vásquez
Chief Equity Officer
KIPP

Sharon Wolder
Chief Officer
Student Support Services
Brockton Public Schools
Brockton, MA

About the Authors

Award-winning author and educational leader **Alan M. Blankstein** served for twenty-five years as president of the HOPE Foundation, which he founded and whose honorary chair is Nobel Prize winner Archbishop Desmond Tutu. A former "high-risk" youth, Alan began his career in education as a music teacher. He worked for Phi Delta Kappa, March of Dimes, and Solution Tree, which he founded in 1987 and directed for twelve years while launching Professional Learning Communities beginning in the late 1980s. He is the author of the best-selling book *Failure Is Not an Option®: Six Principles That Guide Student Achievement in High-Performing Schools*, which received the Book of the Year award from Learning Forward. Alan is senior editor, lead contributor, and/or author of eighteen books, including *Excellence Through Equity* with Pedro Noguera. He also authored some twenty articles in leading education print including *Education Week*, *Educational Leadership*, *The Principal*, and *Executive Educator*. Alan has provided keynote presentations and workshops for virtually every major educational organization in the United States, and throughout the United Kingdom, Africa, and the Middle East. Alan has served on the Harvard Principals' Center advisory board, and the board of the Jewish Child Care Association, where he once was a youth in residence.

Marcus J. Newsome is the director of the Virginia Superintendents Leadership Academy. Previously he served for sixteen years as an award-winning school superintendent in Newport News, Chesterfield County, and Petersburg City (Virginia). In 2015, his work was recognized by the United States Office of Educational Technology during a White House ceremony as a leader in transforming schools from a print to a digital learning environment. He has served as a consultant to governors, members of Congress, and both national and international business leaders on solutions for closing achievement gaps, narrowing the digital divide, assessment design, professional development, and twenty-first-century teaching and learning. Newsome has earned doctorate degrees in educational leadership and religious education. He began his career as an art and mathematics teacher in the District of Columbia, and later served as a curriculum writer, principal, and district administrator. He has also served as an associate professor for several universities, including Harvard University and Virginia Commonwealth University. An ordained minister, and dedicated husband and father, he has dedicated his career to the service of children.

CHAPTER 1

Out of the Crisis

The virus began in China, moved across Asia, and hit Europe hard. Not long after arriving in the United States, the virus was properly given status as a pandemic; the stock market plummeted, bringing on a recession; students were shut out of schools, which had closed; and the death toll began to mount.

According to the *Seattle Times*:

Scattered through the news stories and the mimeographed weekly CDC reports . . . were accounts of tragedy: A 2-year-old toddler dying in his mother's arms on the way to the hospital in Tangipahoa Parish. A 12-year-old camper who died on a hike in San Diego. A 16-year-old exchange student dying of "fulminant hemorrhagic pneumonia" days after arriving in New York." (Brown, 2009)

This didn't begin in 2019–2020; this wasn't coronavirus, or COVID-19. This was a different pandemic.

On April 17, 1957, Maurice Hilleman realized a pandemic was on its way to the United States. That day The New York Times *reported on a large influenza outbreak in Hong Kong. One detail in particular caught the doctor's eye: in the long waiting lines for clinics, the paper said "women carried glassy-eyed children tied to their backs." He quickly got to work, putting out the word that there was a pandemic coming and pushing to develop a vaccine by the time school started again in the fall.* (Little, 2020)

By the time Dr. Hilleman read the *New York Times* article, some 250,000 Hong Kong residents had already contracted the virus. He reached out to the United States Army medical general in Japan to further investigate and in return received the saliva of a serviceman who'd become infected. Hilleman realized that this strain of influenza was one for which we had no cure.

As the chief of respiratory diseases at the Walter Reed Army Institute of Research in Washington, DC, Hilleman had access to other flu serum and the scientific data needed to begin round-the-clock efforts to work on a vaccine in time for his predictive date of the virus's arrival in the United States: September 1957.

While working tirelessly to develop a vaccine, Hilleman also enlisted the initially grudging support of major corporations in preparing for mass development and distribution of the serum yet to be created.

Hilleman's work was intertwined in his own upbringing. He was born in Miles City, Montana, to parents who had survived the Spanish flu pandemic, and he credited much of his success to his rural childhood experience of raising chickens. His vaccines since then had often been derived from fertilized chicken eggs, so he foresaw the need to inform company CEOs whose help he'd enlisted to remind farmers not to kill their roosters at the end of hatching season.

The virus arrived as he'd anticipated in September 1957, as did the first allotment of vaccines. He had begun six months earlier, working first on a hunch after having read the *New York Times* article that April. After nine 14-hour days, Hilleman and a colleague found that it was a new strain of flu that could kill millions in the United States alone. Instead, some forty million doses of vaccines were prepared and distributed in September, and the death rate was held at sixty-nine thousand Americans, and almost two million people worldwide. Hilleman was awarded the Distinguished Service Medal from the United States Army for his work.

> *Robert Gallo, co-discoverer of HIV, the virus that causes AIDS, once said, "If I had to name a person who has done more for the benefit of human health, with less recognition than anyone else, it would be Maurice Hilleman. Maurice should be recognized as the most successful vaccinologist in history."* (Maugh, 2005)

Although Hilleman invented a total of forty vaccines, saving millions of people from mumps, hepatitis B, and scores of other deadly diseases, he remained humble throughout his life. He did not use his name on even one of his vaccines.

LEADERSHIP MATTERS

Adaptive Leadership

The challenges brought about by the 1957 flu are somewhat different from those we face in a COVID-19 or post-COVID-19 world. Yet the lessons of great leadership endure.

Maurice Hilleman saw the need to act and did so for the greater good. He did not await official authority, instructions from President Dwight D. Eisenhower, or an infusion of additional capital from the Walter Reed Army Institute of Research. He started without the answers as to whether there was even a new virus that was spreading. He had no idea as to whether he could apply an existing cure or, if not, how he would invent a new one.

Even before COVID-19, educators were increasingly being placed in positions for which there is no easy answer and no script to follow. In the Petersburg, Virginia, case study first brought to light in Chapter 2 (page 30), the new superintendent discovered shortly after arriving that the city had not paid its bills to the schools in months and funds weren't available to meet staff payroll that week; the health insurance had ceased on teacher and staff medical claims; utility payments were delinquent, and the stoppage of services was imminent; meals for students were at risk of discontinuance; and the city had cut school funding by more than 30 percent. Dealing with these matters wasn't taught in grad school! Nonetheless, strong leadership and teamwork resulted in a turnaround that both pulled the district out of debt and was recognized nationally.

> ▶ *The adaptive demands of our time require leaders who take responsibility without waiting for revelation or request. One can lead with no more than a question in hand.* (Heifetz & Laurie, 2011, p. 78)

In 2020, the world was thrown a COVID-19 curveball. The demands of schools closing challenged teachers and leaders at all levels to solve problems they didn't even know they had. How will we deliver online instruction when students have no internet access? How will we ensure food students need to survive will arrive in a safe and timely manner each day? What will we do to provide high school seniors with the courses they need to graduate?

In addition to finding adaptations to meet new challenges, educators were called on to be transformative, inspiring staff to perform beyond their perceived capabilities (Steinmann et al., 2018). Millions of educators valiantly rose to the challenges COVID-19 posed, commandeering school buses for delivery of student supplies and sending out tens of millions of meals each week to children who would otherwise not eat. The value of fundamentals, and even the often overlooked staff, became apparent:

We've focused on taking care of and feeding our families and staff; people's well-being; communicating with families with signs saying "we miss you"; and alerts to them from the principal. The true heroes became our food service staff—they came in to make food, while others were sent home. I was impressed that food service workers knew all the kids by name, what students like and don't like to eat, and worried about many of the children when they go home. They have great pride in the work they do. (Amy Griffin, personal communication, April 10, 2020)

Courageous Leadership

The educators spotlighted in this book exemplify what has been named throughout recorded history, and even prior among Indigenous Americans, as the virtue above all others: courage (Lassiter, 2017). The written word comes from the French *le cœur*, or "the heart." Most educators entered the profession in concert with the first principle of courage, by starting with the intersection of their passion and life mission—what we term the *core*.

Maurice Hilleman's tireless hours of dedication came from deep within his own life experiences as well. He was born, as noted, to two Spanish flu pandemic survivors; but he lost his twin sister at birth, and his mother two days later. This fueled his passion for finding cures to prevent premature death in others. His intellect, meanwhile, was nurtured by his father, the education afforded him, and even chickens!

The educators whose experience we draw on in this book, likewise, are morally rooted in ensuring success for each of their students. Their deep connection to the importance of the work allows leaders, from the classroom to the boardroom, to overcome enormous obstacles to meet the needs of the young people they serve.

Many frontline employees didn't even know if they were still getting paid, and with my time I've been working fourteen hours, seven days a week, for three weeks. Who has access to internet? Who has parental support? Who has a computer for more than one student in the house? How are we teaching homeless kids? If we hadn't taken inventory prior, this certainly makes us now. (Aaron Spence, personal communication, March 23, 2020)

We needed first to know where every student was. Teachers made personal calls to check on every student. If they couldn't get through, social workers went to their doors. Professionals networked online to talk about how many and which students have and haven't been reached and to share strategies on what each had tried, what was working, and what was not. The whole community got involved, including the sheriff's department, to make sure each child was well.

Academics had to wait. Many parents who work in health care had to minimize contact with their children to keep them healthy; others after finally seeing their children might easily skip the work, and just hug them! (Dena Keeling, personal communication, April 15, 2020)

Together, in this book, we will encourage readers to continue to find and act in concert with their "core," as we provide examples of school, district, and state leadership teams that are rooted in their individual and collective purpose. One of the six vital principles of courageous leadership is exemplified in the next section (for all six principles, see Blankstein [2013]).

COURAGE: FACING THE FACTS AND YOUR FEARS

The degree to which we inaccurately see health care and education as expenses instead of a vital human right, we will continue to see human needs sacrificed, and needless suffering and despair. (Pedro A. Noguera, personal communication, April 8, 2020)

The reality of a forthcoming pandemic was immediately grasped and communicated by Hilleman, even though other leaders were loath to accept that. Yet he persisted in persuading them rather than backing away from the data.

What are the facts that COVID-19 has laid bare for us about which children have access to health care and which do not; about who does and does not have Wi-Fi and tutors to advance their academics; and about the essential and heroic role schools play in mitigating the often forgotten, hidden, or ignored truth that more than half of all school-aged children in America are officially poor, and would go hungry without the nutrition that schools provide?

Facing Facts About Racism, Food, and Housing Instability

While *facing the facts* is often inconvenient as they don't always tell the story we wish to hear, not doing so can be deadly as outlined in the "Lessons of Willful Blindness" section of this chapter. More recently, we are again grappling with the outcome of ignoring centuries of systemic racism that must be addressed forthrightly if we are to quell a civil meltdown and progress to a higher ground of equitable treatment and outcomes for children and families of color. This, too, will be discussed in subsequent chapters.

It is becoming increasingly clear that addressing the surface issues like food sustainability, as schools have, is plugging a roof whose gaping holes of inequity become only more apparent during national catastrophes like Columbine, Katrina, and corona. They beckon us to use our ingenuity, commitment, and moral outrage to not only solve the surface problem *du jour*, but also provide millions of desperate students a place in which they belong—one that provides safety, security, love, acceptance, and dignity as worthy human beings; a "home" that does not wash away when the rain begins to fall.

Yet our students are increasingly at risk, and home itself is ephemeral. The fastest-growing segment of the student population is no longer Hispanic; it's homeless, with some 1.5 million students *reporting* homelessness in 2017–2018, an 11 percent increase over the prior year and the largest number ever reported. The biggest increase, of 103 percent, came in the number of children now living in unsheltered environments like cars, parks, and streets (Keystone State Education Coalition, 2020; National Center for Homeless Education, 2020). If these students all attended one district, they would far surpass the number of students in New York and Chicago—the largest and third-largest districts in the United States—combined.

Homelessness is clearly on the rise, but so is an array of issues facing children, including divorce, poverty, obesity, and depression, among others. While an argument can be made for the fragility of nearly all students nowadays, there is no denying their diversity of needs, all of which becomes apparent as each school day begins.

It is true that many students are still doing well, for example, and that others who might be expected to be "at risk" due to their demographic profile somehow beat the odds. Still others from backgrounds of low socioeconomic status receive the consistency and support from home and/or school that are necessary to thrive, as described in forthcoming chapters.

Yet educators are stretched to the limits in the demands placed on them by policymakers who don't seem to understand the value of frontline professionals caring for and educating our nation's children, or the depth of their diversity and needs. No wonder the United States was exploding in a series of teacher strikes leading up to the most recent crisis (Smith & Davey, 2019; Wolf, 2019).

This book will present examples of schools "beating the odds" before COVID-19, as well as a process for determining newly created approaches to educating children in a post-COVID-19 world. Perhaps more importantly, *breakthrough leadership* spotlights leaders at all levels now leveraging crises like this to shape local and national priorities toward a more equitable and healthy society for our children.

Courageous leaders at all levels have a unique opportunity in advancing an agenda of equitable and successful outcomes for students. The facts about what is at stake couldn't be starker. Good leadership saves lives both in pandemics and in our profession.

The actions that Hilleman, his team, and ultimately the nation took saved millions of lives. The role educators play, likewise, for our nation's children makes a difference in the trajectory of their lives: the difference between survival and malnourishment; between a future career and prison; and between young people who are socially, emotionally, and academically prepared for life and those who are on the road to a low-wage or impoverished existence (Valdez & Broin, 2015). Educators have the ability to affect students' life trajectory through relationships, attitudes, social and emotional competence, contributions to learning conditions, and responses to student behavior (Coggshall et al., 2013). What will happen if we only *respond* to this and the civil rights crisis and return to "normal" afterwards?

LESSONS OF WILLFUL BLINDNESS AND ITS DEADLY OUTCOME IN THE PANDEMIC OF 1918

The COVID-19 pandemic provides a perfect example of why we need a real leader in place during bad times even more than in good times.
(Dan Domenech, personal communication, April 6, 2020)

The horrific scale of the 1918 influenza pandemic—known as the "Spanish flu"—is hard to fathom. The virus infected 500 million people worldwide and killed an estimated 20 million to 50 million victims— that's more than all of the soldiers and civilians killed during World War I combined. (Roos, 2020)

One example of a pandemic that shook the world is the Spanish flu that first emerged in February 1918. This had all of the characteristics of a seasonal flu, although it was highly contagious and extremely harmful. The virus spread rapidly throughout the United States Army installation, after one of the first cases was confirmed for an Army cook. As the month came to a close, 1,100 troops had unfortunately been hospitalized, causing 38 people to perish after developing pneumonia (Roos, 2020).

While virulent, this flu, like its 1957 "Asian" flu successor, might have been brought under control a great deal more quickly had the nation's leaders been focused on that. Instead of protecting citizens, and particularly the armed forces, United States troops were deployed to France, England, Italy, and Spain, where the virus spread freely. Within months, three-quarters of the French troops were infected as was half of the British Army.

Spain was neutral in this war and actually had fewer incidents of infection. Yet the misnomer of "Spanish flu" arose out of the country's free and open reporting of the virus's existence while the American and other media quashed such reports, further exacerbating the pandemic.

Rather than quarantine and treat servicemen, the leadership at the time pursued an aggressive war campaign by moving soldiers throughout the European continent and America, often in close proximity to one another.

> *In Britain, for example, a government official named Arthur Newsholme knew full well that a strict civilian lockdown was the best way to fight the spread of the highly contagious disease. But he wouldn't risk crippling the war effort by keeping munitions factory workers and other civilians home.* (Roos, 2020)

The dearth of nurses and plans for treatment were also exacerbated by racism. Well-trained Black nurses who were prepared to work were only permitted to assist German prisoners of war.

Ironically, at the end of World War I, President Woodrow Wilson himself was apparently infected during his Paris treaty negotiations (Roos, 2020). The terms of the treaty suffered as a result of his inability to focus and maintain mental acuity, and this set the stage for the next world war.

A NEW WAY FORWARD: *BREAKTHROUGH LEADERSHIP*

Our choices are clear. As a nation, continent, and world, we can turn a collective blind eye to the interconnected equity issues that COVID-19 and the blatant murder of our citizens of color lay bare, or use our understanding of these issues to make a better and more equitable society. The breakthrough leadership model is rooted in the principles of courage, and is consistent with, but not reliant on, adaptive leadership, which is focused on innovating to address emerging challenges. At the root of breakthrough leadership, however, is a fundamental shift in perspective regarding the root cause of the challenge at hand, the solution to which is a new set of actions that often require going beyond one's current "boundaries." Whereas adaptive leadership might lead a team to mobilize in finding and delivering meals to homeless students and families, breakthrough leadership would in addition call for a deeper analysis to determine why they were homeless in the first place, and what set of alliances, resources, and common understandings and commitments are necessary to address this issue at its root, definitively and systemically. Both are rooted in courage, as indicated below.

FIGURE 1.1 Breakthrough Leadership

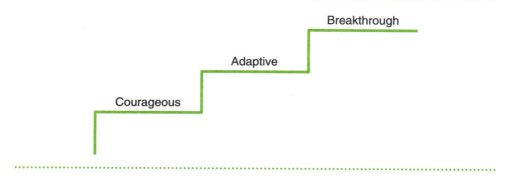

This COVID-19 and civil rights crisis calls for the kind of breakthrough leadership described in Chapter 2. The viral breakout and civil unrest have led to a breakdown, which in turn can become a breakthrough for our collective commitment to a new level of equity.

Adaptive and courageous leadership at all levels is now becoming the norm in assisting and educating children during this pandemic. Next, we are called on to understand and to change the underlying conditions that have led to a secondary crisis for our children that may far surpass the toll taken by the virus itself. At the heart of this leadership is an unflinching and profound look at the needs of our children and their families, and a steadfast commitment to actions to change the conditions accordingly.

By contrast, in the Spanish flu example, the Allied forces were seen as expendable, and their well-being was sacrificed by their leadership to further other priorities. Moreover, the truth of the pandemic underway was hidden to the detriment of these same soldiers, and up to fifty million other victims, ultimately including the commander-in-chief, President Wilson.

Similarly, consider the news, as reported to NPR by Jim Zarroli on April 13, 2020, that "a Smithfield Foods plant in Sioux Falls . . . has become the latest meat processing facility to shut down as COVID-19 sickens plant workers." Zarroli reports that "one of the country's largest pork-producing plants closed indefinitely after nearly 300 of its employees tested positive for COVID-19. And the company's CEO warned that the coronavirus pandemic is pushing the nation's meat supply 'perilously close' to the edge."

The backstory of this closure, and many more to come, is the poor and unclean working conditions of this company's impoverished workforce. As we write this chapter, another plant in Iowa is closing down (Jackson, 2020). The employees, in turn, haven't enough funds or health insurance coverage to forgo a day's or week's pay. Working, and thereby chancing infection of their colleagues, seems the only way forward for these employees (Grabell, 2020).

The "smallest cog" has led to the closure of one of the largest and oldest meatpacking companies worldwide, which in turn affects the entire supply chain and availability of food for us all. If we don't pay attention to the health, education, and well-being of the least among us, even the most powerful will be affected:

> *We are dependent on one another. Some feel they can escape COVID-19, but they can't escape destruction of our planet. Impacts of climate change were already dictating movements of people. Maybe some have a fantasy that they will pay their way on a rocket ship. We always were codependent as humans, and locking down Florida doesn't mean they can escape that. It isn't the "others" that are the problem. It further highlights our interdependence.* (David Osher, personal communication, April 1, 2020)

Beating the Odds, or Changing Them?

As this book demonstrates in the coming chapters, educational leaders have often beaten the odds stacked against even the poorest schools and their students. Their successes with "those children" were alternatively admired, extolled, or sidelined in the "turnaround" section of the educational literature, much the way Black history is relegated to the month of February in the United States. More recently, however, there is a greater spotlight on both the undeniable and the aching needs of perhaps a majority of our students and the extraordinary lessons of perseverance, adaptability, and courageous convictions the professionals who succeed with them have to share with colleagues, who are, by necessity, now thrust into the role of "transformational leaders" (Allen et al., 2015; Klocko et al., 2019, p. 9; Northouse, 2013).

> ▶ *If we had been asked to move to distance learning under other circumstances it would have taken twenty years to do what we have done in three weeks.* (Atkins, personal communication, April 9, 2020)

The opportunity to addresses systemic issues that advance equitable outcomes for *all* of our children is before us. Yet many will prefer going back to what they know, especially if it worked for them, their children, their clients, or their constituents: "Everyone who is happy with what they have now wants no change, and those who don't have what they want rarely have a voice" (John Malloy, personal communication, April 14, 2020).

Best Practices Pre-COVID-19

The possible ways forward can be found within the following pages of this book. Best practices for equitable outcomes in schools as they existed before COVID-19 are described in coming pages as a baseline. Many of these insights, guiding principles, and strategies remain relevant no matter the context.

Adaptive Changes Post-COVID

How schools are managing this crisis by adapting to the new constraints are described as well (using online technologies and decoupling seat time from student requirements, for example), as are plans for moving some of these adaptations into mainstream practice when the pandemic is over. Yet, as Michael Fullan (personal communication, April 10, 2020) cautions: "If the post-COVID opportunity is one in which technology dominates, it will have been a wasted crisis."

Ultimately, advancing equity or learning through new efficiencies and delivery methods, or tighter collaboration among professional teams, will be of benefit. Yet this alone will not bring about the sea change required to dismantle centuries of structural inequities now being exposed at the surface level.

Breakthrough Opportunities Post-COVID

The only thing we have to fear is fear itself. (Franklin D. Roosevelt)

Deeper questions are also addressed in coming chapters about the value of grades, "catching up" when actually *everyone* is "behind," and how to act on our collective understanding that students' most common complaint about school is that it's "boring" (Michael Fullan, personal communication, April 10, 2020). This sentiment has been fueled by a testing regimen that has consistently disadvantaged certain groups of students, that is not currently valid for *any* student, and whose future value can be more carefully considered at this juncture.

> ▶ *A modern education should be preparing students for transfer—to be able to apply their learning within, and across, disciplines. We currently focus excessively on "covering" content and preparing students for multiple-choice, standardized tests. Those are narrow and impoverished educational goals. Instead, we should be preparing today's learners to deal with unpredictable opportunities and challenges . . . now more than ever.* (Jay McTighe, personal communication, May 11, 2020)

Both processes for advancing these conversations toward action, and examples of such visionary actions underway in schools and districts, await the reader. We now have a once-in-a-century opportunity to create a "cure" for inequity. This will be neither an easily attained nor a foregone conclusion to the story. The history of the underserved gaining access to true decision-making power, even over their own lives, is fraught. The use of breakthrough leadership is meant to provide both the best practices underway to address current inequities and a powerful guiding light for changing the conditions leading to them.

Many have heard the story of the wise old man and the mischievous boys. One day, a mischievous group of boys were idly looking for something to do when they saw an old man sitting on a park bench. He had the reputation of being the wisest man in town. The boys plotted to prove the old man unwise. They caught a bird that had been trapped in a bush. They said to one another, "Let's hide it behind our back, take it to the old man, and ask him if it is alive or dead. If he says it is dead, we will show him the living bird. It he says it is alive, we will smother it until it is dead. Either way, we will prove him wrong." So, the mischievous boys approached the wise old man, and told him they had a bird behind their back. They asked him, "Is the bird dead or alive?" The wise old man responded, "His life is in your hands."

We have an opportunity to address a crisis beyond COVID-19 that can't be ignored or explained away. The decision to act is in our collective hands. The possibilities and opportunities to transform schools to meet the needs of every student stand before us.

REFERENCES

Allen, N., Grigsby, B., & Peters, M. L. (2015). Does leadership matter? Examining the relationship among transformational leadership, school climate, and student achievement. *International Journal of Educational Leadership Preparation*, *10*(2), 1–22.

Blankstein, A. M. (2013). *Failure is not an option: Six principles that advance student achievement in highly effective schools*. Corwin.

Brown, D. (2009, August 26). Lessons to be learned from 1957 pandemic. *The Seattle Times*. https://www.seattletimes.com/seattle-news/health/lessons-to-be-learned-from-1957-pandemic/

Coggshall, J. G., Osher, D., & Colombi, G. (2013). Enhancing educators' capacity to stop the school-to-prison pipeline. *Family Court Review*, *51*(3), 435–444. https://doi.org/10.1111/fcre.12040

Grabell, M. (2020, March 28). *What happens if workers cutting up the nation's meat get sick?* ProPublica. https://www.propublica.org/article/what-happens-if-workers-cutting-up-the-nations-meat-get-sick

Heifetz, R. A., & Laurie, D. (2011). The work of leadership. In *Harvard Business Review's 10 must reads on leadership* (pp. 57–78). Harvard Business School Publishing Corporation.

Jackson, S. (2020, April 21). Pork Producers cite need for packer operations. *Ottumwa Courier*. https://www.ottumwacourier.com/news/pork-producers-cite-need-for-packer-operations/article_fde9cc76-836a-11ea-8b45-3bae0ca18a86.html

Keystone State Education Coalition. (2020, January 31). *It's School Choice Week in Pa. Don't buy what its advocates are selling* [Opinion]. http://keystonestateeducationcoalition.blogspot.com/2020/01/pa-ed-policy-roundup-for-jan-31-2020.html

Klocko, B. A., Justis, R. J., & Kirby, E. A. (2019). Leadership tenacity and public-school superintendents. *Journal of Leadership Education, 18*(1). https://journalofleadershiped.org/jole_articles/leadership-tenacity-and-public-school-superintendents/

Lassiter, C. (2017). *Everyday courage for school leaders.* Corwin.

Little, B. (2020, May 6). *How the 1957 flu pandemic was stopped early in its path.* History. https://www.history.com/news/1957-flu-pandemic-vaccine-hilleman

Maugh, T. H., II. (2005, April 13). Maurice R. Hilleman, 85; scientist developed many vaccines that saved millions of lives. *Los Angeles Times.* https://www.latimes.com/archives/la-xpm-2005-apr-13-me-hilleman13-story.html

National Center for Homeless Education. (2020, January). *Federal data summary school years 2015–16 to 2017–18: Education for homeless children and youth.* https://nche.ed.gov/wp-content/uploads/2020/01/Federal-Data-Summary-SY-15.16-to-17.18-Published-1.30.2020.pdf

Northouse, P. G. (2013). *Leadership: Theory and practice* (6th ed.). SAGE.

Roos, D. (2020, April 29). *Why the second wave of the 1918 Spanish flu was so deadly.* History. https://www.history.com/news/spanish-flu-second-wave-resurgence

Smith, M., & Davey, M. (2019, October 31). Chicago teachers' strike, longest in decades, ends. *The New York Times.* https://www.nytimes.com/2019/10/31/us/chicago-cps-teachers-strike.html

Steinmann, B., Klug, H. J., & Maier, G. W. (2018). The path is the goal: How transformational leaders enhance followers' job attitudes and proactive behavior. *Frontiers in Psychology, 9,* 2338.

Valdez, M., & Broin, A. (2015). *Untapped: Transforming teacher leadership to help students succeed.* New Leaders.

Wolf, Z. (2019, February 23). *Why teacher strikes are touching every part of America.* CNN. https://www.cnn.com/2019/02/23/politics/teacher-strikes-politics/index.html

Zarroli, J. (2020, April 13). *U.S. meat supply is "perilously close" to a shortage, CEO warns.* NPR. https://www.npr.org/sections/coronavirus-live-updates/2020/04/13/833110486/u-s-meat-supply-is-perilously-close-to-a-shortage-ceo-warns

CHAPTER 2

Breakthrough Leadership

Nations do not die from invasion. They die from internal rottenness.
(Abraham Lincoln)

It is in your hands to create a better world for all who live in it.
(Nelson Mandela)

Since the word *breakthrough* entered the English lexicon in 1912, it's been used to depict new inventions or dramatically different thinking in science, business, and psychology. Breakdowns can lead to break*throughs* (Benny Vásquez, KIPP, personal communication, April 14, 2020), and the psychotherapeutic "aha" experience from personal insight can happen in a remarkably short time. "Part of the evidence for this . . . is emerging from brain science . . . human beings aren't driven by our ability to analyze and cogitate about our lives. Instead, we're moved by our viscerally immediate, bottom-up responses to events and relationships . . . our emotional responses to lived experience" (Simon, n.d.).

IS THE WORLD FLAT?

Pythagoras first proposed that the earth is flat sometime around 500 BC. A century and a half later, Aristotle affirmed this theory. Both of them experienced for different reasons a *breakthrough*—the discovery of a fundamental and profound truth that challenged what they had previously believed. Had either of them been brought to their discovery with the help of another person, they would have experienced *breakthrough leadership* on a *personal* level. Had they or their guide used this new discovery to change others' thinking and/or actions (like beginning a shipping industry that circled the world since the world is indeed round), we would have seen breakthrough leadership *taken to scale*.

A breakthrough is a new discovery or epiphany about a fundamental truth that challenges previous beliefs. Breakthrough leadership is the facilitation of this discovery and actions that can be taken accordingly.

Martin Luther King's Breakthrough

Martin Luther King Jr. was under threat of assassination shortly after he became part of the civil rights movement in 1955. After his home was blown up, he sought protection, in part, by arming himself. William Worthy, a journalist who covered the Southern Christian Leadership Conference, reported that once, during a visit to King's parsonage, he went to sit down on an armchair in the living room and, to his surprise, almost sat on a loaded gun. Glenn Smiley, an adviser to King, described King's home as "an arsenal" (Winkler, 2011).

Yet after intensive conversation with activist Bayard Rustin one evening, Dr. King decided to relinquish his firearms. He later wrote: "I was much more afraid in Montgomery when I had a gun in my house. When I decided that I couldn't keep a gun, I came face-to-face with the question of death and I dealt with it. From that point on, I no longer needed a gun nor have I been afraid" (Carson, 2001, p. 82).

Dr. King had a personal breakthrough, guided by Rustin, and used his new insight and breakthrough leadership to help others experience similar understandings. He then took breakthrough leadership to scale by leveraging this growing enlightenment of those in the movement to courageously and strategically confront the old paradigms of violent subjugation of a race of people. His chosen tactic to further enlighten others to join the movement while forcefully confronting a system of racism through direct unarmed actions changed the nation and the world.

WHY BREAKTHROUGH LEADERSHIP NOW?

Breakthrough leadership is called on to tap into and guide these "viscerally immediate, bottom-up [breakthrough] responses" for individuals who experience it—whether at the school, district, community, state, provincial, or national level. Such leadership is needed to act on the gaping and profound inequities we always *knew* about but now *see* in real time when we "Zoom into" a student's kitchen for a lesson and happen to see that the cupboards are bare, or finally find a "missing" student and enter a homeless shelter armed only with a Chromebook, passion, and determination to make a difference for that child. For many, it was one thing to *hear about* such conditions, and yet another to *see* them firsthand.

We are also witnessing a rare eruption of protests on streets throughout the world in a culminating response to centuries of violent, racist oppression of people of color. Hundreds of thousands of people of all nationalities, ages, and ethnicities are linking arms to collectively say "Enough is enough!" following the most recent spate of slayings of innocent people due to the color of their skin. It is time to reexamine our role in institutions as maintainers of systems that are damaging the very people they are *ostensibly* employed to be helping.

The COVID-19 pandemic didn't create the inequities it has exposed. Nor has the catalytic murder of George Floyd while facedown with an officer's knee on his neck been an outlier of the racism it represents. The confluence of these events, however, calls loudly for breakthrough leadership to harness our visceral, collective realizations in order to dramatically change the systems and institutions that are harming those whom they should be helping.

The new visceral "aha" reality can spark change beyond the individual level. Rather, it can be leveraged to impact the culture and policies of the school, district, community, or nation. To do this will require unrelenting pressure, a strategy that fits each leader's context, and an "invitation" to others to join the movement.

CASE STORY 2.1

South African Breakthrough Leadership Ends Apartheid Era With Truth and Reconciliation

"We didn't struggle [to dismantle apartheid] in order just to change the complexion of those who sit in the Union buildings: it was to change the quality of our community and society . . . [to one] that was a compassionate society, a caring society, a society where you might not necessarily be madly rich, but you knew that you counted," shared Nobel Peace Prize winner Archbishop Desmond Tutu (2016, p. ix).

Instead of keeping an inherently flawed and inequitable caste system that was explicitly racist, this leader, along with Nelson Mandela and others, opted *not* to put one of his own in charge of it, but to dismantle the system itself. More strikingly, these leaders negotiated the historic peaceful change of power, in part, by allowing the perpetrators of heinous crimes under apartheid to have amnesty if they would face the victims of their crimes and the nation as a whole in a process called Truth and Reconciliation.

This leadership created a major breakthrough never before seen: the peaceful relinquishing of control over a vassal nation by a colonial power. The concept of granting restitution in exchange for complete truth and admission of guilt in order to gain peace nationally was novel; it placed humanity and the *greater* good above individuals' desires for revenge.

Breakthrough leadership is now essential at all levels to marshal and collectively focus individuals' visceral and palpable realizations about the truth we've silently agreed to ignore for centuries. The profound inequities before us are unsustainable and must be eradicated at their root.

The Genesis of This Book

This book is born out of urgency. It reflects a deep dive into the best practical research worldwide on effective leadership from the classroom to the boardroom for equitable outcomes. In addition, this book reflects the wisdom of some of the greatest leaders who've successfully harnessed breakthrough leadership to navigate historic turning points. Finally, this book is informed by recent interviews with scores of noted thought leaders and hundreds of practitioners coping with, and leading through, crisis and uncertain times.

This chapter begins with adaptive leadership recently displayed by professionals. The next section "takes stock" of the considerable achievement professionals have already made in confronting the COVID-19 crisis. Much of what has been learned in this period is critical for future planning.

The final two sections demonstrate breakthrough leadership already underway, and then strategies for bringing such leadership to scale. Specifically, how can we leverage this moment at local, regional, state and provincial, and national levels? These strategies can be used to catalyze thinking about systemic change and maximum impact.

Educators, like all professionals, can always "do better" and in fact have developed "school improvement plans" more than anyone would care to admit or to remember. Yet there is now a breakthrough moment that leaders can and must seize to fundamentally uplift all of our children, at every possible level. This rare collective moment of truth is akin to another such moment in America's history in which the Founding Fathers were moved to pen "We hold these truths to be self-evident, that all men are created equal."

In 1979, Ron Edmonds boldly and accurately stated: "We can, whenever and wherever we choose, successfully teach all children whose schooling is of interest to us; we already know more than we need to do that; and whether or not we do it must finally depend on how we feel about the fact that we haven't so far" (p. 23).

Now is the moment for educators to coalesce and vociferously share their expertise and newfound breakthrough understandings with one another, and then in unified manner with families, community partners, school boards, policymakers, and the public at large in order to expand the "We" who are collectively responsible for the success of the next generation.

The light has shown clearly on our collective reality. Those who direct this light wisely will shape the future.

CASE STORY 2.2
Zooming In to New Realities
April 21, 2020, 2 p.m.

When Ms. Lewis's Zoom call to Sam seemed to be connecting, she was at once excited and uneasy. She'd managed the technology before on her end, yet meeting her student in this way came only after weeks of challenges in even locating Sam, and then in connecting him to Wi-Fi. Ultimately, success came via coordinated actions by the school social worker, the administration, the technology team, and a local Burger King manager, who allowed for a hot spot location near Sam's home.

At the same time, Ms. Lewis had her doubts about Sam's having done any work at all since the school closed in March. She was a leader among a group of veteran teachers who didn't allow students an "easy pass" when it came to either "dodging" their work responsibilities or misbehaving in class. She perceived Sam to be one of these students.

Shortly after they began reviewing the math lesson, Ms. Lewis heard sounds coming from behind Sam. She could see an altercation come into focus, which quickly exploded into a physical fight between what appeared to be Sam's mother and his older sister. He turned his head to gauge the level of conflict and then turned back to Ms. Lewis with a knowing look of resignation, slightly tinged with embarrassment, as he tried to ignore the scene and continue on with his lesson.

Ms. Lewis was stunned at what she saw. In order to reduce the discomfort Sam must have been feeling in having her view this scene, Ms. Lewis created an out: "I need to check on something that's come up for my daughter. Can we schedule for tomorrow please, Sam?"

When Ms. Lewis later debriefed with her principal, she was clearly shaken. She shared her deep empathy for Sam's situation as well as a personal moment of clarity: "From now on I will never ask a student 'Why haven't you done your homework?' I'll ask instead, 'How can I help you complete this assignment?'" (Katrise Perera, personal communication, April 29, 2020)

(Continued)

It would be almost impossible for a professional working with children for any length of time not to have experienced or at least heard about home situations like this. They are often used to give credence to writing students off as "unable" to do the work. This view would doom millions of children to failure.

Statistically speaking, even before COVID-19, massive civil unrest, and the toll this has taken, a majority of students in the United States were poor, receiving free or reduced-price lunch (National Center for Education Statistics, 2020). More students are homeless throughout the nation than are enrolled in New York City and Chicago public schools combined (Sparks, 2020). The numbers of single-parent families and two-working-parent families are at historic highs, leaving many who are struggling to make ends meet looking to their older children to pick up the slack in caring for younger siblings and take on adult responsibilities (Edwards et al., 2020). Schools serve as a bastion of hope for many, especially in American schools. Yet other schools are increasingly the modern depiction of Dickens's *Tale of Two Cities* that presaged the French Revolution, as Black children are five times more likely than White ones to attend schools segregated by race and ethnicity and more than twice as likely to attend a high-poverty school (Emma Garcia, personal communication, February 12, 2020).

None of this is new. What *is* new, however, is that we are at a crossroads just as millions of frontline professionals—from educators, to child care workers, to health care professionals—are now directly viewing, in real time, the fallout that these children once bore alone and in the shadows. Their cries for help were sometimes heard and tended to by a caring professional; in other instances, they were addressed systematically within an exceptional school like Brockton High School in Massachusetts, whose extraordinary turnaround is documented in Case Story 2.3. There are many such outliers including the Toronto District School Board (TDSB) in Ontario and the Gresham-Barlow School District in Oregon, whose exceptional practices are referenced throughout this book. They value and augment the rich cultures and strengths of students and their families who have in other instances been discounted and discarded.

More frequently, the needs of students have been dealt with by each professional differently within a school, depending on how those needs were perceived by the teacher or administrator (creating cohesion using the six principles of courageous leadership [Blankstein, 2013] is addressed in the following chapters). Moreover, students with the greatest needs have typically received the heaviest dose of punishment (Desautels, 2018). One has only to review *which* students are punished most severely vis-à-vis their peers, and *which* are most likely to be seen as "gifted," "college material," or "capable" of doing Advanced Placement work, in order to understand the enormous odds students of color, English learners, and students receiving special education face in even making their way *to* school, much less *through* school and on to college or a career. Such disproportionalities have been fixtures of our education systems for generations.

In addition, school professionals' "to-do" list—teaching, student and parent relationship building, counseling, lunchroom duty, attending evening meetings and school sporting events, meeting state testing mandates, and shelling out on average $500 worth of personal capital for supplies that their own students could never afford (Akhtar, 2019)—has left many emotionally and physically too drained to add one more thing to their work. This is true even if that "one more thing" is a deeper understanding of the lives of the students with whom they share most of their days. As the beleaguered city bus driver, likewise, shared with his "boss" after arriving late: "I would have been on time if it hadn't been for all those darned passengers!" It's easy to forget one's purpose when overwrought, undersupported, and serving too many masters.

COVID-19 Calls for Courage and Adaptability

We are now on the edge of a new frontier. Never before have millions of educators been pressed into so many different roles so quickly. The adaptations professionals have made are stunning. Adaptive leadership as described in Chapter 1 calls for finding new responses to situations for which there is no script (Rowe & Guerrero, 2012), and educators have risen to this challenge.

Never before have schools acted as first responders in delivering millions of meals to students' homes; tracking down students who can't be found; and making daily personal phone calls home to work with both students *and* their families, on whom they now heavily rely as partners. Veterans and those opposed to a "flat screen" as a potential substitute for delivering instruction in person have within weeks mastered technologies they would have successfully dodged for decades in the past.

A relatively traditional profession has turned into one that is filled with adaptive and courageous leaders at all levels, continuously solving problems never before seen while staying rooted in their "core purpose." Courageous leadership principles begin with finding one's purpose, and courage itself has been deemed by visionaries and leaders throughout time and across geographies—including the Oglala Sioux, Aristotle, Maya Angelou, Martin Luther King Jr., and Winston Churchill—as the most important of all virtues, without which there would be no other.

Before COVID-19, the value of educators and other child and youth care professionals was increasingly being called into question by a confluence of profiteering prison providers, policymakers, and private school entrepreneurs whose "competition" is publicly accessible and *successful* education for all children. Even steadfast parents who lauded their *local* educators were beginning to follow the drumbeat of devaluing the quality of education in their assessment of schools *nationally*. Just 19 percent of Americans gave the nation's schools an A or B grade, while many more gave an A or B to their local schools—44 percent, which is still less than half, and down from a high of 53 percent six years prior (PDK Poll, 2019).

Yet public school principals remain among the most trusted of all officials (Pew Research Center, 2019), and no one can deny the value of what our public education servants have brought to children worldwide at this moment in history. If New York City mayor Bill De Blasio indeed delivers on a ticker-tape parade for first responders, educators and youth professionals deserve to join hands with health professionals at the front of the line. Parents of all stripes—especially those economically challenged—can attest to this, as they have now found themselves "acting as teacher, counselor, and sometimes the principal!" (Katrise Perera, personal communication, April 29, 2020).

It's incumbent upon us all to reassert our crucial contribution to what is fundamental to our democracy: *public* education. This has been well understood and articulated for centuries:

> *The Whole People must take upon themselves the Education of the Whole People and must be willing to bear the expenses of it. (President John Adams in a letter to John Jebb, September 10, 1785)*

Today, education is perhaps the most important function of state and local governments. Compulsory school attendance laws and the great expenditures for education both demonstrate our recognition of the importance of education to our democratic society. (Supreme Court Chief Justice Earl Warren, 1954)

Now is the opportune moment to name, claim, and direct that goodwill for the betterment of our students' lives. This is one of the strategies for advancing equity and children's overall well-being shared in the section on "taking stock" to leverage current gains, and again more expansively at the end of this chapter.

WHAT'S NEW, AND WHAT CAN WE DO?

The COVID-19 pandemic is a world health crisis that has affected, and will continue to affect, generations to come. This is true of what has been sparked worldwide by the murders of George Floyd and Rayshard Brooks as well. Yet, as with any action, it is our *reaction* to it that will determine our future.

As we have learned from scores of psychologists beginning with Robert Ellis, according to the ABCs of cognitive psychology, in between the *action* and the *consequence* is the *belief* about that action, and this is *ours* to determine. If we change our belief, we change the consequence or outcome (Ziegler & Smith, 2004).

The fact is that many began changing their actions *first* during the pandemic. This has always been a valid means of changing people's beliefs as well: changing one's actions through some type of intervention (say, a new instructional approach) leads to a different, tangible consequence (say, low-performing students begin to excel), and finally beliefs change ("Wow, all students really can learn!").

During a crisis, this process is potentially expedited. "In normal times, I'm balancing between the accelerator and the brakes when it comes to change. During a crisis, I say, 'OK, I hear you, but the time for asking questions is done, and the time for a decision is now. We can't let perfect get in the way of great'" (Aaron Spence, personal communication, June 8, 2020). This has led to millions of educational converts: "Ah, I really *can* do things differently!" Or "I never really understood why Johnny couldn't bring his homework on time or at all. Now I do!"

Capitalizing on these new understandings will be the next great leap forward. Likely all teachers and principals miss the routine of seeing their students in school each weekday, and grieving that loss is appropriate.

Time, space, and support for this is called for in Chapter 3. Some teachers and principals may also find the level of change and uncertainty required by this crisis to be emotionally overwhelming and can in turn affect their teams' sentiments as well. In some larger cities like Minneapolis, it is estimated that this may affect as many as a third of the principals in the district (Eric Moore, personal communication, May 8 and June 5, 2020).

Adaptive leaders are less inclined to find solace in the idea of "things going back to normal." They are more oriented toward adapting new lessons learned to a new vision of education, and asking questions like "What should the new school look like? Why do kids come to school? What are they gaining from the prior paradigm? From the new one? What should we bring forward in a newly constructed environment?" (Rosa Atkins, personal communication, April 9, 2020). See Chapter 5 for how to build this into a new vision for your school.

Some powerful opportunities for *action* have been put before us by coronavirus. If we *believe* it is within our power to leverage these to create a more dynamic, thriving, and equitable learning environment for all of our students, then this is more likely to become the outcome, or *consequence*, of this pandemic.

Taking Stock of Coronavirus-Catalyzed Accomplishments and Opportunities

- *Determining what matters.* Throughout North America, scenes like the one described in Case Story 2.2 were repeated, and professionals set about finding a certain segment of missing students. Parents of other students unable to get online struggled with engaging their children using worksheets. Still others decided that education was larger than subject-specific test preparation and provided their own ad hoc, project-based learning while walking to a park or nearby creek. Clearly, students' physical and emotional safety became the number-one priority for schools to tend to, while the modality of instruction students received was wildly uneven at best. "After all of this, what is the purpose of grades?" asked Dan Domenech (personal communication, April 6, 2020). "Especially if only 40 percent of the students are going on to college, and for the rest it has no significance?"

- *What do students really need to learn?* In questioning the Massachusetts Comprehensive Assessment System standards, Sue Szachowicz (personal communication, April 26, 2020) asks: "Could we lead a good life without knowing about the Tokugawa Shogunate in Japan?" Fundamental questions can now be raised: What really matters? What do students need to survive *and* thrive? How can we best support *all* students' learning? What are the conditions that will enable their success in school *and* in life, and how can we create them? What should students know and be able to do, and how do we provide this in an equitably responsive manner?

Many schools and districts were beginning to ask such questions prior to the pandemic. Others began including underrepresented student and family voices in the determination of what is taught and how, how it is evaluated, and what supports are in place to ensure success. For others, as in Toronto, the protocols for gathering this information from a representative group of stakeholders and then systematically acting on it were already in place. In 2018, the TDSB's Enhancing Equity Task Force heard some of these underrepresented voices for the first time. They heard commentary that was difficult to listen to, but also became the basis of dynamic actions shared in Chapter 4 (John Malloy, personal communication, April 14, 2020).

- *Slaying sacred cows.* It's not all about adding more to our agendas. It's about narrowing our focus to what counts and getting rid of what doesn't—like seat time. Now that we have spent months educating students at a distance, doesn't it make sense to decouple seat time from determining a student's learning? "Seat time is the wrong end of the kid to be measured anyway," shares Katrise Perera (personal communication, April 29, 2020), superintendent of Gresham-Barlow School District in Oregon.

  Determining why students need to come to school, and how that need can best be met, is a good start. How can school schedules be revisited to reflect the new reality? At a cost of $120 million per building and a major financial shortfall ahead (Burnette, 2020), some are even considering the option of schooling happening at sites provided by partnering organizations (Rosa Atkins, personal communication, April 9, 2020), as referenced in Chapter 1. Yet if these or any other decisions are addressed in the absence of thorough consideration and planning for the most vulnerable students, we will have allowed the COVID-19 crisis to lead us further backward.

- *Acting on empathy and awareness regarding inequities.* It's one thing to know that a student shares a two-bedroom home with grandparents and six siblings; it's another thing to walk into that home. As educators "Zoomed" and sometimes *walked* into homes to connect with their students, if they hadn't already known, they became starkly aware of the circumstances in which those students lived—a world divided by inequities. The question is how to process this so that it is used to find solutions for reaching and teaching students and not as an excuse for pitying them and lowering expectations.

(Continued)

(Continued)

As mentioned in the debrief to Case Story 2.2, empathy is quite different from sympathy. Empathy is required for a principal in the Minneapolis Public Schools when he brings a computer to a homeless shelter to get a student started on a lesson, instead of dismissing the need for the student to do the work since he doesn't have the ideal setting in which to do it (Eric Moore, personal communication, May 8 and June 5, 2020). School plans may include gathering teams to digest what has been learned, modeling the adaptive leadership (problem-solving approach) needed to advance this into formalized actions, and building these new understandings into an improved set of protocols and the school culture (see Chapter 5).

- *Enhancing teamwork.* In the best cases, leadership has become more collaborative by necessity, rank has gone out the door, and everyone speaks their mind in real time (Aaron Spence, personal communication, June 8, 2020). Crystalizing what was learned about collaboration and turning it into new guiding protocols and expectations regarding direct and healthy communication is a way to transfer this gain beyond the crisis.

- *Nurturing new alliances.* New and often ad hoc partnerships, like those described in Case Story 2.2, have stretched the normal boundaries both outside of education and across networks within and between states. These can be grown among schools, community agencies, and businesses, which will be extremely helpful in the near future, especially as budget shortfalls loom (see Case Story 2.3).

- *Collaborate across regions to solve problems.* New, profession-alike networks have come into existence. In Virginia, for example, State Superintendent James F. Lane meets weekly with all superintendents to determine how best to support their needs. These new alliances can be solidified and intentionally grown as schools look ahead to the fall and beyond.

- *Crystalizing the value of caregivers and families as partners.* Reaching students, and planning for their participation in learning, has opened up a new vista of contact between school officials and many parents and caregivers. While home involvement in a child's education is a major factor in student learning and success (Đurišić & Bunijevac, 2017), it has not always been successfully nurtured, especially for families of lower socioeconomic status and those of color (Jensen, 2009). COVID-19 period contacts have changed this dynamic, and how this is handled can conceivably lay the groundwork for much success for those students in the future.

- *Traditional constraints are out the door.* Testing, instructional times, means of delivering instruction, and much more have become "negotiable." This leads to great opportunities for organized and visionary leaders and professionals at large to work with community and family partners to shape their futures.

- *The political capital of our profession is at a record high.* As indicated earlier, families are now taking on homeschooling, and the general population at large is aware of the actions of heroic educators making home deliveries of computers, academic lessons, clothes and food, and even self-styled entertainment to cheer up home-bound children. How this political capital is focused and spent in coming months and years will determine a great deal regarding the future of our profession and the students we serve.

CASE STORY 2.3

New Alliances Are Tapped in Supporting Students and Readying for Their Return

Wraparound services at Brockton High School were many and were easier to use when students were coming to school. Though the school staff set up hotlines for families in need, they couldn't physically assist in delivering an array of services: "We have no cleaning supplies. Can you help?" "We don't have Tylenol, and our child is sick." The school's security monitoring system flags emails that indicate the potential of high risk for a student, and the staff follow up immediately through crisis partners or directly. In this part of Massachusetts, COVID-19 is rampant, and some families think they will die anyway, so avoid the stigma of going to a doctor. It's easy to become hopeless here, as one student's note indicates: "Why should I do homework, when I probably won't survive this anyway?" On a follow-up call, the student's mother confirmed, "I'm more afraid for my child minus the structure of school, than I am of the virus."

The staff enlisted support of scores of local agencies, police, and others to create the most comprehensive and rapid response plans possible. Likewise, they are compiling a list of grief-related and culturally sensitive resources and supporting agencies in their planning for students now and upon their return. "We need to help students with loss of their grandparents, for example, who haven't had a ceremony or funeral to mark their passing," shared Sharon Wolder (personal communication, April 20, 2020), Brockton's

(Continued)

(Continued)

chief officer of student support services. "Different cultures have differing ways to grieve, and we have one hundred languages spoken here that we have to consider as well."

"When people do return to school," Wolder added, "we will not have 4,500 children show up on day one! We will stagger this, and this will be the same for staff, who will have to return earlier than the students and also will need grief counseling. Everyone's emotional well-being will come first, and there will be teams of people ready to address children's abuse, neglect, and/or anxiety related to their time away from school."

Breakthrough Leadership Already Underway

After a lecture at Indiana University, Cornel West (personal communication, February 5, 2004) once shared: "There have always been light-skinned brothers and sisters in the struggle with us . . . just not enough of you." Similarly, when faced with the exigency of an urgent situation, some educators have always found breakthrough solutions.

The mobility rate at McCarver Elementary School in Tacoma, Washington, hit a high-water mark of 200 percent, disrupting schooling for everyone. A new level of leadership was called for that went beyond the school boundaries to engage the Tacoma Housing Authority and ultimately to collaborate with fifty families to ensure housing stability, counseling, and job-training support for those families in exchange for them sending their children consistently to McCarver. The children, in turn, received International Baccalaureate classes to deepen their engagement rather than a remedial curriculum. Three years after the program was piloted, forty-five families were still participating, the mobility rate of McCarver Elementary School dropped to 75 percent, and both the students within the program *and* their peers who were not suffering housing insecurity made academic gains (Blad, 2014). Breakthrough solutions often come from "reframing," as seen in Case Story 2.4.

CASE STORY 2.4

Educators Become "Talent Scouts" to "Grow" *Emerging Scholars*

The Baltimore Emerging Scholars program has recently emerged as yet another breakthrough experiment and partnership—in this case between the Baltimore City Public Schools and the Johns Hopkins Center for Talented

Youth. It is designed to mine untapped potential in a school system where student test scores are nearly two grade levels below the national average.

In twenty-one schools across the city, the program introduces second-, third-, and fourth-grade students to above-grade-level lessons in architecture, engineering, and astronomy. Most of these schools rank in the bottom quartile in the state of Maryland, and even the schools' principals had to be convinced that they had any "gifted" students with "talent." The dialogue has since changed as the "talent scouts" shared new ways of looking at students, based on their strengths and potential.

The Center for Talented Youth sought out the partnership with the city schools because certain students—mainly Black and low-income—had largely been shut out of its programs, which benefit academically talented students in all fifty states and more than ninety countries.

Leaders there decided the key to finding a more diverse pool of students was not testing more children or lowering the bar for participation; it was finding another way to identify them. "Our focus is on those kids who have the strength in academics that we just have to try and uncover," said Amy Shelton, the center's interim executive director (Mitchell, 2019).

The leadership in Case Stories 2.3 and 2.4 was founded on breakthrough realizations that include the following:

1. All students have talents and can succeed at high levels.

2. Conditions can be altered to facilitate that success.

3. It is the job of the adults, not the children, to alter those conditions and disrupt the past stigmas, broken relationships, and backward thinking that has impeded these children.

4. New alliances and resources that include but are not limited to schools often need to be tapped to create these conditions for student success.

5. It is incumbent upon leadership at all levels to obtain and deploy resources necessary to accommodate all students' needs.

6. A primary resource for students' success is adults around them who see themselves as talent scouts, not gatekeepers, for those young people.

Resources will indeed be front and center in fiscal year 2020 and beyond in the United States if not in many countries worldwide. Yet, as underscored in a recent piece by Daarel Burnette, titled "Devastated Budgets and Widening Inequities: How the Coronavirus Collapse Will Impact Schools," the unique system of funding American education will exacerbate the problem for half of the nation's schools. Meanwhile, the other half will be left in far better financial stead. If left to chance, or its "natural" conclusion, this will be disastrous for a nation that already pales in international tests and other health indicators next to other major industrialized countries due to exactly this type of inequity. According to Burnette (2020),

> *Almost half of the nation's 13,000 school districts may be forced to make the deepest cuts to education spending in a generation—slashing programs and laying off hundreds of thousands of administrators, teachers and other staff—to fend off financial collapse brought on by the coronavirus.*
>
> *But while the economic impact on schools will be historic, it will not be random.*
>
> *The districts most at risk share demographic profiles—student populations that are heavily black, Latino and low-income—and one crucial trait of their budgets: They get more than half their revenue from state aid.*

In Case Story 2.5, we see how one such district beat the odds in coming back from the financial abyss. The breakthrough leadership in response to a profound crisis depended heavily on purposeful collaboration with state- and local-level bipartisan political officials as well as other community stakeholders. Students participated in the district's fundraising effort by gaining practice in grant writing. Like so many children in our educational system, these students required more in the way of resources to realize the district's promise of equity. While this is extremely inspiring and instructive at this juncture, we also have an even larger question to squarely face as numerous districts and schools must work with shrinking budgets in the coming year: Do we want to continue to disrupt our underlying systems, policies, and practices that keep our students from becoming their best selves? The end of this chapter addresses that question with nine breakthrough leadership strategies.

CASE STORY 2.5

Petersburg Rising: Out of Economic Ashes

Petersburg, located in central Virginia on the Appomattox River, is a city of thirty thousand residents who share a proud history. It had struggled for decades, however, by the time I (Marcus) had arrived as the new superintendent. Financially, things were about to get worse.

In an April 2016 *Progress Index* article titled "'Higher Powers' May Be Called On to Fix School System," Michael Buettner explained the saga of

Petersburg, its schools of 4,300 students, and the challenges facing the new school leadership team. The Petersburg challenges are similar to those in many other cities and states—West Virginia; Detroit, Michigan; Gary, Indiana; Camden, New Jersey—that have suffered departing industries and a declining tax base.

Financial Collapse

Petersburg was on the verge of financial collapse. Interim City Manager Dironna Moore Belton faced the City Council and a packed hall of angry residents to announce drastic cuts to city services, starting with schools, whose students were already among the lowest-performing in the state. Budget cuts would also include fire and police services in a city with an exceedingly high violent crime rate.

One month into the job, I learned the school district was unable to pay its bills; the city government was unable to make its funding transfers to schools. The contracted health insurance company refused to pay employee medical claims, the district was unable to make legally required employee retirement payments, utilities were delinquent, equipment and supplies were cut off, the contractor responsible for supplying school meals had threatened to discontinue deliveries, and the district was struggling to make payroll.

To make matters worse, just days before the opening of the new school year, the City Council cut the school district's budget by more than 30 percent of its approved allocations. This was how the school year began, much in the same way that the 2020–2021 school year will begin coast-to-coast for so many educators, children, and families.

Restoring Faith in the Leadership

The Petersburg City School Board was set to hire its ninth superintendent within fifteen years. When a school system is experiencing a superintendent turnover every two years or less, it does not have a superintendent problem; it has a school board problem. In an effort to stabilize the school system, state and local officials would take a different approach. They would make every effort to recruit, hire, and support an experienced leader with a solid track record.

Before going to Petersburg, I had a brief three-minute hallway conversation meeting with then Virginia governor elect, and 2016 Democratic vice-presidential nominee, Tim Kaine. That meeting led to my appointment as vice chair of Kaine's education policy transition team. Later I had opportunities to interact with Kaine's wife, Anne Holton. Holton would later become a pivotal influence in my transition to Petersburg.

(Continued)

(Continued)

Those who have worked closely with me saw attributes that helped me build enduring relationships, necessary to earn substantial support for Petersburg. They knew I viewed education as a ministry to children and families, had a results-driven work ethic, and was an empathic listener willing to embrace and implement ideas of others without compromising core values.

The governor, the secretary of education, and members of the general assembly (both Democrats and Republicans) wanted Virginia schools to be the best in the nation. In order to achieve their ambitious goals, they would need to provide better support for the state's lowest-performing schools. They believed Petersburg schools could be a model for others. During a presentation I made before the Virginia Senate Education and Health Committee, Senator Tommy Norment said, "I have seen a lot of Petersburg superintendents come and go, but this is the first time I have been encouraged about the future of Petersburg schools." The first step was agreeing to a memorandum of understanding that addressed the school board role and a plan for district improvement (please see the resources available at https://resources .corwin.com/BreakthroughLeadership).

Addressing Financial Shortfalls

The financial crisis required both immediate and sustained interventions. These were the steps taken:

1. *Reach out to committed allies.* Having built credibility and connection with those who could intervene quickly, the first calls were placed to top-level allies committed to this work in Petersburg. During my introductory press conference, State Secretary of Education Holton promised me and Petersburg, "From the governor's office on down, we're going to roll up our sleeves and help you."

   I placed a phone call to State Superintendent Steve Staples to inform him of the crisis and to seek assistance. Governor Terry McAuliffe invited state and local officials, to include members of his cabinet and staff, the Petersburg mayor, the city manager, the superintendent, the school board chair, and others, to brainstorm solutions. One solution was to modify the state lottery funding process to allow Petersburg schools to receive their allotment immediately in September as opposed to January of the following year, which is when the other 131 school districts in the state receive their funds.

   Over the next few months, the governor's office scheduled several additional meetings with members to address other shortfalls. State officials played an important role in support of teacher recruitment and retention. The Virginia Department of Education worked collaboratively with the Virginia Retirement System to change its policies to allow retired teachers to return as full-time teachers, and receive a teacher salary and maintain their full retirement benefits. The governor sent a letter to approximately five hundred recently retired teachers living within a twenty-mile radius of Petersburg, encouraging them to work in Petersburg schools.

2. *Enlist partners and volunteers.* Our partnerships with local organizations grew from thirty-five to two hundred (see Case Story 9.4 in Chapter 9) and filled many financial and human resource holes, including the following:

   - Mega Mentors and Petersburg Promise volunteers read to students, support classroom instruction, help provide basics like food, and so on.

   - The YMCA provided a Power Scholars summer program, which reversed the "summer slide" effect for our students.

   - Virginia State University provided teacher internships and recruitment.

   - Churches and other agencies assisted in upgrading our school facilities.

   - United Way provided a coordinator for the umbrella Petersburg City and Schools Partnership, which in turn collectively helped ensure student success.

3. *Turn structural weaknesses into strengths.* Once the pride of this community, our Peabody Middle School was in poor condition and flooded regularly as well. We had access to a better building, and despite community opposition, we closed Peabody and opened, with the help of thousands of volunteer hours, a newer and better school. This sent a positive message of pride and improvement overall, and better served our students.

4. *Turn political support into financing.* The state legislature helped to finance Petersburg at multiple points in this journey. To his credit, Emmett Hanger, co-chair of the Finance Committee and representative of a rural, White, relatively impoverished district, understood that they had more in common with Petersburg than they had with wealthy suburban districts.

5. *Engage students and access grants.* Students helped write grants and launch GoFundMe campaigns for band uniforms and instruments, which we also received from those the military bands and prior alumni donated. We received many grants, including one for technology from the state legislature, and funds from many philanthropies.

From Fiscal Instability to Award-Winning Budgets

While the city's financial stability improved, Petersburg was never able to fully restore funding cuts to schools. Yet staff were able to organize a "best practice" budgeting process and enforce a disciplined payment plan for debtors and monitored with surgical precision every expenditure. Three primary

(Continued)

(Continued)

strategies were used to ensure efficient and effective best budget and operations practices: (1) Conduct an audit of the budget, finances, and human resources. The audit revealed misalignment of resources. (2) Reorganize staff to better align with the corrective action plan. (3) Develop a five-year budget aligned to the five-year strategic plan. (4) Freeze hiring of nonessential vacant positions. (5) Collaborate with debtors to create a long-term plan to pay bills.

Within eighteen months, every bill was brought up-to-date and paid on time, and employees were able to receive pay raises. In 2018 and again in 2019, the Association of School Business Officials International presented Petersburg City Public Schools with the Meritorious Budget Award for excellence in school budgeting and reporting. This would not have been possible without the support and collaboration among state and local officials.

The Petersburg case is part of an extraordinary story that has become an award-winning film, *Petersburg Rising*, about how this district and community and the state of Virginia pulled together to change the trajectory of these students' lives. The end of this chapter provides strategies for advancing breakthrough leadership creatively with individuals and to shift entire systems.

Potential Breakthrough Leadership Strategies Moving Forward

It shouldn't be wholly on schools to figure out food issues and who eats, or mental health issues. We as a society need to do a better job of tackling these systemic problems. Hopefully, the prior oversimplification and magical thinking that schools will somehow make up for all the inequities of society is now seen for what it is: untrue. (Paul Reville, personal communication, April 21, 2020)

We need to be honest: We cannot reform something this monstrous; we have to abolish it. (Bettina L. Love)

The following is a list of successfully utilized strategies for augmenting and advancing breakthrough thinking and equitable outcomes for our students, their families, and society as a whole. The "aha" moments are coming at a rapid pace now as evidenced by hundreds of thousands of citizens worldwide marching in the streets for justice and against blatant and violent racism. The alchemy between seeing the ravages of inequities exposed by

COVID-19 and the rampant and ruthless violence perpetrated against people of color by those who are hired and paid to protect those same citizens has become an explosive force that can lead to enlightened actions to route the underpinnings of inequity and oppression.

Here are nine strategies to advance this work. They begin with optimizing simple "aha" moments that an individual may have in an interpersonal interaction, and move on to transforming a society.

1. *Use crisis as an opportunity to channel student energies.* Teachers have long taken advantage of "teachable moments" in which there is a student "aha" that can be leveraged to change behavior. Such moments have also been used to spark movements led by students such as Emma González and other Parkland, Florida, student activists; environmental activist Greta Thunberg; and Nobel Peace Prize winner Malala Yousafzai, to name a few.

   To demonstrate how to facilitate turning crisis into opportunity thinking, consider this as one of many possible strategies:

   While working with Rudy Espinoza, a gang interventionist in the Humboldt Park section of Chicago, Alan met a thirteen-year-old new Deuces gang inductee named Angie. When asked why she'd joined the gang, Angie replied: "Everyone is in the gang: my uncle, my friends, and my boyfriend." She nodded her head toward a young man standing a half-block away. A few minutes after we left, a Latin Kings posse drove by and took her boyfriend's life. When Rudy saw her at the funeral, he used the crisis to get her out of the gang: "I'm sorry about your boyfriend. I was close with him too. But this is what you signed up for. It will be you one day, unless you quit the gang. Here's how we can get you out together." She took Rudy up on the opportunity he offered, shortly after the crisis became clear.

   The combination of seeing the stark reality clearly and taking a better alternative forward can be used with individuals, as well as groups, in processing both what the realities are and what the options for moving forward could be.

2. *Leverage the moral high ground.* There is perhaps no other time in recent history when the population at large valued educators more than it does now. Collectively, educators have saved millions of lives since March 2020. It behooves professionals to leverage this attending goodwill toward ensuring positive changes and necessary resources to support all of our children and those who educate and care for them. Being rooted in a noble mission for the greater good of children allows professionals a strong foundation for vociferous advocacy for resources commensurate with the job at hand.

3. *Tap into enlightened self-interests.* The *Petersburg Rising* case demonstrates that rural White legislators voted to fund this city's schools, which were 99 percent African American, because they understood they had more in common with that locality than they did with wealthy suburbs. When business and policy leaders can see how their interests are connected to others who may not look like them, we will have fewer meatpacking plants closing due to an impoverished workforce, and fewer schools fighting *alone* for survival as well.

4. *Take the legal route.* An April 23, 2020, ruling by the United States Court of Appeals for the Sixth Circuit in Cincinnati "was a real breakthrough," stated Michael A. Rebell, professor at Columbia Teachers College. "This is the first time in more than four decades that there may really be an opening for some kind of broad-based federal right to education." The suit was brought by a handful of Detroit schoolchildren against the state of Michigan due to the horrendous conditions in which they were forced to learn (Walsh, 2020). What is the lesson for other breakthrough leaders?

5. *Refuse to pay for services not rendered.* At the moment this book is being written, there is a reassessment around paying for police protection by many who feel instead *threatened* by those services. There is a "defunding" movement taking place in cities, and nationally, while at the same time school districts facing tight budgets and seeking peaceful campuses have begun canceling their contracts with police departments (Beckett, 2020). Boycotts, similarly, have been a powerful and successful strategy to advance breakthrough thinking throughout the world for centuries. This is a very helpful strategy to consider alongside budgeting.

6. *Clarify the inexorable alternatives.* When Nelson Mandela was first offered his freedom after twenty-seven years of imprisonment, he declined. He knew that the alternatives for the ruling party weren't attractive: a growing and restless Black population, economic sanctions by an increasing number of nations, and potentially explosive civil unrest and violence were all predictable. The terms and conditions for accepting his own freedom were his: a fair and free election where the majority candidate rules. What should be our collective terms for shoring up the health of our children, and what will naturally occur if we stay on our current trajectory?

7. *Pass legislation that has financial impact.* The prison population began to climb exponentially in the United States following the passage of legislation in 1980 (Blumstein & Beck, 1999) allowing prisons to operate for profit (Southern Poverty Law Center, 2019; Stevenson,

2015). The outrage around the killing of George Floyd and others is being harnessed locally to defund police contracts with schools and city police departments, as well as advance legislation around protocols for policing nationally.

8. *Focus on high-leverage items.* Housing, for example, determines where children will go to school in much of North America, and what the tax base will be for schools in the United States. The Tacoma Housing Authority case demonstrates the power of stable housing in the lives of our children. Other countries, such as Singapore, have figured this out writ large. We could as well.

   Instead of redlining and other legally sanctioned exclusionary practices notably used in the United States (Rothstein, 2017), all neighborhoods or "housing estates" in Singapore were built to include comparable access to supermarkets, food courts, recreational facilities, hospitals, good schools, Mass Rapid Transit stations, and bus stops. Housing, likewise, was integrated, and battles for an exclusive flat to live in were minimized. Residents became acquainted with and friendly toward those from other nationalities or ethnic groups. Some fifty years later, Singapore society is one of the most equitable in the world, and the country's students rank among the top three in the Programme for International Student Assessment exams in all categories (Schleicher, 2019).

   For the first time in the last century and a half, Harvard University and numerous other Ivy League schools celebrated Juneteenth in 2020. In the months prior to these announcements, the United States government issued billions of dollars to sustain corporations closed down due to COVID-19. Anything is possible at this juncture, including full funding of schools and support systems such that equity is realized.

9. *Vote for children!* Education is barely on the ballot in many nations, especially during the pandemic. Yet every teacher strike in the recent past in the United States has led to better outcomes for educators and students. The issue isn't always about "not having enough money." It's about "not wanting to prioritize children and those dedicated to caring for and educating them." It's time to reprioritize.

WHAT IF WE DON'T SEIZE THIS MOMENT?

We are experiencing a collective "aha" moment like no other in modern-day history, the outcome of which has yet to be decided. Teachers can reach vulnerable students like never before and change their lives. Principals can tap into the newfound understanding of their staff and students and change their school cultures. District administrators can put systems into place to codify and extend these gains throughout the district and beyond. Collectively, and including newfound family, business, organizational, and policy partners, we can reconceive of the *real* needs of all our students and prioritize resources accordingly. (Read how others are planning and use the tools in Chapter 3.)

While COVID-19 has made clear both the crisis and the opportunity before us, there are many who would use this moment to consolidate power, and further disable the weak and voiceless among us. The *New York Times* article "Pandemic Tempts Leaders to Seize Sweeping Powers" (Gebrekidan, 2020) documents how even democratically elected governments worldwide have seen this as an opportunity to encroach on personal liberty and freedoms in the name of "safety." The future will no doubt be determined by those who adamantly proclaim and shape it.

Courage—the virtue considered above all others by visionaries, poets, civil rights advocates, ancient societal elders, and world leaders—was originally not about vanquishing the "enemy" or giving up one's life on the battlefield. It was about sacrificing one's immediate desires for the common good of those in the village in greatest need (Eastman, 1902). Children were, and no doubt still are, among those in greatest need. If you're in education or youth care, you've already displayed great courage. Who better than you to use the power of this virtue and our breakthrough awakenings to speak and act on the truth and thereby help reshape the future?

> *If not* you, *then who? If not now, then* when? (Hillel the Elder)

REFERENCES

Akhtar, A. (2019, August 15). 31 teachers across the US reveal their exact salary, and how much of it goes to paying for school supplies like chalk and pencils. *Business Insider*. https://www.businessinsider.com/how-much-teachers-spend-on-basic-school-supplies-2019-8

Beckett, L. (2020, June 1). Minneapolis public school board votes to terminate its contract with police. *The Guardian*. https://www.theguardian.com/us-news/2020/jun/01/minneapolis-public-school-end-police-contract

Blad, E. (2014, December 9). K–12, housing partner to aid homeless students. *Education Week*. https://www.edweek.org/ew/articles/2014/12/10/housing-partnership-aids-homeless-students.html

Blankstein, A. M. (2013). *Failure is not an option: 6 principles that advance student achievement in highly effective schools*. Corwin.

Blumstein, A., & Beck, A. J. (1999). Population growth in U.S. prisons, 1980–1996. *Crime and Justice, 26*, 17–61. www.jstor.org/stable/1147683

Buettner, M. (2016, April 16). "Higher powers" may be called on to fix school system. *The Progress Index*. https://www.progress-index.com/article/20160416/news/160419716?template=ampart

Burnette, D., II. (2020, May 8). Devastated budgets and widening inequities: How the coronavirus collapse will impact schools. *Education Week*. https://www.edweek.org/ew/articles/2020/05/09/devastated-budgets-and-widening-inequities-how-the.html

Carson, C. (Ed.). (2001). *The autobiography of Martin Luther King, Jr.* Warner Books.

Desautels, L. (2018, March 1). Aiming for discipline instead of punishment. *Edutopia*. https://www.edutopia.org/article/aiming-discipline-instead-punishment

Đurišić, M., & Bunijevac, M. (2017). Parental involvement as a important factor for successful education. *Center for Educational Policy Studies Journal*, 7(3), 137–153.

Eastman, C. (1902). *Indian boyhood.* McClure, Phillips & Company.

Edmonds, R. (1979, October). Effective schools for the urban poor. *Educational Leadership*, 37(1), 15–24. http://www.ascd.org/ASCD/pdf/journals/ed_lead/el_197910_edmonds.pdf

Edwards, K., Evan, G., & Schwam, D. (2020, April 8). Parenting through the pandemic: Who's working, who's caring for the kids, and what policies might help. *The RAND Blog*. https://www.rand.org/blog/2020/04/parenting-through-the-pandemic-whos-working-whos-caring.html

Gebrekidan, S. (2020, March 31). Pandemic tempts leaders to seize sweeping powers. *The New York Times*, A1.

Jensen, E. (2009). *Teaching with poverty in mind: What being poor does to kids' brains and what schools can do about it.* ASCD.

Love, B. L. (2020, June 12). An essay for teachers who understand racism is real. *Education Week*. https://www.edweek.org/ew/articles/2020/06/12/an-essay-for-teachers-who-understand-racism.html

Mitchell, C. (2019, December 12). Mining for gifted students in untapped places. *Education Week*. https://www.edweek.org/ew/articles/2019/12/12/mining-for-academic-talent-in-untapped-places.html

National Center for Education Statistics. (2020, May). Concentration of public school students eligible for free or reduced-price lunch. In *The condition of education 2019* (NCES 2019-144). U.S. Department of Education. https://nces.ed.gov/programs/coe/indicator_clb.asp

PDK Poll. (2019, September). *Frustration in the schools: Teachers speak out on pay, funding, and feeling valued.* The 51st Annual PDK Poll of the Public's Attitudes Toward the Public Schools. https://pdkpoll.org/wp-content/uploads/2020/05/pdkpoll51-2019.pdf

Pew Research Center. (2019, September 19). *Why Americans don't fully trust many who hold positions of power and responsibility.* https://www.pewresearch.org/politics/2019/09/19/why-americans-dont-fully-trust-many-who-hold-positions-of-power-and-responsibility/

Rothstein, R. (2017). *The color of law: A forgotten history of how our government segregated America.* Liveright.

Rowe, W. G., & Guerrero, L. (Eds.). (2012). *Cases in leadership.* SAGE.

Schleicher, A. (2019). *PISA 2018: Insights and interpretations.* OECD. https://www.oecd.org/pisa/PISA%202018%20Insights%20and%20Interpretations%20FINAL%20PDF.pdf

Simon, R. (n.d.). *The in-session breakthrough fantasy.* Psychotherapy Networker. https://www.psychotherapynetworker.org/blog/details/80/the-in-session-breakthrough-fantasy

Southern Poverty Law Center. (2019, December 9). *Prison by any other name: A report on South Florida detention agencies.* https://www.splcenter.org/20191209/prison-any-other-name-report-south-florida-detention-facilities

Sparks, S. D. (2020, February 10). Number of homeless students hits all-time high. *Education Week*. https://www.edweek.org/ew/articles/2020/02/12/number-of-homeless-students-hits-all-time-high.html

Stevenson, B. (2015). *Just mercy: A story of justice and redemption*. One World.

Tutu, D. (2016). Foreword. In A. M. Blankstein & P. Noguera (Eds.), *Excellence through equity: Five principles of courageous leadership to guide achievement for every student* (pp. vii–ix). ASCD.

Walsh, M. (2020, April 29). Right to education ruling jolts education advocacy world. *Education Week*. https://www.edweek.org/ew/articles/2020/04/29/right-to-education-ruling-jolts-education-advocacy-world.html

Winkler, A. (2011). *Gunfight: The battle over the right to bear arms in America*. Norton.

Ziegler, D. J., Smith, P. N. (2004). Anger and the ABC model underlying rational-emotive behavior therapy. *Psychological Reports*, *94*(3), 1009–1014.

CHAPTER 3

The First Hundred Days—A Pandemic Reentry Plan

It was a difficult time for everyone. The stock market had plunged, nearly one-fourth of the workforce was unemployed, many parents didn't know how they were going to feed their children, in rural areas farmers were talking openly of a revolution, and protest crowds were growing in the streets. The year was 1929, the lowest point of the Great Depression, which would last for ten years. On March 4, 1933, the crowd that assembled in Washington, DC, in front of the Capitol to watch the inauguration of President Franklin D. Roosevelt had given up on America. However, it turned out to be the beginning of a transformation.

During the first hundred days of Roosevelt's presidency, he presented a series of initiatives to the Seventy-Third United States Congress to counter the impact of the Great Depression. He began to move with unprecedented speed to address the problems facing the nation in his inaugural address, declaring: "I am prepared under my constitutional duty to recommend the measures that a stricken nation in the midst of a stricken world may require" (Walsh, 2009). Roosevelt's specific priorities at the outset of his presidency were getting Americans back to work, protecting their savings and creating prosperity, providing relief for the sick and elderly, and getting industry and agriculture back on their feet (Keith, 2017).

On the hundredth day of his presidency, Roosevelt recited a list of his accomplishments during one of his famous radio fireside chats before an audience of sixty million listeners, resulting in a remarkable turnaround of public trust. The legislation included the creation of federal deposit insurance to reopen banks and institution of the New Deal—a variety of projects and programs designed to provide relief, recovery, and reform. He created the Securities and Exchange Commission, the National Labor Relations Act, the Federal Deposit Insurance Corporation, Social Security, and the Fair Labor Standards Act of 1938. He also signed legislation to end Prohibition and provide assistance to farmers (to produce wheat, dairy products, corn, and tobacco, among other crops). These actions produced mixed results. Following a remarkable turnaround, the economy relapsed into a deep recession in 1937 and 1938. Even so, much of the legislation enacted in Roosevelt's first hundred days is still in operation almost a hundred years later.

It should be mentioned that, along with his many accomplishments, Roosevelt had moments of extraordinary bad judgment—not the least of which was Executive Order 9066 calling for the internment of more than 112,000 Americans of Japanese ancestry following the invasion of Pearl Harbor. In 2019, the United States government paid more than $1.6 billion in reparations to survivors of the internment camps and their heirs.

Recovery from the COVID-19 pandemic is a unique opportunity for our nation to offer its students a New Deal, where every student can have an equal and equitable opportunity to experience the Declaration of Independence's recognition that everyone is "endowed by their Creator with certain unalienable Rights, that among these are Life, Liberty and the pursuit of Happiness." This is not a time for small tweaks or adjustments to our education systems, but a time for big, bold, ambitious, innovative, courageous, and breakthrough leadership. Ideally, government, business, civic, and education institutions will work collaboratively to develop a New Deal for education. However, it may be more realistic for grassroots local school communities to take the lead in working with these institutions.

President Roosevelt's most famous quote is "The only thing we have to fear is fear itself." Leaders cannot be afraid of change or failure. Public health and economic experts agree that the key to post-COVID-19 economic recovery begins with reopening day care centers and schools. Other countries, including China, Germany, France, and South Korea, have recognized that reopening schools when it is safe to do must be a national priority (Francis, 2020). Planning for your first hundred days should begin weeks before the first day of the plan, and must include first and foremost the health and emotional well-being of staff and students. Consider Case Story 3.1 from the Brockton Public Schools in Massachusetts.

CASE STORY 3.1

Brockton's Approach to Reopening Schools

by Sharon R. Wolder, Chief Officer of Student Support Services

One of the first steps taken by our district was establishing a call team of nurses, counselors, and bilingual liaisons. These professionals were issued phones and asked to reach out to families in need. Members of our call team speak the languages of most of our students and families. They also understand the cultures of the families so that they can identify the right resources or approaches to support them. The district is committed to having people available to communicate directly with families and help them navigate all of the changes related to learning from home as well as accessing resources and coping with loss.

Brockton has the second-highest rate of COVID-19 cases in the state, which necessitated the closure of most businesses, mandatory masks, and a 9 p.m. curfew. The school district is seeing the impact on adults, as well as the trauma children are experiencing, as they grapple with the impact of this virus. During the closure, the system has struggled to provide technology resources, keep students engaged, and ensure they have adequate amounts of food. In the midst of learning how to run the district remotely, we became aware of students whose families were battling the virus and then of those who lost a member because of COVID-19. Immediately, we had to determine how to provide meaningful support from a distance. Our approach has been to enlist district administrators to deliver food and hygiene products to families in need. Counselors, principals, and teachers call and speak with students or family members to share condolences, ask about their needs, and encourage students to honor their loved one by sharing positive memories or using creative expression such as pictures, songs, and poems in tribute to the person they lost. Most importantly, this outreach is ongoing: the counselors or members of the call team stay in continual contact with students and their families in the absence of school buildings where, in normal times, students would find support from faculty and peers.

Students and families have emerged with different needs in the face of the crisis. Keep in mind that as some move forward with adjusting to the changes caused by this pandemic, those who have suffered personal loss require higher levels of support. Therefore, schools need to be aware of individual students' experience, understand where each student is in the grieving process, and develop a thoughtful and individualized approach to supporting the social and emotional needs of all students while moving them forward academically. This district has designated grieving students as *Handle With Care* to ensure the educators who work with them next school year are aware they have experienced a greater level of trauma during the shutdown.

Several resources used to inform our thinking and practices can be found at https://resources.corwin.com/BreakthroughLeadership.

In some cases, entire states are coordinating trauma relief. James F. Lane, Virginia's superintendent of public instruction, said that as schools reopen, "ameliorating this trauma will be at the core of their mission. I also think that there is a need for us to focus on social and emotional learning for students, and not only how we can provide the academic support, but how can we provide the mental health support and the wraparound supports for students when they come back, to help them recover and bring back that safety net of schools" (Kamenetz, 2020).

For a growing number of districts, equity is at the core of their reopening plans. Eric Moore, chief of accountability, research, and equity for Minneapolis Public Schools, builds equity-mindedness in the district leaders using an "Equity Consideration Process" (ECP) in which all new initiatives require completion of a form to answer key questions: What is the change? Who is impacted by it? What will be the positive and negative impacts? How can we mitigate any negative ones? The ECP forms are reviewed by an equity, diversity, and impact assessment committee of sixteen organizations that address issues for students of color. The process is designed to build capacity by making people who are leading change consider equity issues before beginning the change process.

Case Story 3.2, from the Orange County Schools in North Carolina, demonstrates another multifaceted and interlocking team-planning approach for which the overarching steering committee is focused on ensuring equity and voice for those often underrepresented in such critical decision making.

CASE STORY 3.2

Planning to Reopen More Equitable Schools

by Dena Keeling, Chief Equity Officer

I have five subcommittees to the Closing the Gap and Acceleration Committee, respectively addressing each of the following:

1. Intensive summer and remote learning with a focus on students who are difficult to reach (Our state is requiring all districts to have a remote learning plan.)

2. School reentry, including all state guidelines, logistics, pedagogy changes, busing, food, safety protocols, temperature checks, equipment, and procurement of masks, sanitizer, and other personal protective equipment

3. Accessibility via technology for *all* students, including English learners and students with disabilities

4. Human resources/human capital (When we take into account existing staff shortages, staff absences on account of illness, budget cuts, and early retirements, we face a personnel shortage.)

5. Communication at district and school levels, including plans conveyed to community partners and parents, new alliances with mental health organizations and professionals who are constantly on the ready, and other needs not yet determined

The Closing the Gap and Acceleration Committee coordinates and reviews plans from all five subcommittees to ensure a focus on our "Center Students." Equity-minded, diverse, and innovative, this guiding committee developed questions for each of the subcommittees to address. For example, the state required that every student have access to a device. The appropriate subcommittee then added: What accommodations are needed for students with disabilities or who speak other languages?

Our curriculum needs to have evidence that it will work for our African American students, our homeless students, and other marginalized groups. Normally, the district would come up with a plan for 80 percent of students and then tweak it for our Center Students. We've reversed that.

Think About It

Who is involved in creating your plan for school reopening? Are those involved representative of all stakeholders and students? Do they bring the necessary contacts and experience to engage the larger community and financial supporters? What is your paradigm for decision making?

One major consideration at the forefront of planning for reopening schools is referenced in Chapter 2: What do students need to know, and how can we best meet that need? The tendency following this world pandemic may be to rush into reopening schools, yet the case stories just told would caution a more thoughtful approach.

Another area in which we might miss an opportunity is in attempting to meet the basic needs of staff and students, at the expense of attending to their more robust needs and abilities. "Robust equity" addresses this.

Robust Equity: From Surviving to Thriving

by David Osher, Jill Young, and Rob Mayo

▶ Equity is more than equal access to shallow learning. *Robust* equity is multidimensional. It builds on our best knowledge that all children and youth can and should thrive—socially, emotionally, cognitively, physically, economically, and spiritually. It is not only mindful of thriving but sets thriving as the goal for young people. It recognizes that well-being in one domain contributes to well-being in others. Robust equity addresses individual and collective dimensions of thriving.

Within educational settings, this means addressing students' academic needs through culturally responsive after-school tutoring or small-group sessions in multiple languages that also support students' emotional well-being during moments of local or global crisis. This might include small-group sessions with bilingual staff in an after-school setting and collaborating with community-based organizations and public agencies (see, for example, Osher et al., 2018). Robust equity intentionally counters inequality and institutionalized privilege and prejudice, and creates conditions that support overall well-being.

For example, far too many students, particularly those of color and those with disabilities, disproportionately experience the negative effects of harsh exclusionary discipline, due to stress, attitudes, and mindsets of staff and a lack of support for students. Similarly, providing equal access to Advanced Placement (AP) classes is not enough. We must also provide social and emotional support and mental health services to address challenges that limit meaningful participation in AP and International Baccalaureate, including identity, stereotype threat, implicit bias, unmet mental health needs, and unequal opportunities to learn.

Robust equity is possible (see Darling-Hammond et al., 2020). We can design and support conditions that focus on opportunities to learn and develop, including *the quality of instruction* (see Chapter 8). Development-rich environments are culturally responsive and provide opportunities for students to wonder, think critically and deeply, develop their identity, express themselves, develop their social and emotional skills, and experience meaning and spiritual engagement.

We can also realize equity by improving *school climate*—that is, the conditions for learning and development, such as physical and emotional, connectedness and belonging, challenge and adult engagement, peer and adult social and emotional competence, restorative approaches to discipline, and cultural competence and responsiveness.

The quality of content and *the amount of learning time* are additional factors in achieving equity in a school. Young people benefit from environments that can help them realize their full potential as intelligent, creative, socially responsible, critical thinking whole persons.

Learning from and with students, we find that many youth of color, as well as students who are economically disadvantaged, students with disabilities, and students who are LGBTQIA+, face barriers to learning that limit their opportunities to reach their potential in general, or in particular areas, which has been amplified by COVID-19. *Necessary supports* may be physical, social, emotional, and psychological.

These supports post-COVID-19 will include mental health services as needed that avoid stigma, labeling, and segregation, and are (1) culturally competent, responsive, and humble; (2) child centered and youth, consumer, and family driven; (3) individualized; (4) strengths based and building; (5) contributory to thriving; and (6) family, school, and community based. Effective wraparound approaches provide a useful framework.

We must avoid a simplistic notion of just focusing on the basics and catch-up because resources are tight. This approach will be counterproductive and reinforce inequity during a historical moment when mental health needs are likely to rise universally along with poverty. Given the pandemic, we will need to double down on relationship and community building, norms setting, and restorative practices, which include but are not limited to culturally responsive social and emotional learning strategies, opportunities for healing and repairing harm, and attention to minimizing suspension and eliminating corporal punishment and racial harassment and microaggressions.

Triaging efforts away from well-being supports—including trauma-sensitive mental health services—will contribute to health ill-being. Triaging efforts away from deeper education and creativity and culturally responsive social and emotional learning will undermine the ability of our graduates to be entrepreneurial, to be socially responsible, and to gain good jobs at a time when jobs will continue to be replaced by artificial intelligence and robotics and when community economic development is particularly important. This is the moment to go beyond minimizing what our students need and can do. Instead, we must support their identity development, critical thinking, and civic engagement in order to provide the individual and collective skills to work for change that eliminates inequality and promotes equity.

Table 3.1 is a planning tool for you and your team to consider for the first hundred days of school.

TABLE 3.1 Pandemic Reentry Plan: Recommendations for the First 100 Days

Phase I Preentry	Organize your team to create a new vision for change	• Coordinate reopening plan with local government officials. • Clearly define shared purpose and direction for innovative change. • Develop a unifying purpose statement that the entire community can understand, including students.
	Listen and learn	• Commit to scheduling between 50 and 100 meetings to include employees at all levels, families, and professional organizations. • Use a combination of face-to-face and digital meetings to engage education stakeholders.
	Review and analyze budget	• There is a direct correlation between successful school systems and a strong local economy. Collaborate with your local government to advocate for education and appropriate funding. In most communities, education is the largest funding allocation category. School systems employ the largest workforce, transportation system, and food service system, and maintain the most facilities. During financially challenging times, local governments make the largest percentage of budget cuts to school budgets to help fund other local government agencies like health and human services, safety, and streets. *Fight for fair funding for your students.* • The federal government has authorized funding to assist K–12 and higher education to help mitigate the negative impact of COVID-19 on schools. Use these funds in a creative and innovative way to help ensure you close equity, opportunity, and achievement gaps. • **Study strategies of successful school leaders and innovators.** *Consider breakthrough strategies from Chapter 2!*
	Engage the team in asset mapping	• As opposed to focusing on what you have lost or do not have, focus on your assets—your organization's gifts and talents. • Maximize use of community resources. There are countless community organizations that want to help, but no one from the school district may have ever reached out to them. Don't be afraid or embarrassed to ask for help. • Frequently, there are redundancies in school programs and resources. Taking inventory of your assets and eliminating redundancies can result in significant savings.

| Phase II Entry Plan | Conduct equity audits | • Schools experienced inequities prior to COVID-19, and they have widened during the pandemic.
• When students return to school, conduct equity audits to determine student needs and opportunities for growth.
• Identify barriers to equity.
• Conduct visual audits:
  ○ Observe demographics of students enrolled in honors and advanced classes.
  ○ Observe demographics of students enrolled in career and technical education classes.
  ○ Observe demographics of students enrolled in special education classes.
  ○ Observe demographics of community committees, parent-teacher association, and teacher leaders.
• Conduct listening audits:
  ○ Listen and talk to students about classroom diversity, discipline, and fairness.
  ○ Listen to teachers speak to determine if they are communicating high or low expectations and equity or inequity.
  ○ Listen to what school board and other elected officials are saying.
• Review equity data:
  ○ Monitor and review equity opportunity and achievement gaps.
  ○ Monitor and review discipline, attendance, and referral data by subgroup.
  ○ Monitor and review human resources data by race, gender, and ethnicity.
  ○ Implement a real-time data dashboard. |
| | Build trust through honest, transparent, and consistent communication | • You can never overcommunicate. You cannot count on the media or anyone else to communicate your message. Be proactive. President Roosevelt earned the trust of the American people in part by conducting 30 national fireside chats in his first year. Use a variety of tools to communicate frequently:
  ○ Face-to-face communication with individuals and focus groups
  ○ Social media
  ○ Digital conferencing
  ○ Digital newsletters
  ○ Key communicators—parents and community advocates who can help share your message |

(Continued)

TABLE 3.1   (Continued)

		• Be visible and responsive. Ensure that people know how to contact you. • Remain open to new ideas. • Bury your ego, and be willing to accept good and bad feedback. • Communicate progress and setbacks. • Treat everyone with respect, even your critics.

	Provide a safe place for students and staff	• Anticipate the basic physical and psychological needs of students and staff.
		• Follow Centers for Disease Control and Prevention guidelines for reopening:
		  ○ Train all students and staff in appropriate safety precautions (handwashing, social distancing, etc.).
		  ○ Sanitize and disinfect surfaces.
		  ○ Encourage students and staff to stay home if they are sick.
		• Establish a strong relationship with your local health department.
		• Order supplies as soon as possible (face masks, sanitizer, disinfectants, gloves, etc.). Some of these items are in short supply, so plan extra time for shipment and delivery.
		• Visually observe and monitor students for stress or signs of unhealthy behaviors, and seek assistance from support professionals (counselors, social workers, psychologists, school nurses, etc.).

	Assess academic needs of students	• Assess the academic status of every student to determine a baseline necessary to create personalized learning plans for every student aligned to state standards and performance indicators. • Revisit tiered interventions for supporting individual academic needs of students. • Review and update individualized education plans.
	Act and implement	• Implement your version of the New Deal. • Reorganize district leadership structures based on evolving needs of students and available resources. Given the national economy, educators may be required to do more with less. Determine how you will ensure student growth with fewer resources. • Hire innovators and divergent thinkers. • Shift professional development focus to support digital learning.

- Monitor and evaluate the success of your initiatives, and don't be afraid to eliminate them if they are not producing results.

- Anticipate new challenges and opportunities before they occur.

- Report progress.

- Establish a network with school leaders in other districts. During COVID-19 school closures, superintendents and other leaders engaged in weekly Zoom meetings, webinars, and strategic planning sessions to remain up-to-date on new information and recommendations. Maintain these relationships.

Schools are starting to look very different. To make up for learning loss, some districts have converted to a year-round schedule. As James F. Lane, the Virginia superintendent for public instruction, told NPR, "I think there will be opportunities for us to discuss different ways to approach calendars." He has also encouraged school officials to develop school calendars with multiple options that consider opening, closing, and reopening if future outbreaks of COVID-19 occur (Kamenetz, 2020).

Maria Litvinova, a researcher at the Institute for Scientific Interchange in Turin, Italy, argues that without treatments or a vaccine, "there is no such thing as 'safe' reopening" (Kamenetz, 2020).

Nevertheless, it is important to balance safety with the impact on families and the economy. Some schools are limiting social contact by bringing students to schools in shifts, thus decreasing class sizes. At the Copenhagen International School in Denmark, students are grouped in classes of ten (Kamenetz, 2020). COVID-19 risk to healthy children is very low. However, the risk to students with preexisting conditions and their teachers is much greater.

The need for remote or distance learning is likely to continue, even after school reopenings. The challenge will be to maintain equity for students learning in school buildings and at home.

Art Stellar, former superintendent of the Burke County Public Schools in western North Carolina, strongly believes an entry plan ought to serve as a reality check. A well-thought-out entry plan will pay huge dividends in the long term.

Chapter 4 lays the foundation for "relational trust" using six principles proven effective in developing high-performing and equitable schools.

REFERENCES

Darling-Hammond, L., Flook, L., Cook-Harvey, C., Barron, B., & Osher, D. (2020). Implications for educational practice of the science of learning and development. *Applied Developmental Science*, 24(2), 97–140. https://doi.org/10.1080/10888691.2018.1537791

Francis, L. (2020, May 13). Schools reopening will likely be different in every state. In *Fatherly*. Yahoo! Life. https://www.yahoo.com/lifestyle/schools-reopening-likely-different-every-170435855.html

Kamenetz, A. (2020, April 24). 9 ways schools will look different when (and if) they reopen. In *All things considered*. NPR. https://www.npr.org/2020/04/24/842528906/what-it-might-look-like-to-safely-reopen-schools

Keith, T. (2017, April 21). President Franklin D. Roosevelt set 100-day standard. In *All things considered*. NPR. https://www.npr.org/2017/04/21/525110119/president-franklin-d-roosevelt-set-100-day-standard

Osher, D., Moroney, D., & Williamson, S. (Eds.). (2018). *Creating safe, equitable, engaging schools: A comprehensive, evidence-based approach to supporting students*. Harvard Education Press.

Walsh, K. (2009, February 12). The first 100 days: Franklin Roosevelt pioneered the 100-day concept. *U.S. News & World Report*. https://www.usnews.com/news/history/articles/2009/02/12/the-first-100-days-franklin-roosevelt-pioneered-the-100-day-concept

CHAPTER 4

Relational Trust as a Foundation for the Equitable Learning Community

Change is technically simple, but socially complex. (Michael Fullan)

In the past, the technical aspects of a given model (like differentiated instruction) or process for shaping cultures (like professional learning communities) have gained widespread acceptance. The relationships and human side of change, however, are often left to chance (Batista, 2018; Osher et al., 2020). This chapter is focused on recent data that correlate "relational trust" with student success. In essence, every effective, sustainable professional learning community (PLC) and high-performing school that we have worked with in the past twenty-five years was founded on a consensus of what it means to be such a community and on relational trust.

The issue of trust has become both more fraught and more crucial for students' well-being than at any time in recent history. Incidents of bullying, discrimination, racism, and violence involving adults as well as children have been increasing dramatically since 2016 (Hassan, 2019). Students and families, meanwhile, are arguably more vulnerable than at any time since the Great Depression and need a sense of physical and psychological security, continuity, and belonging. They need to feel they can count on those who are assisting them, including educators and caregivers of all varieties. These professionals have, by default, often become first responders in giving the lifeline of hope and sustenance that they had come to be counted on to provide prior as well. Destiny, a homeless student, clarifies:

I'm on edge all day long. . . . Everything was really good until recently. I'll survive. It's just actually really hard. . . .

School was my outlet. . . . It's just a really small, loving community. Everyone goes above and beyond to help. (Morton, 2020)

Under these circumstances, it is essential for professionals to understand the dynamics of building and sustaining trust. The next section addresses the meaning, importance, and development of *relational trust*.

RELATIONAL TRUST ACROSS DIVIDES

Relationships are at the core of successful learning communities as well as student success (Aceron & Guerrero, 2018; Bryk et al. 2010; Burden, 2020; Konishi & Wong, 2018). This is particularly true for students of color in their schools (Brooms, 2019; Ferguson, 2002; Hackett et al., 2018). A study of middle schools concluded "one of the most striking features identified by teachers and administrators in higher-performing middle schools and credited as the primary reason for their success is 'respectful' and 'trusting' relationships" (Wilcox & Angelis, 2009, p. 7). As one administrator stated, "the single, most important thing . . . is to build trust with your faculty" (Wilcox & Angelis, 2009, p. 12). Positive relationships have been found to be significantly "essential to a child's ability to grow up healthy and achieve later social, emotional, and academic success" (Ewing Marion Kauffman Foundation, 2002, p. 1; see also Adams, 2014).

Those positive relationships begin with the adults in the school building and district (Bryk & Schneider, 2002). The personal rapport among teachers, students, and parents influences students' school attendance and their sustained efforts at difficult school tasks (Van Eck et al., 2017). The history of relationships between the principal and the teaching staff determines teachers' willingness to take on new initiatives, and the relationships among adults in the school greatly influence the extent to which students in that school will succeed academically (Aceron & Guerrero, 2018; Bryk et al., 2010; Kutsyuruba et al., 2015; Scales et al., 2020). In essence, if the adults in the building get along, so will the students.

The relationship among adults is an area for potential improvement in a great many schools. This is true of industry as well; a 2009 international study revealed that the majority of people trust a stranger more than they do their boss! (Segalla, 2009; Sturt & Nordstrom, 2018). The corollary to schools in terms of performance in high-trust companies is similar: high-trust organizations outperform their low-trust peers by 286 percent total return to shareholders (Zalabak et al., 2010). While it is relatively easy to install the technical aspects of a PLC—systems to collect data, time for teams to meet, and so on—the tough part is subtler, less scripted, and more human (Blankstein et al., 2007).

Building meaningful and productive relationships with people is complex; people are less predictable, and their emotions can be scary! How many school leaders have been trained in the many nuances of dealing with an angry parent, a disgruntled staff member, or a crying teacher? Where is the how-to manual for these tasks? Moreover, who has time for these things when the "real" work of increasing student achievement awaits?

Another complicating factor is that educational staff do not resemble the students they are teaching (Boisrond, 2017; Miller, 2018). At the same time, numerous studies have affirmed that students of color achieve at higher levels and are significantly more likely to graduate from high school and go on to college if they have teachers of color (Darling-Hammond et al., 2020; Rosen, 2018).

Recruiting and retaining faculty of color, likewise, requires more than placing "Equal Opportunity Employer" at the bottom of the advertisement. In Petersburg, Virginia, for example, the school district worked closely with a nearby historically Black university, Virginia State, to bring in interns, and to co-host job fair recruitments. Many districts are putting in place plans for retention of diverse staff as well (Susan Enfield, personal communication, May 13, 2020).

Think about what your school or district can do to recruit and retain staff who have a variety of experiences and cultures that support their ability to relate to and speak for their students. How can you most effectively utilize the talents of these staff members to sensitize other staff to the needs of all students? What special supports will be needed to ensure all on staff feel welcomed and heard?

Building trusting relationships in tense and otherwise "untrusting" times requires great sensitivity and awareness of "the other." Yet relationships *are* the real work of school improvement! Without people, whom exactly will administrators be leading, and how far will followers be willing to go?

Defining Relational Trust

The concept of "relational trust" came from a five-year study of achievement in math and literacy in twelve Chicago public schools by the Center for Urban School Improvement at the University of Chicago. As discussed in Bryk and Schneider (2002), these systematic case studies were augmented by researchers' clinical observations and field notes. The research results demonstrated that high-trust schools were three times more likely to improve in reading and math than those with very weak levels of trust, and *those that remained low-trust over the course of the study had virtually no chance of improving* in either reading or math.

The concept of *relational* trust in schools focuses on distinct role relationships and the obligations and expectations associated with each. When these expectations are met, trust is enhanced. When one person's expectations of another person are not met, trust is diminished.

There are four components of relational trust:

1. *Respect* for the importance of another person's role, as well as viewpoint. Listening carefully augments a sense of respect and builds trust (Leis et al., 2017).

2. *Competence* to administer one's role. This includes the ability to act on what was heard. On the building level, it is also associated with having respectful discipline, an orderly and safe school, and meaningful instruction and assessment.

3. *Personal regard for others.* Highly associated with reducing others' sense of vulnerability and with general caring, this is especially demonstrated by extending oneself beyond the requirement of one's role or normal duties—finding out about a staff member's personal challenges, helping teachers develop their careers, and so on.

4. *Integrity*—in this context, alignment of words, actions, and ethics. Do others keep their word, and are their intentions ethical? (Bryk & Schneider, 2002, pp. 23–26)

Communication is multifaceted and can be enhanced with an understanding of the framework shown in Figure 4.1. Thus, if the adults in the building cocreate a project with one another and/or with students, the shared reality

FIGURE 4.1 Communication Framework to Enhance Affinity

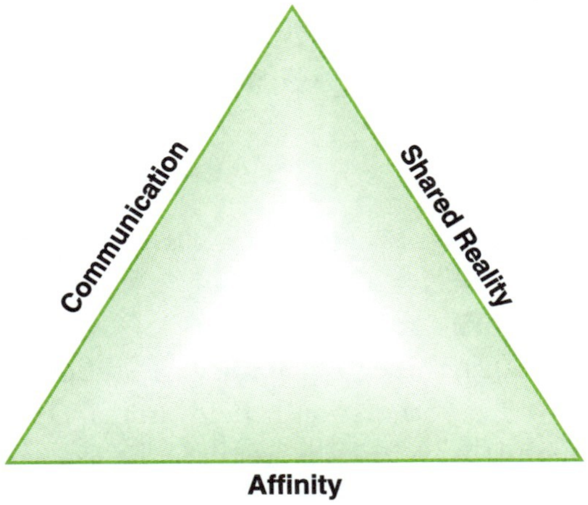

SOURCE: Blankstein, A. M. (2013). *Failure is not an option: Six principles that advance student achievement in highly effective schools* (3rd ed.). Corwin.

is expanded, leading to more communication and greater affinity. If any side of the triangle is activated, then there is a greater chance to strengthen the other two sides.

Relationships During and Following a Crisis

The challenge of building trust in general often comes in *listening* to others (respect) and their beliefs about your behavior (competence, personal regard, and integrity). For this reason, it is best to check in with people to determine their perspective of a given situation.

It is especially likely during and directly following a crisis that people's true feelings and opinions are not heard, or even voiced. This may not seem to be the case as those with stronger personalities may weigh in even more during a crisis than at other times.

Still others will not express their sentiments, fears, or sense of inadequacy to address the tasks at hand. In many situations, like wartime, expression of one's feelings is not even encouraged, and processing time isn't available to anyone.

Leaders need to find a way to tap into people's real thoughts and feelings, if not during the immediacy of the crisis, then soon thereafter. Making a literal space and time for this with "no fault" and "no assumptions" protocols in which each person has the opportunity to speak without interruption will be helpful. Having each person choose a partner to debrief a question prior to sharing with the group is also a valid technique.

Currently, school leaders are faced with an immediate crisis of shrinking budgets. The following account details breakthrough leadership responses to extreme budgetary cuts that were made during the 2008 recession.

Building Trust Over Time

▶ During the recession that began in 2008, when the budget in Chesterfield County, Virginia, was cut by over $100 million, the school district used six strategies to help build staff and community trust:

1. Transparency in communications, planning, and forecasting—consulted with economists to project trends and communicated them with weekly updates to all employees

(Continued)

(Continued)

2. Staff and community voice—posted a survey for the staff and community, allowing everyone a voice in prioritizing their funding and budget cut preferences, with results published by local media

3. Community budget advisory committee—organized to include teachers and staff; parents; business, civic, and faith representatives; and elected officials to inform them and listen to their recommendations and concerns

4. "Myth busting"—posted on the district's home web page any myth or rumor (both of which during times of crisis run rampant) brought to administrators' attention and corrected it with empirical facts

5. "Budget 101"—visited every school and department to provide a session to educate employees on the budget process, share rationale for decisions, and respond to concerns

6. Counseling—met with individual employees most impacted by budget cuts or experiencing stress and anxiety to provide support

Think About It

What kind of communication strategies seem helpful in this case? How could they become embedded in your school culture?

Strategies for Building Trust

Building relational trust with the staff is a precursor to sustainable success. In our work in thousands of schools and districts, this trust has been built by the leader using various approaches.

One-on-One Strategies

Build one-to-one relationships: Invest consistent time in building one-on-one relationships. For example, schedule weekly or monthly lunch meetings with the mayor, city manager, school board members, union leaders, and other community members.

Look for the good in others: Appeal to the moral and noble motives in everyone. Help others see what they have to offer and validate them, especially those who have been hurt or disappointed.

Listen first: It's essential to recognize that everyone wants to be heard. The new-leader syndrome, however, often entails changing things quickly to establish authority. Many veteran leaders, on the other hand, may feel they already know what is best and may move forward without building consensus. In both cases, the "slow" part—listening—of going fast is cut out of the process, and initiatives are short-lived.

The "listen first" strategy has many components:

1. *Show appreciation via understanding the other point of view.* Surprisingly, effective communication has more to do with emotions than with logic, or intellectual "clarity" (Fisher & Shapiro, 2006). Most often problems arise when people don't *feel* understood. In addition to using simple paraphrasing and checking for understanding (e.g., "I am hearing you say XYZ"), the effective listener will tap into meta-messages that are not directly spoken and then inquire further. For instance, "There are too many mandates!" may also mean "I don't feel capable of meeting new standards." Listening to "the music as well as the words" (Fisher & Shapiro, 2006) means tapping into the emotional tenor of the speaker: "I am *not upset*, thank you!" would indicate a message that belies the words.

2. *Finding merit in what the person does, thinks, or feels is important in showing appreciation.* This is true even if you don't agree with the speaker's point of view. In Chapter 2, we saw a change process that involved getting naysayers engaged. In practice, it looks something like this: "I know how hard you worked on the past initiative, only to see it abandoned. I appreciate that kind of effort, and understand how it might be difficult to see a new direction enter on the heels of all that work. I only ask that you consider this new approach for now, see how it unfolds, and advise me of your feelings and thoughts about it."

3. *Communicate understanding in words and actions.* We can accomplish this not only by listening to, accurately identifying, and then voicing the concerns of our staff people, but also by taking many actions, such as the following example of a breakthrough response to crisis.

   When I (Marcus) began to discuss achievement gaps in Chesterfield County almost twenty years ago, segments of the community immediately became defensive, seeing it as a racial initiative, where students in middle-class communities would be penalized. We framed the discussion using subgroups defined by the federal government: racial and ethnic groups, economically disadvantaged, students with disabilities, and students with limited English proficiency. We did not compare subgroups against one another, but we measured the success of every group using a standard of 100, demonstrating that every group had gaps, regardless of race or socioeconomic status. Then we communicated a plan to support closing gaps for every group. Instantaneously, the fears of the community were put to rest.

4. *Show appreciation for yourself as well!* This can be done in a positive way that puts you and the listener on the same side: "Like you, I worked very hard on student achievement using the prior set of standards. I don't know how you feel about it, but on my worst day, I feel like I may have wasted a lot of time. It's not easy to move forward, but I feel good that I have made that decision . . ."

5. *Make the work about doing what is in the best interest of* all *students.* Educators go into this business because they want to make a positive impact on children. Every parent wants to know that you want what is best for their child.

Find common ground: Finding areas of commonality may be the best way forward—even when they are few in number. Uncovering the underlying issues helps. In practice, one might say something like this: "The research indicates that holding students back in early grades does not work, but I can see your point about the need for there to be some 'rework' in the instruction before Johnny can advance . . ."

Overcommunicate: As the Chesterfield recession story indicates, it is best to do a lot of listening in the relationship-building process. Checking in with people to align their perceptions and your intentions as a leader is also critical. To that end, it helps to clearly communicate your own perspective or point of view—and to do it often. If this is vague for people, or if there is a void of communication, it is often filled in with other fears, worst-case scenarios, and rumors.

Confront inappropriate behaviors: There is little that will undermine a leader more than to ignore inappropriate behaviors. While it enables people to avoid a short-term conflict, it also erodes trust in the leader. The outcome is that respect for the leader and confidence in the school community's ability to succeed is diminished among those who *are* adhering to the agreed-upon norms.

Organizational Strategies

Create fail-free zones: While confronting behaviors is necessary, so is indicating in advance the rules by which people will be judged. Failing in a pilot project or doing poorly in a new instructional practice, for example, should be off-limits. Refusing to be coached, to collaborate, or to modify one's instruction when data reveal the need to do so, by contrast, may be among the areas in which a learning community would require intervention. Here are some specific ways to create fail-free zones:

- Adopt a "never finished" stance and expectation in which the new norm is that there is always a better way and continuous improvement is our job (Wilcox & Angelis, 2009, p. 13).

- Eliminate blame as a recourse or conversational option.

- Clarify expectations collaboratively with staff, and ideally students, so that everyone is in agreement and fear of failure or fault is reduced.

- Engage staff on a voluntary basis initially to gain support and build capacity. In the past, leadership teams we worked with often introduced learning walks in a nonthreatening manner beginning with volunteers, calling it peer-to-peer, and avoiding any formal evaluations initially. Beginning with the few and the willing in massive change efforts has been leapfrogged. Now the issue is about codifying the changes already made in a participatory and inclusive manner that builds trust and equitable results.

Enlist student voice: In every major community- and district-wide convocation and assembly, spotlight selected elementary and secondary students to serve as master and mistress of ceremonies to demonstrate and showcase the talents and gifts of students.

Share bad news: Earn trust by creating a culture where the school system is the first to report bad news to the community, when possible, on issues such as school assaults, weapons violations, threats, environmental issues, and so on.

Process Tools for Building Trust

Another example of going slow to later go fast is to develop the staff's capacity for making the change by creating a common language and knowledge base. This can be facilitated by teams working on a meaningful project together using a structured format. For an example of this, visit this book's companion website (https://resources.corwin.com/BreakthroughLeadership) and under Chapter 4 resources locate "Creating a Common Rubric for Defining Excellent Instruction."

DEFINING A TRUE "LEARNING COMMUNITY"

> *School districts should not try to simply build a learning community that has as many definitions as there are people defining it. The emphasis should be on restructuring how people work together. That's what ultimately has an effect on the classroom.*
> (Nelda Cambron-McCabe, quoted in LaFee, 2019)

For more than a decade, a growing confluence of research and practice has indicated that our best hope for success in schools is through the creation of

PLCs (Brown et al., 2018; Burden, 2020; Washington, 2018). This is very good news indeed. It seems to provide clear direction for educators who are contemplating substantive school change. At the same time, it invites as many questions as it answers.

- What is a learning community in practice?
- What are the key elements for making such a community succeed?
- How do I know if I have succeeded in creating such a community?
- What are my next steps in the process of creating and sustaining a learning community?

There are many definitions of a *professional learning community*. We include a summary of these, as well as a brief background on the rise of interest in this area, in the next section. We also introduce readers to the concept of *equitable learning communities*, or ELCs, later in this chapter.

More important than the use of one definition or another, however, is the common understanding of what such a community looks and feels like, how one behaves in this context, what the mutual commitments are, and how all of this affects students in general and their academic achievement in particular. It is more common to find school professionals who say they are part of a "learning community" than it is to actually find a PLC in operation, much less an ELC. In fact, a shadow version of true learning communities, "performance training sects" (Hargreaves, 2003, p. 176), provides intensive pressure and support for teachers in a limited number of instructional priority areas. While student performance is enhanced, it is rarely sustained and comes at the expense of other instructional areas, though this can be combated (Darling-Hammond et al., 2017). Moreover, the research indicates that teachers dislike such highly prescriptive programs (Kiemer et al., 2018), which often diminish their long-term commitment to their work (Lambersky, 2016). There are many possible reasons for the disparity between the number of schools that see themselves as PLCs and those that actually are. In contrast to such shadow versions of learning communities, Hargreaves and Fullan (2015) have advocated for PLCs that undertake collaborative inquiry as a way to provide teachers with greater agency in improving their practice. As we saw in Chapter 1, making fundamental changes and shifts in assumptions, beliefs, and actions is difficult. It is far easier to make slight modifications to old behaviors and then give the effort a new name. Moreover, this can be reinforcing, because some of these modifications actually *do* bring about modest changes. For example, it would be easier to schedule times when teams meet—a technical "fix"—than to build a true collaborative culture in the school—an adaptive shift (see Chapter 1). One is structural, easily implemented, and *may* still have the benefits of creating a more motivated staff. The other, however, would require more time, an effective school mission (defined in Chapter 5), and deeper conversations about the meaning and focus of the collaboration. This *collaborative culture* would also require discipline to maintain a focus on student learning.

Clarifying terminology *alone* requires time and effort. W. Edwards Deming (1986) wisely called for developing "operational definitions" before undertaking a new project. One might ask whether the dishes are clean, but answering the question operationally depends on knowing why the dishes are needed and why they must first be clean. A plate may be clean enough to eat from but still be stained. Operationally, which definition is more important?

Many schools striving to become ELCs, for example, are challenged to reach a common understanding of what that means.

What Is Equity?

In this book, we define *equity* as providing all students what they need to succeed (Blankstein et al., 2016; Center for Public Education, 2016). Since everyone is different, professionals would be required to reach and teach students differently as well. As parents, we do this naturally—each child doesn't get the same clothes, food, and drink at the same time. This is because they all have different interests and needs, *and because we know them*. In Chapter 6, we share in greater depth the implicit biases, systems, and structures that lead people astray of ELCs.

What Is Community?

The schools that I have observed usually share a strong motivation to learn new teaching practices and a sense of urgency about improving learning for students and teachers. What they lack is a sense of individual and collective agency, or control, over the organizational conditions that affect the learning of students and adults in their schools. (Richard Elmore, 2002, p. 24)

This sense of *collective* agency and control over organizational *conditions* is embodied in the *community* of ELCs. Many schools—especially high schools—lack these qualities. These schools do not often benefit from the deeper meaning implied in the term *community*.

Cohesive Communities

There are several definitions of the word *community*. Here are two:

1. Common character, similarity, or likeness, as in *community* of spirit
2. The people living in the same district, city, or other area under the same laws

The second definition is more commonly used. It is easier for a group of school professionals to achieve this definition since they generally work together, under the same rules, in the same location.

The first definition, however, is closer to how we would describe the ideal school community—one that leads to sustainable student achievement. "Community is concerned with the deep-structural fabric of interpersonal relations" (Gardner, 1991). "Soundly woven, this fabric permits a shared frame of reference and supports mutual expectations" (Rossi & Stringfield, 1997, p. 3). More recently, cohesive communities have been found to be very beneficial (Wepner & Gómez, 2020).

Relationships and trust are the glue that holds this kind of community together. A professional community is built on more than a pay-for-service contract in which adults and children run for the exits when the final school bell rings. It is built on more than common geography. It goes beyond symbiosis, common rules, or policies that bind all to *minimum* behaviors. This kind of community is founded on mutual respect, concern, caring, reliability, and commitment to a common, larger cause. In short, it is founded on relational trust as described in the previous section.

Creating common understandings, therefore, is hard work. Getting commitment from the school community is even more difficult. And changing fundamental assumptions or beliefs is harder still. Yet, these are the challenges inherent in building a true learning community, and the payoff for doing so is enormous. The chapters on building a courageous leadership imperative and overcoming common pitfalls provide a foundation for beginning an enduring, sustainable learning community. The next sections of this chapter indicate the evolution of learning communities and more definition around the terms used in defining such a community.

ORIGINS AND DEFINITIONS OF THE "LEARNING COMMUNITY"

Peter Senge (1990) first used the term *learning organization* in his best seller, *The Fifth Discipline*, and the term soon made its way into the education literature. Thomas Sergiovanni (1992) translated one of Senge's five principles—"team learning"—to an educational context: "The idea of school as a learning community suggests a kind of connectedness among members that resembles what is found in a family, a neighborhood, or some other closely knit group" (p. 47).

The terms continued to evolve, as noted in Table 4.1.

TABLE 4.1 Evolution and Research Base for Principles Guiding High-Performing Learning Communities

DATE	AUTHOR	TERMINOLOGY	GUIDING PRINCIPLES
1997	Shirley Hord	Professional learning community	1. Supportive and shared leadership 2. Shared values and vision 3. Collective learning and application 4. Shared personal practice 5. Supportive conditions
1998	Richard DuFour and Robert Eaker	Professional learning community	1. Shared mission, vision, values, and goals 2. Collective inquiry 3. Collaborative teams 4. Action orientation and experimentation 5. Continuous improvement 6. Results orientation
2004, 2010	Alan Blankstein	Failure is *not* an option	1. Shared mission, vision, values, and goals 2. Prevention and intervention 3. Collaborative teams 4. Data-based decisions 5. Family and community engagement 6. Sustainable leadership capacity
2013	Wallace Foundation	Five key principles	1. Shaping a vision of academic success for all students 2. Creating a climate hospitable to education 3. Cultivating leadership in others 4. Improving instruction 5. Managing people, data, and processes to foster school improvement

(Continued)

TABLE 4.1 (Continued)

DATE	AUTHOR	TERMINOLOGY	GUIDING PRINCIPLES
2015	National Policy Board for Educational Administration	Professional Standards for Educational Leaders	1. Mission, value, and core values: Effective educational leaders develop, advocate, and enact a shared mission, vision, and core values of high-quality education and academic success and well-being of each student.
			2. Ethics and professional norms: Effective educational leaders act ethically and according to professional norms to promote each student's academic success and well-being.
			3. Equity and cultural responsiveness: Effective educational leaders strive for equity of educational opportunity and culturally responsive practices to promote each student's academic success and well-being.
			4. Curriculum, instruction, and assessment: Effective educational leaders develop and support intellectually rigorous and coherent systems of curriculum, instruction, and assessment to promote each student's academic success and well-being.
			5. Community of care and support for students: Effective educational leaders cultivate an inclusive, caring, and supportive school community that promotes the academic success and well-being of each student.
			6. Professional capacity of school personnel: Effective educational leaders develop the professional capacity and practice of school personnel to promote each student's academic success and well-being.
			7. Professional community for teachers and staff: Effective educational leaders foster a professional community of teachers and other professional staff to promote each student's academic success and well-being.
			8. Meaningful engagement of families and community: Effective educational leaders engage families and the community in meaningful, reciprocal, and mutually beneficial ways to promote each student's academic success and well-being.

DATE	AUTHOR	TERMINOLOGY	GUIDING PRINCIPLES
			9. Operations and management: Effective educational leaders manage school operations and resources to promote each student's academic success and well-being.
			10. School improvement: Effective educational leaders act as agents of continuous improvement to promote each student's academic success and well-being.
2019	Dion Burns, Linda Darling-Hammond, Caitlin Scott, et al.	Common strategies of 7 "positive outlier" districts in California	1. A widely shared, well-enacted vision that prioritizes learning for every child 2. Continuous leadership from instructionally engaged leaders 3. Strategies for hiring, supporting, and retaining a strong, stable educator workforce 4. Collaborative professional learning that builds collective instructional capacity 5. A deliberate, developmental approach to instructional change 6. Curriculum, instruction, and assessment focused on deeper learning for students and adults 7. Use of evidence to inform teaching and learning in a process of continuous improvement 8. Systemic supports for students' academic, social, and emotional needs 9. Engagement of families and communities
2020	Alan Blankstein and Marcus Newsome	Equitable learning communities	See the six principles in this chapter below.

Equitable Learning Communities

Synthesizing the research from the sources in Table 4.1, and factoring in research on effective schools, the United States Department of Education's criteria for excellent schools, and our own practice in the field, we have distilled the essence of ELCs into the following six principles:

1. Common mission, values, vision, and goals toward equitable outcomes for all students

2. Comprehensive systems for prevention and intervention

3. Data-based decision making for continuous improvement

4. Collaborative teaming toward engaging and culturally responsive curriculum, instruction, and assessment

5. Meaningful engagement with families and community

6. Sustainable leadership capacity at all levels

These principles encompass the focus on student learning and collaboration emphasized in the research. In addition, these principles are inclusive of the Professional Standards for Educational Leaders (PSEL) (National Policy Board for Educational Administration, 2015). Our sixth principle explicitly calls for the development of sustainable leadership capacity. Given the extraordinary rate of turnover in educational leadership and the tendency toward "launching" versus "sustaining" learning communities, we have found this principle to be critical to the success of our work with schools throughout North America. Similarly, as cited in Wood and Bauman (2017), "circles of support" research, and the PSEL, we have found that actively engaging family and communities (our fifth principle) is essential for long-term support and sustainability of school initiatives. This has been particularly true in times of great change, economic downturn, or intense media pressure on schools. Chapter 9 provides an abundance of research correlating enhanced student achievement and family support. Figure 4.2 summarizes "look-fors" in ELCs.

The prior synthesis of research and our own relevant experiences are presented as an explanation of how we arrived at these working principles for ELCs. Having "one best definition" for this or any other school improvement effort is counterproductive and defies all that we know about change efforts. In fact, there is danger in becoming too attached to one certain speaker, program, or set of principles. It is far more important that whatever is practiced is internally aligned, consistent with the research, and focused on student success. "Various definitions exist . . . but they all feature a common image of a professional community where teachers work collaboratively to reflect on their practice, examine evidence about the relationship between practice and student outcomes, and make changes that improve teaching and learning" (McLaughlin & Talbert, 2006, pp. 3–4).

Taking a cue from the medical profession, it is advisable to continually scan for new best practices and to stay current with changes in the research:

Here on our first day of med. school, we were presented with the short white coats that proclaim us part of the mystery and the discipline of medicine. During that ceremony, the dean said some-thing that was repeated throughout my education: "Half of what we teach you here is wrong—unfortunately, we don't know which half." (Sanders, 2003, p. 29)

FIGURE 4.2 Equitable Learning Communities: Trust and the Learning Community

How do you know if you are working in an equitable learning community? Consider (with a smile) these possible indicators:

You know you are in an equitable learning community when . . .

- You enter the school building and are warmly greeted by a parent volunteer, regardless of their or your race, color, or creed.
- Staff help make decisions about issues affecting them.
- There are means of policy creation and dispute resolution that are informed by the larger community including credible organizations representing traditionally marginalized people.
- You see articles with highlights all over them posted in the teacher lounge, or posted online.
- You are actually *happy* to see another teacher or an administrator visiting your classroom to observe instruction.
- Colleagues have a safe space in which to discuss sensitive issues, and do so regularly.
- Those who are making key decisions are representative of the student body and include student voice in many direct and indirect ways.
- Colleagues stop by your home on the weekend . . . to talk about work!
- Enhancing student learning is the primary focus of team meetings, and best practices for enhancing their achievement as well as sense of safety and belonging drive decisions.
- SMARTER goals (see Chapter 5) are set, regularly assessed, and achieved.
- Last year's "worst behaved" fourth grader is tutoring a second grader this year.
- During professional development days, the *last* rows of seats are the ones left empty.
- You cannot tell the difference between an Advanced Placement and core content class by instructional approach or which students are in attendance.
- The principal says, "I don't know. Let's research this together."
- When the final bell rings, the teachers and principal aren't the first ones out the door!

MOVING FORWARD

This chapter was meant to serve as a final checkpoint. In this chapter, we provided you with the framework and system for moving forward with a foundation of trust. Now, you are prepared to take action. The rest of this book will emphasize specific processes for building such a sustainable, equitable learning community, beginning with Chapter 5 on creating a common mission, vision, values, and goals.

REFERENCES

Aceron, L. O., & Guerrero, J. G. (2018). Principals' relationships towards teachers: Its impact to schools' management and success. *International Journal of Recent Innovations in Academic Research*, 2(6), 178–185. https://www.ijriar.com/docs/volume2/issue6/IJRIAR-12.pdf

Adams, C. M. (2014). Collective student trust: A social resource for urban elementary students. *Educational Administration Quarterly*, 50(1), 135–159. https://doi.org/10.1177/0013161X13488596

Batista, M. (2018). *The moderated relationship between emotional intelligence and burnout in K–12 teachers* [Unpublished doctoral dissertation]. Capella University.

Blankstein, A. M. (2004). *Failure is not an option: Six principles that guide student achievement in high-performing schools*. Corwin.

Blankstein, A. M. (2010). *Failure is not an option: Six principles that guide student achievement in high-performing schools* (2nd ed.). Corwin.

Blankstein, A. M., Cole, R. W., & Houston, P. D. (2007). *Engaging every learner* (Vol. 1). Corwin.

Blankstein, A. M., & Noguera, P. (with Kelly, L.). (2016). *Excellence through equity: Five principles of courageous leadership to guide achievement for every student*. ASCD.

Brooms, D. R. (2019). "I was just trying to make it": Examining urban Black males' sense of belonging, schooling experiences, and academic success. *Urban Education*, 54(6), 804–830. https://doi.org/10.1177/0042085916648743

Brown, B. D., Horn, R. S., & King, G. (2018). The effective implementation of professional learning communities. *Alabama Journal of Educational Leadership*, 5, 53–59.

Bryk, A. S., Bender Sebring, P., Allensworth, E., Luppescu, S., & Easton, J. Q. (2010). *Organizing schools for improvement*. University of Chicago Press.

Bryk, A., & Schneider, B. (2002). *Trust in schools: A core resource for improvement*. Russell Sage Foundation.

Burden, P. (2020). *Classroom management: Creating a successful K–12 learning community*. John Wiley & Sons.

Burns, D., Darling-Hammond, L., Scott, C., Allbright, T., Carver-Thomas, D., Daramola, E. J., David, J. L., Hernández, L. E., Kennedy, K. E., Marsh, J. A., Moore, C. A., Podolsky, A., Shields, P. M., & Talbert, J. (2019, September 10). *Closing the opportunity gap: How positive outlier districts in California are pursuing equitable access to deeper learning*. Learning Policy Institute. https://learningpolicyinstitute.org/product/positive-outliers-closing-opportunity-gap-report

Center for Public Education. (2016, January). *Educational equity: What does it mean? How do we know when we reach it?* https://cdn-files.nsba.org/s3fs-public/reports/10901-4496-16_CPE_%20Equity%20Symposium_FINAL.pdf?LKIv6zrRE08mxahlArLZ8PdfeQzWahY2

Darling-Hammond, L., Burns, D., Campbell, C., Goodwin, A. L., Hammerness, K., Low, E. L., McIntyre, A., Sato, M., & Zeichner, K. (2017). *Empowered educators: How high-performing systems shape teaching quality around the world*. Jossey-Bass.

Darling-Hammond, L., Flook, L., Cook-Harvey, C., Barron, B., & Osher, D. (2020). Implications for educational practice of the science of learning and development. *Applied Developmental Science*, 24(2), 97–140. https://doi.org/10.1080/10888691.2018.1537791

Datnow, A., & Castellano, M. (2000). Teachers' responses to Success for All: How beliefs, experiences, and adaptations shape implementation. American Educational Research Journal, 37(3), 775-799.

Deming, W. E. (1986). *Out of the crisis*. MIT Center for Advanced Engineering Study.

DuFour, R., & Eaker, R. (1998). *Professional learning communities at work: Best practices for enhancing student achievement.* Solution Tree Press.

Elmore, R. (2002). Hard questions about practice. *Educational Leadership, 59*(8), 22–25.

Ewing Marion Kauffman Foundation. (2002, Summer). Set for success: Building a strong foundation for school readiness based on the social-emotional development of young children. *The Kauffman Early Education Exchange, 1*(1). http://dx.doi.org/10.2139/ssrn.2355477

Ferguson, R. (2002). *What doesn't meet the eye: Understanding and addressing racial disparities in high-achieving suburban schools.* North Central Regional Educational Laboratory.

Fisher, R., & Shapiro, D. (2006). *Beyond reason: Using emotions as you negotiate.* Penguin Random House.

Gardner, J. (1991). *Building community.* Independent Sector.

Hackett, E. M., Ponterotto, J. G., Zusho, A., & Jackson, M. A. (2018). Rising out of the gap: Early adolescent black males and academic success. *The Qualitative Report, 23*(10), 2561. https://nsuworks.nova.edu/tqr/vol23/iss10/19/

Hargreaves, A. (2003). *Teaching in the knowledge society.* Open University Press.

Hargreaves, A., & Fullan, M. (2015). *Professional capital: Transforming teaching in every school.* Teachers College Press.

Hassan, A. (2019, November 12). Hate-crime violence hits 16-year high, F.B.I. reports. *The New York Times.* https://www.nytimes.com/2019/11/12/us/hate-crimes-fbi-report.html

Hord, S. M. (1997). *Professional learning communities: Communities of continuous learning and improvement* (ED410659). ERIC. https://eric.ed.gov/?id=ED410659

Kiemer, K., Gröschner, A., Kunter, M., & Seidel, T. (2018). Instructional and motivational classroom discourse and their relationship with teacher autonomy and competence support—findings from teacher professional development. *European Journal of Psychology of Education, 33*(2), 377–402.

Konishi, C., & Wong, T. K. Y. (2018). Relationships and school success: From a social-emotional learning perspective (pp. 103–122). In B. Bernal-Morales (Ed.), *Health and academic achievement.* IntechOpen.

Kutsyuruba, B., Klinger, D. A., & Hussain, A. (2015). Relationships among school climate, school safety, and student achievement and well-being: A review of the literature. *Review of Education, 2*(2), 103–135. https://doi.org/10.1002/rev3.3043

LaFee, S. (2019). *Professional learning communities: A story of five superintendents trying to transform the organizational culture.* AASA, The School Superintendents Association. https://www.aasa.org/SchoolAdministratorArticle.aspx?id=9188&terms=A+story+of+five+superintendents+trying+to+transform+the+organizational+culture

Lambersky, J. (2016). Understanding the human side of school leadership: Principals' impact on teachers' morale, self-efficacy, stress, and commitment. *Leadership and Policy in Schools, 15*(4), 379–405.

Leis, M., Rimm-Kaufman, S. E., Paxton, C. L., & Sandilos, L. E. (2017). Leading together: Strengthening relational trust in the adult school community. *Journal of School Leadership, 27*(6), 831–859. https://doi.org/10.1177/105268461702700603

McLaughlin, M. W., & Talbert, J. E. (2006). *Building school-based teacher learning communities: Professional strategies to improve student achievement.* Teachers College Press.

Morton, N. (2020, May 24). Homeless students set adrift by school closures face crisis after crisis. *The Hechinger Report.* https://hechingerreport.org/im-on-edge-all-day-long-schoolwork-a-mere-afterthought-for-homeless-youth/

National Policy Board for Educational Administration. (2015). *Professional standards for educational leaders*. https://www.npbea.org/wp-content/uploads/2017/06/Professional-Standards-for-Educational-Leaders_2015.pdf

Osher, D., Cantor, P., Berg, J., Steyer, L., & Rose, T. (2020). Drivers of human development: How relationships and context shape learning and development. *Applied Developmental Science, 24*(1), 6–36. https://doi.org/10.1080/1088869 1.2017.1398650

Rosen, J. (2018, November 12). Black students who have one black teacher are more likely to go to college. *The Hub*. https://hub.jhu.edu/2018/11/12/black-students-black-teachers-college-gap/

Rossi, R. J., & Stringfield, S. C. (1997). *Education reform and students at risk*. Office of Educational Research and Improvement, U.S. Department of Education.

Sanders, L. (2003, March 6). Medicine's progress, one setback at a time. *The New York Times Magazine, 29*.

Scales, P. C., Van Boekel, M., Pekel, K., Syvertsen, A. K., & Roehlkepartain, E. C. (2020). Effects of developmental relationships with teachers on middle-school students' motivation and performance. *Psychology in the Schools, 57*(4), 646–677. https://doi.org/10.1002/pits.22350

Segalla, M. (2009). How Europeans do layoffs. *Harvard Business Review*. https://hbr.org/2009/06/how-europeans-do-layoffs

Senge, P. (1990). *The fifth discipline*. Currency.

Sergiovanni, T. (1992). *Moral leadership: Getting to the heart of school improvement*. Jossey-Bass.

Sturt, D., & Nordstrom T. (2018, March 8). 10 shocking workplace stats you need to know. *Forbes*. https://www.forbes.com/sites/davidsturt/2018/03/08/10-shocking-workplace-stats-you-need-to-know/#60c4750af3af

Van Eck, K., Johnson, S. R., Bettencourt, A., & Johnson, S. L. (2017). How school climate relates to chronic absence: A multi-level latent profile analysis. *Journal of School Psychology, 61*, 89–102. doi: 10.1016/j.jsp.2016.10.001

Wallace Foundation. (2013). *The school principal as leader: Guiding schools to better teaching and learning*. https://www.wallacefoundation.org/knowledge-center/pages/overview-the-school-principal-as-leader.aspx

Washington, B. A. (2018). *Perspectives of professional development and related experiences of K–12 school administrators* [Unpublished doctoral dissertation]. Wingate University.

Wepner, S. B., & Gómez, D. W. (2020). *Entrepreneurial leadership: Strategies for creating and sustaining partnerships for K–12 schools*. Rowman & Littlefield.

Wilcox, K. C., & Angelis, J. (2009). *Best practices from high-performing middle schools: How successful schools remove obstacles and create pathways to learning*. Teachers College Press.

Wood, L., & Bauman, E. (with Rudo, Z., & Dimock, V.). (2017). *How family, school, and community engagement can improve student achievement and influence school reform*. American Institutes for Research & Nellie Mae Education Institution. https://www.nmefoundation.org/wp-content/uploads/2020/05/Final-Report-Family-Engagement-AIR.pdf

Zalabak, P. S., Morreale, S., & Hackman, M. Z. (2010). *Building the high-trust organization: Strategies for supporting five key dimensions of trust*. Jossey-Bass.

CHAPTER 5

Principle 1—The Pillars of an Equitable Learning Community

Mission, Vision, Values, and Goals

> *It takes more than toughness to keep going when the going gets tough. It's vital that you find purpose and significance in what you do.*
> (James M. Kouzes & Barry Z. Posner, 2010, p. 35)

AUTHOR'S NOTE

When I (Alan) founded, and then ran, Solution Tree for more than a decade, the work we endeavored was implicitly around social justice. This included the creation of professional learning communities, as my thinking was that learning communities would be democratic and inclusive by definition and then all would benefit accordingly.

It is clear now that implicit intentions of inclusion of people who have been explicitly excluded for centuries is not sufficient. During the writing of this book alone, so many innocent Black and Brown men and women in the United States have been slain in the streets by those who are employed and paid to protect them that those same streets have finally erupted in desperate protest. The "last straw" of George Floyd's execution has in turn set off protests throughout the world.

(Continued)

Whether viewing the extraordinary thirteenth-century iconic mosque in Djenné, Mali, or the Parthenon in Athens, Greece, one can see that enduring structures are built on solid foundations. Standing on a strong foundation of relational trust, as described in Chapter 4, we can now add four pillars essential to lifting the equitable learning community (ELC): mission, vision, values, and goals (MVVG) (Mombourquette, 2017; Taylor, 2018). The architects of such a sustainable organization are the leadership teams. They are essential to a thriving learning community, as is the inclusion and commitment of the entire community, as it is the people in this community who will live and work there.

Though most schools by now have established their MVVG, reviewing, renewing, and recommitting to them—if not reimagining and reconstructing them—would be wise at this juncture. As the previous chapters indicate, we all know a great deal more than we did when 2020 began, and we've grown our collective efficacy beyond what anyone could have imagined. This new depth of knowledge and capacity can best be deployed when working in concert on a common agenda as outlined in the next section.

THE LEADERSHIP TEAM

Nothing will advance the school and overall student achievement more than an effective leadership team. This team, supported by the district and composed of the building leader and lead teachers, shapes the school culture and enhances instruction school- and system-wide (Portin et al., 2009;

Wallace Foundation, 2013). For more than a century, educational leaders have not been prepared to effectively play the role of facilitative team leader (Louis et al., 2010), and teachers as well have a long history of going into the classroom at the beginning of their careers and coming out at the end! Even among the most successful districts in North America, one of the biggest holes has for decades been in "facilitative leadership" necessary to build the school culture and advance instruction system-wide.

Yet, as noted in previous chapters, adaptive leadership and teamwork are likely at an all-time high in our field. Capitalizing on this and the individual and collective breakthroughs underway can be done using processes described in this chapter.

A key insight that has emerged in recent years is that for leaders to be successful leader*ship* is essential. Creating a high-performing team, able to shape school culture and guide improvement in instruction, is the key to sustainable student success (Fullan, 2018; Hargreaves & Fullan, 2012; Rosenfield et al., 2018). Moving leadership forward from the managerial role that was expected for the prior decades (Leithwood et al., 2020; Louis, 2015; Murphy & Louis, 2018) to creator, convener, and leader of high-performing teams able to act on new breakthroughs is the challenge now, and the payoffs are enormous, as this approach

- builds collective teacher efficacy (Donohoo et al., 2018; Leithwood, 2018) and closes teacher performance gaps (Darling-Hammond et al., 2017; Penner et al., 2019);

- enhances student performance in math and literacy (Ash & Hodge, 2016; Burns et al., 2017; Leithwood & Azah, 2017);

- eliminates a sense of isolation and "brings out the energy that exists naturally within people" (Mintzberg, 2004, p. 214; see also Carter, 2017);

- fully engages staff and students who move from compliance to collective commitment;

- spreads the responsibility of leadership to a team that is better able to lead the enterprise than is any *one* person;

- engages voices representative of children, families, and professionals previously marginalized; and

- saves money on external, off-the-shelf "solutions," replacing them with internal capacity to take on virtually *any* challenge.

The four pillars forming the foundation of school success addressed in this chapter are core to defining the school culture. Culture reflects the collective commitment and values of those in the organization. These, in turn, drive adult behaviors, which determine student outcomes. This chapter, therefore, begins with bringing some clarity to the word *culture*, and then provides direction in formulating the leadership team essential to creating the school and district MVVG.

Clarifying Culture

Some schools have productive cultures; others have problematic ones. But *every* school *has* a culture, whether one is aware of it or not. How would you categorize these three different approaches to introducing the idea of a four-day workweek and other cost-cutting measures?

Scenario 1

In her excitement to save the district money and allow plenty of time for student learning, the superintendent studied the four-day workweek underway in other districts. She returned from visiting schools in Massachusetts to share the good data and announce district plans to make the switch, which would clearly be to everyone's advantage.

Later, in the parking lot, one teacher shared with another: "Another change, and less time to improve students' test scores?! Look at these scores from my history class. They're just terrible. Quite a few Fs . . . most of the students got Ds. We've been over and over this material, but they just don't seem to care. They don't do their homework, and they don't participate in class. I have no family support. I am overwhelmed and don't know what to do!"

Scenario 2

In an effort to balance a shrinking budget, the district leadership decided to do a scan of best practices. They locked in on one that was neutral in every way except that it reduced costs—a four-day workweek! They hosted meetings and training of key staff to get their buy-in and help deliver the message system-wide. If they began the following academic year, no layoffs would have to occur.

Scenario 3

Leadership teams throughout the district had been meeting for more than a year to develop a common language and instructional focus and strengthen processes for advancing improvements at their respective schools. Based on decisions made during their last meeting, they had brought with them artifacts of their work around closing achievement gaps in several target areas.

There was news that derailed the scheduled agenda, however, and it involved cutting $15 million of the budget in this fifty-school district. There were many ways to proceed, and most would likely be painful. The mood and the severity of the challenge did not allow for continuing with the scheduled agenda of that meeting as planned. The first order of business—for all stakeholders in the room—was now to tackle the challenge together. Several possible plans emerged. In keeping with protocol, the leadership teams created a "reentry" plan so that all members of their school communities would be able to process the same information using identical techniques displayed by the facilitators of this meeting.

How would you categorize each of the three cultures based on the differing leaders' approach to a similar problem? While the leader in Scenario 1 is clearly enthusiastic and well intentioned, there would likely be an ultimate disconnect between intent and impact. The enthusiastic, charismatic leader may move the organization forward almost singlehandedly, but it is at best unsustainable in her absence, and at worst likely to alienate enough people to stall the effort at some point early on.

In Scenario 2, there is a more "enlightened" approach to the change effort enlisting one leadership team, researching the challenge, and attempting to get "buy-in" through training and communication. The problem is that people rarely commit to someone else's solution by virtue of getting training, and "buy-in" becomes acquiescence or compliance with the final outcome. Moreover, asking for people's input and then proceeding with the predetermined plan is a surefire way to diminish trust.

In Scenario 3, the groundwork had been laid to deal with this and virtually any other crisis or opportunity. Lead teams were intact and had an infrastructure and the tools for problem solving. District leadership was transparent, and the challenge was *everyone's* to solve. Since everyone was using a common language and framework for analysis, conversation, and action, the district was able to work through this effectively, and come to consensus in record time.

The more leaders include the staff in meaningful ways, the better the outcome for students. A number of research studies support this simple principle: "the more willing the principals are to spread leadership around, the better for students" (Wallace Foundation, 2013, p. 10). Moreover, "effective leadership from *all* sources—principals, influential teachers, staff teams and others—is associated with better student performance on math and reading tests" (Wallace Foundation, 2013, p. 10; see also American University School of Education, 2020; Louis et al., 2010).

By contrast, leaders who "go it alone," failing to trust staff or develop their collective efficacy, foster cultures of blame and hopelessness. One high school staff was asked to analyze a situation in which 25 percent of their students were not passing state tests. After much deliberation, the staff reached a consensus: *It's that middle school! They were sending us students who were unprepared!*

A corollary to a culture of blame is a shift in responsibility for ensuring student learning. Consider the following often-heard statements:

- It's not *my* job to ensure that students *learned* the lesson—my job is to teach it!

- We believe all students can learn, but some learn better than others.

- In general, all students will learn, but *those* kids from *that* neighborhood aren't as smart or as motivated as the rest.

- If we had more [discipline, resources, time, parental support, and so on], *then* I would be successful!

What these statements have in common is that they shift accountability *away* from school professionals. What could be more demotivating for the members of a school community than to believe that they have no power and that what they do makes no difference? "The research literature over the last quarter century has consistently supported the notion that having high expectations for all . . . is one key to closing the opportunity gap between advantaged and less advantaged students, and for raising the overall achievement of all students" (Porter et al., 2008, p. 13; see also Cardona, 2020; Choyce, 2019; Ijei & Harrison, 2010). Moreover, having teachers of color lifts success for students of color (Carter Andrews et al., 2019; Kohli et al., 2019), and having leadership that supports belief in all students increases their rates of graduation, sets them up for success on standardized tests, and reduces suspensions and other disciplinary actions (Cardichon & Darling-Hammond, 2017; Gregory & Skiba, 2019; Stanford, 2017).

In this chapter, direction is provided for shaping the school culture and collective beliefs and actions of the school community by development of the four pillars of an organization: mission, vision, values, and goals. Together they establish the common base on which all of our efforts will be built. The six principles of ELCs are not implemented in a concrete sequential manner. Thus, the way in which the MVVG are created can also serve as a means of developing leadership capacity, for example. It will be the leadership team that guides the development of this foundational pillar. Thus, we begin with a focus on developing that team.

Developing the Leadership Team

Leadership teams are formed at the school level and ideally are networked with like teams throughout the district using a common framework and language for dialogue and action. When this powerful strategy is utilized, leadership teams have been found to be very effective (Cotter, 2019).

Although the biggest gains come from district-wide use of the strategies mentioned as follows, it behooves school principals to develop these leadership teams to enhance student gains regardless. The elements of constituting such teams are outlined here and taken up throughout the rest of this book.

- *Select team members*—the team should be representative of the school community rather than a reflection of the leader alone. The latter is great for an early and quick launch . . . and a crashing thud later on as those not represented help put on the brakes. Specifically, if we are to achieve success for all of our students, then professionals and community members of color, from non-English-speaking countries, who identify as LGBTQIA+, or who have low socioeconomic status, and students themselves, among others, must have a voice. While it can be onerous to include "naysayers," as long as they are not CAVE people (Citizens Against Virtually Everything), it is a good idea to have the "yeah buts" show up during the leadership team meetings, rather than in the parking lot. Team members must make the necessary time commitment and be open to the process that will unfold.

- *The team creates meaningful protocols* for determining its norms— how team members will interact with one another, resolve conflicts, and so on. This corresponds on an organizational level with the "Values" section of this chapter.

- *Focus is determined*—the team aligns its focus with SMARTER goals (described later in this chapter) for the organization, and chooses a starting point.

- *Process and framework for action are determined*—having the common language and means of making cohesion out of the cacophony often found in schools is critical to coordinated action by the team (see, for example, "Creating a Common Rubric for Excellent Instruction" in the Chapter 4 resources on the companion website, https://resources.corwin.com/BreakthroughLeadership). This is one tool that follows the same principle: the team needs clarity, common language, and a well-researched system or framework for coordinating action.

- *Tools are chosen and aligned with the focus and framework*—there are many such tools to draw on, and they are selected based on what the team needs to get done and the manner in which the team operates (i.e., culture). Tools that are "cost-effective," the latest craze, or sold by a good friend would not necessarily fit with what the team members need to clearly define as their objective and means of proceeding.

- *Engagement or reentry plans are created*—to avoid the inside-outside syndrome in which those not attending the team meetings feel left out, a plan to return and effectively engage others is needed at the end of each lead team meeting.

- *Returning, reporting, and refining the new learning becomes the norm*—ultimately, both the process of change and the new changes themselves become embedded in the culture.

This infrastructure, in combination with an equity lens, will assist in the development of high-performing leadership teams that remove barriers to student success. Along with specific tools to advance the dialogue, it has been continuously refined and served as the mainstay of success for numerous districts since 2001. The team can now move forward on developing, refining, or totally rethinking the organization's MVVG.

THE MISSION

The mission of an organization is essential to its success. A mission statement should be created and published as a means of giving those involved with the organization a clear understanding of its purpose for existence.

Mission statements are found everywhere—in schools, big businesses, small businesses, nonprofit organizations, organized religion, and all levels of government. They are a popular management tool used by corporations to motivate stakeholders and keep everyone on the same page. A quick survey of mission statements reveals a common pattern: they use superlatives and absolutes. Such an approach leaves people feeling as though they had cotton candy for lunch: happy but still hungry for the real meal! Phrases like *world's best, premier, largest*, and *first choice of customers everywhere* abound. How "premier" status will be attained and how "best" will be measured are rarely clarified or discussed.

Schools and school districts also have mission statements—and they should. Unfortunately, education is not exempt from the tendency toward generic, vague, and meaningless mission statements. Effective schools move beyond stating generic hopes for our students.

The four critical questions to be addressed in the mission statement are, by and large, *not* new:

1. If we expect all students to learn, *what* is it we expect them to learn?
2. *How* will we know if they are learning it?
3. *How* will we ensure an engaging, relevant pedagogy?
4. What will we do when they *don't* learn?

An effective mission statement must be specific enough to address all four of these questions. If it does not, it will lack resonance for staff members, and it will quickly be forgotten or written off as meaningless. Because most schools already have a mission statement, it is best to review it in light of these criteria, and with the larger community defining twenty-first-century educational needs. Chapter 2 includes fundamental questions around what students need to know that can facilitate a good dialogue. Note the clarity and specificity of the following mission statement, and the corresponding actions taken to ensure it is fulfilled.

Mission of Highline Public Schools (outside of Seattle, Washington)

▶ *OUR PROMISE: To know every student by name, strength, and need, and graduate all students prepared for the future they choose.*

"We've done a lot to live this mission; now the community holds us to it," explained Susan Enfield, superintendent of schools. "For example, we put every student's photo on the table in the cafeteria, and every faculty put a note next to photos of each student they knew. Then we looked to see who *doesn't* have a note next to their photos, and make sure those students have adults who know them. Sometimes it's the coach, or bus driver, or other paraprofessional," shared Dr. Enfield, who herself was en route to seeing a sixth grader she's known since kindergarten who is now living in a hotel. This is the DNA of their system. They make decisions based on a data system that goes beyond test scores (Susan Enfield, personal communication, 2020, May 13, 2020).

At Highline, there is vertical articulation so the previous year's grade-level teachers talk to the next year's grade-level teachers, for the same students, about *each* student. Principals and staff know a student's *story*—and have moved away from labeling and using a deficit model to categorize students. "We have more

(Continued)

(Continued)

than formal expectations; it comes down to *people* doing that work, and this has in turn become a powerful recruiting tool. Human resources lead with this selection in mind. They need people for whom *our promise* is in their bones" (Susan Enfield, personal communication, May 13, 2020).

They've prioritized hiring and retention. Potential teachers have to do a demo lesson, and the recruitment team asks about their commitment to equity. Principals make the selection, and there's a rigorous process for that, which includes staff, students, and community members. Human resources replaced an onerous process that yielded hundreds of applicants who weren't a good fit for one or another school seeking staff. Now the schools define their needs and help screen applicants. They are not facing the teacher shortages seen throughout the country.

"I start with getting and cultivating great building leaders," shared Dr. Enfield (personal communication, May 13, 2020). "Teachers need a great principal and will walk through fire for one."

What Is Mission?

In effective schools, the mission statement goes far beyond an expression of "wishful thinking." The mission statement can serve as the bedrock of the school's daily activities and policies. It should be fundamental to every decision at every level. An effective mission statement expresses the school's purpose—its essential reason for educating in the first place. It expresses why a school *exists*.

The mission serves as a polestar, or guiding principle, for a school. Just as a ship sails toward but never actually reaches its guiding star, we too strive toward but never actually fulfill our mission. Why? Because as long as the world continues to change and evolve, our students' needs will change, and we will need to develop new ways to respond.

What Good Looks Like

The best mission statements are clear about why the organization exists and what will be done to ensure that the purpose is met. The mission statement serves the organization by providing specifics:

1. What do we want to do?
2. How will we know if we are succeeding?
3. What will we do to ensure success?

Given these three questions, which of the following would you consider effective? Mark each mission statement with an *E* for effective or an *I* for ineffective, and note why you made the selection.

Mission 1 _____

The mission of this school district is to ensure that each and every student is prepared to succeed in life. This is accomplished in an environment of trust and respect that fosters positive attitudes toward self, others, work, and responsible citizenship. We are dedicated to maximizing individual potential and developing lifelong learners who will be contributing members in a global society.

Mission 2 _____

The mission of our school is to create and maintain an environment that ensures that every member of the school community reaches a high level of twenty-first-century skills development and academic achievement as determined by state and national standards. Students will both graduate and go on to a career that pays a living wage or to an institution of higher learning. We commit to a comprehensive system of support to ensure this outcome.

Mission 3 _____

It is our mission as a school district to educate students to be creative, responsible, self-sufficient citizens who have the capacity and motivation for continued individual growth and who will have the ability to make a positive contribution in our society.

Mission 4 _____

We are committed to the academic excellence of all students by empowering them with the means for the successful completion of high educational standards and by challenging them to become productive members of society.

What's your analysis? Consider the following.

Example missions 1 and 3 do not attempt to clearly define *success* in measurable ways. "Success in life" would demand that we wait too long for feedback on how a school community is doing in fulfilling its mission. Similarly, terms like *creative* and *responsible* are vague and hard to measure.

Example mission 4 provides more specificity on both the definition of students' success and how it will be measured (by "high educational standards"). However, it lacks the clarity to answer the third question ("What will we do to ensure success?").

TABLE 5.1 Effective Mission Statements

TRADITIONAL MISSION STATEMENTS . . .	EFFECTIVE MISSION STATEMENTS . . .
Are vague or generic	Are clear
Say all kids can learn	Are specific (what exactly are students supposed to learn?)
Do not define learning	Are measurable (how do we know students have learned?)
Do not address the possibility of failure	Provide for failure (how do we respond when students don't learn?)

SOURCE: HOPE Foundation et al. (2002).

Only example mission 2 addresses all three questions. But be aware: photocopying this statement and hanging it underneath the office clock for all to see will not improve your school. It is the process of collaboratively creating a mission and spelling out all the specifics not provided in a generic mission statement that will lead to school improvements and cultural shifts. Table 5.1 summarizes some of the differences between traditional and more effective mission statements, but first, here is another example of an effective mission statement:

> *The mission of Running River Elementary School is to provide an opportunity for every student to master grade-level skills regardless of previous academic performance, family background, socioeconomic status, race, or gender. It is our purpose to educate all students to high levels of academic performance, while fostering positive growth in social–emotional behaviors and attitudes. The entire staff pledges itself to these student outcomes.*

Implementation Guidelines

Most schools have no problem creating a mission statement. A small number of people can sit down at a restaurant and hammer one out before the food arrives. (Or, in our current COVID-19 environment, some might craft one in the course of a Zoom meeting.) The discussions leading to the final document, however, are as important as the final document itself. It is critical that the process involves representatives from all stakeholder groups—teachers, paraeducators, administrators, community members, students, and parents. It is equally important that those involved reflect ethnic and socioeconomic diversity, as well as diverse learning styles. A statement of mission has little meaning or impact unless it reflects the thoughts of the school community and is collectively embraced by those whom it affects.

There are various ways to collaboratively create a mission statement. The first step for any process should be to evaluate what already exists. Using the criteria that have been laid out, ask stakeholders to evaluate and revise the statement, using any of the following methods.

1. *Assemble a task force* made up of representatives from each stakeholder group. In this strategy, the representatives are responsible for soliciting feedback from and accurately representing the views of their constituencies. They are also responsible for sharing drafts of the evolving statements with their respective groups.

2. *Collect the views of each stakeholder group* in a more formal way, perhaps through an online survey instrument. Convene representative focus groups, then examine and discuss the views obtained through the survey. Ultimately, the focus groups report their findings to a task force, which is responsible for drafting the statement.

3. *Small-group work* can begin with representative stakeholders who are first reminded of the four critical questions that their mission statement should address. They then form small groups of five to seven people, and each group drafts a complete mission statement. The groups' statements are posted on the walls around the room, and participants do a "gallery walk," reviewing each statement and offering feedback on sticky notes. At the end of the session, the school's leadership team collects all the drafts and sticky notes and uses them to write a statement—which then goes out for more feedback from all stakeholders.

4. *The "snowball" method* can also yield good results. In this approach, all stakeholders are paired into groups of two. After each initial pair drafts a statement, two pairs join together to share their thoughts and merge their statements into one. That group of four joins with another group of four, and the new group of eight then does the same. The process is repeated until there is one comprehensive statement that incorporates all stakeholder feedback. This statement is then reviewed by a representative group in light of the criteria for a good mission statement. The resulting statement is circulated for final approval.

In smaller schools, these approaches can be, and ideally are, used with the entire school staff. Doing so takes longer, but it deepens the commitment to the outcome. KIPP, the Knowledge Is Power Program, just developed its mission statement with the engagement of five thousand stakeholders! In any case, it is vital to focus the discussion around the purpose and the three questions that ask for the necessary specifics. Collecting feedback from all stakeholder groups helps to ensure that the mission statement provides enough detail and is meaningful. Such an outcome requires plenty of time for thoughtful reflection and response—as well as time for writing, reviewing, and revising the statement.

Sustaining Success

Once you have developed an effective mission, your next challenge will be to establish it in action and keep it alive. In all schools, the entire student body is replaced every three to six years, and in a growing number of schools, staff turnover is even more frequent. How can you ensure that your mission statement remains a living, integral part of the school experience? Here are some strategies:

- Display your mission statement prominently within the school and in places where the school presents itself to the public—for instance, on your website, in press releases, on letterhead, and the like.

- Exemplify effective adherence to the mission in stories affecting the lives of real children and their families.

- Make sure the mission is cited as a guide whenever staff meet to set goals, plan programs, make decisions, or discuss problems.

- Coach teacher leaders in using the mission as a guiding force in their team meetings. Teachers' understanding of their role in maintaining the mission is critical for success.

- Frequently evaluate the school's policies and procedures to ensure their adherence to the mission.

- Schedule time to familiarize new staff and students with the mission. This should include in-depth discussions about the implications for how the school operates.

- Respond quickly and correctively to any and all failures to act in accordance with the school's mission. If we state, for example, all students will succeed, we must intervene when this is not the case (see Chapter 6).

- Formally review and update your mission every four to five years, or sooner in the case of fundamental shifts in educational demands—for example, those brought on by new standards, by requirements of fundamentally different learning outcomes (like twenty-first-century skills), or by major discontinuous change (like a world pandemic)!

Mission statements will invariably commit to success for *all* students, but how the school community responds when this is *not* happening will determine the character and credibility of that school or district. At the Toronto District School Board, members of the stakeholder community demanded action: "We are tired of hearing about an *education solution* when there's an issue of discrimination. Where's your accountability for your staff, like termination?" In response, then TDSB director of education John Malloy (personal communication, April 14, 2020) communicated in effect to thirty-seven thousand staff in a webinar: "Err on the side of caution—report any possible issues of racism and discrimi`nation with specifics. This isn't meant to threaten, but if you fail to report issues of racism and discrimination, it could lead to termination." He shared "The staff now know our expectations and our commitment to providing access to all students, as well as our commitment to ending the disproportionality that exists in the system which favors some students over others."

THE VISION

Like mission, creating a vision is another common part of the planning process in most organizations today. The word *vision* is used as an adjective (the visionary leader), a noun (a vision for the community), and even as a verb (visioning the future). "The capacity to imagine and articulate exciting future possibilities is the defining competence of leaders" (Kouzes & Posner, 2014, p. 46). But what exactly *is* this elusive vision—and where do you get one?

What Is Vision?

Whereas a mission statement reminds us of why we exist, a vision paints a picture of what we can become. Most of us employ vision in our personal lives. We strive toward a better, future version of ourselves that may be wealthier, smarter, more organized, healthier, and so forth. We use that vision to guide our behaviors on both a long-term and a short-term basis.

A school's vision serves the same purpose—that is, it offers a realistic alternative for a better future. It says, "This is what we want to be." Just as our own vision guides the personal or professional course we follow, a school's vision should guide the collective direction of its stakeholders. It should provide a compelling sense of where the school is headed and, in broad terms, what must be accomplished in the future to fulfill the school's purpose. Every decision made, every program implemented, every policy instituted, and all goals should align with this vision.

Without a common vision, decisions are made randomly. At best, policies, procedures, and programs will lack unity and fail to adequately support one another. At worst, they will actually work at cross-purposes. Virtually no school lacks for new initiatives or programs; *most* schools lack cohesion and a unified effort shared between various programs and initiatives. Whereas the mission statement answers the question "Why do we exist?" the vision explains where the school is *headed*.

What Good Looks Like

Like the mission statement, a good vision statement should be detailed enough to carry meaning. The most successful vision statements are vivid and compelling; they motivate us to strive for an improved future. They provide a foundation on which we can assess the areas for improvement—and then plan. Perhaps most important, an effective vision statement describes a *collective* vision and is shared by all stakeholders. Table 5.2 provides a comparison of traditional and more effective vision statements.

TABLE 5.2 Effective Vision Statements

TRADITIONAL VISION STATEMENTS . . .	EFFECTIVE VISION STATEMENTS . . .
Are vague or unimaginable	Are realistic, clear, and compelling
Are created by a select group	Have broad-based buy-in
State hopes and wishes	Describe intended change
Are soon forgotten	Guide action

Using these criteria, how would you rate the following vision statements? Mark each one with an *E* for effective or an *I* for ineffective, and note why you made the selection.

Vision 1 _____

The Roseluxe Unified School District fosters curious and creative learners by setting high academic goals and encouraging critical thinkers to both collaborate and utilize technology to their advantage.

Our teachers and leaders believe all of their students can meet these rigorous standards. All staff together form a supportive learning community where opportunities for professional learning and improvement are always encouraged and made available. By analyzing and refining our instructional practices, we adjust to the needs of our students and ensure the equitable use of our resources.

Families are an essential part of our success. They are active and welcomed in the education of our children. They provide input and help us craft our programs. We rely on our families' funds of knowledge to enrich all members of our learning community.

We believe that our schools are vital to the health of our communities, and we strive to provide classrooms with culturally relevant curriculum that begins with the interests and abilities all of our students already possess. We are committed to cultivating the inner brilliance of each and every child. We offer enriched learning environments and numerous supports for the health and growth of the whole child.

Vision 2 _____

We envision a school where children and adults work productively toward success for all students. This would involve mutual respect, cooperation, and responsibility on everyone's part.

Vision 3 _____

Our vision is increasing reading by 6 percent in the next three years.

What is your analysis of these vision statements? Ours follows.

Example vision 2 fails to provide clarity. From our perspective, it is not compelling. Example vision 3 is very clear, understandable, and communicable. Yet it is not ambitious and likely won't galvanize the school community.

Although example vision 1 does not include any quantifiable data, it is very specific in describing a compelling future that is imaginable and feasible. This example is our preferred vision of the three.

Implementation Guidelines

Rather than choosing or adapting a "canned" vision statement or depending on a single member of the leadership team to craft one, the best vision statements are "grown." Diverse members of the school community devise a process for examining their school, then create together a vision that provides a profound purpose for all members. The collective vision emerges from the personal visions of each member. Like mission, vision is not something that can be handed down from on high. It must be co-created by the entire learning community in order for it to have shared meaning.

Should the vision be developed at the school level or district level? Ideally, both the district leaders and the schools they oversee should have a role in the process.

Should the development process involve only school personnel, or should it involve the larger community, including families? Research calls for (1) developing (emotional) depth or connection to the effort, (2) breadth in terms of who is involved, and (3) sustainability in terms of leadership transition plans for best results (Hargreaves, 2001). In light of this, school leaders gain the best long-term outcomes by deeply involving the broader school community in creating the vision.

The vision should also be rooted in research on best practices and reflect the school's history and existing culture. Ideally, the following information would be gathered in preparation for creating a vision:

- Relevant information about the school or district—that is, data on parent and student perceptions (e.g., inclusiveness and belonging, engagement, student success, and staff and faculty performance); copies of prior vision or values statements; internal and external factors affecting the school or district; findings of visitation teams who evaluated the school and district for accreditation purposes; longitudinal achievement data; and community survey results

- Research on school culture

- Research on characteristics of high-performing schools and districts

- Research on school change and reculturing

- An honest assessment of the current conditions in the school or district

Once stakeholders have had an opportunity to review this background information, they or a subset of the school leadership team can begin drafting the vision. Vision statements tend to be thoughtful, fairly lengthy documents that encompass many aspects of a school. For example, a school's vision might be divided into such sections as "curriculum," "attention to individual students," "personnel," "leadership," "students," "climate," and "community partnerships" (see Case Story 3.2 in Chapter 3). The organization of the statement is not important, but the vision should include the ideas of all stakeholders and touch on all aspects of the school deemed significant to realizing the ideal.

One method involves having all stakeholders make lists of the things that they think are important for a good school. The stakeholders then form groups of eight to ten people, combine their lists, and collaboratively agree on the top ten. The school improvement team takes the top-ten lists from all the groups and clusters the statements by common theme. The school improvement team divides into groups, with each group taking one of the common themes and writing a paragraph that captures all the statements in that theme.

A similar approach requires participants to write their initial statements—as many as they wish—on sticky notes. Participants then work together to group the notes into clusters. Each cluster is assigned a name, which is used as a vision category. As with the previous method, small groups take the various categories and draft mini-visions. Ultimately, all the mini-visions are combined into a single statement and sent to stakeholders for feedback.

A Post-COVID Vision

To get creativity flowing, it is sometimes helpful to provide an expansive or "stretch" vision as a catalyst for thinking and conversation. Dallas Dance, president and CEO of consulting firm The DDance Group and former superintendent of Baltimore County Public Schools, envisions a new personnel allocation structure in which master teachers create fifteen-minute lessons that are taught to all, after which tier 2 teachers reinforce the lessons with all students and act as tutors as well. Those who still need intensive work in those lessons would meet with master teachers. Tier 3 assistants would support all of this through pullouts and various technical assistance (Dallas Dance, personal communication, May 5, 2020).

THE VALUES

What Are Values?

Values are the attitudes and behaviors an organization embraces. They represent commitments we make regarding how we will behave on a daily basis in order to become the school we want to be. They are established and articulated guidelines we live by. "Values are best described in terms of behavior: If we operate as we should, what would an observer see us doing?" (Senge et al., 1994).

Values endure. They do not fluctuate with staffing changes, funding shifts, or trends in instructional methodology. They are never compromised for a short-term gain or a quick solution to a problem. Values express a *shared* commitment to certain behaviors; they do not result from a top-down dictate—that is, they start with "*We* will," not "*You* will."

Ideally, values reflect the attitudes and beliefs of the school community. Ultimately, after they are created, value statements guide the behavior of everyone in the organization. In fact, the change actions more often lead to new outcomes and ultimately changes in belief, rather than the other way around.

School leaders cannot read minds or respond to perceptions of what people in the organization *believe*. Leaders can inquire as to staff members' beliefs on a given topic, but responses may or may not be forthcoming. At the very least, however, after having collectively created values, it is the leader's role to hold people to *behaviors* that mirror those values (as opposed to *beliefs*).

In high-performing schools, eventually the school *staff* will also help bring individuals' behaviors into line with stated values. Acting in accordance with these stated values becomes part of the culture. Lateral accountability for shared commitments and agreed-upon behaviors becomes the province of the entire school community.

Without a shared commitment to a core base of values, schools fall into the "my belief versus your belief" pattern. These schools may have certain individuals or factions that operate as "rogue agents," taking actions that run counter to the school's mission and vision. For example, imagine a school with a mission that states that all students can achieve at a high level and that it will provide an environment to make that happen. Yet many classrooms in that same school have long lists of prerequisite criteria—many of which are quite subjective—that students must meet in order to access the more rigorous curricular offerings. Clearly, such behaviors do not support the school's mission. Therefore, it lacks a *functional* set of values—a school-wide statement that dictates *all* behavior.

What Good Looks Like

A successful statement of values touches on the most pertinent, pervasive principles shared by a school's stakeholders. The statement goes to the core of their beliefs and the depth of the commitment of action by the school community.

A statement of values that captures only core beliefs should be relatively brief. It may contain as many as ten values—but five or six is a more manageable number. Each value should be simply stated so that the general meaning is easy to grasp and remember. It should also relate directly to the vision statement.

The question to consider when articulating values is not just what values are appropriate for your school, but what values *specifically support* your vision statement and are aligned with your mission. For example, the value statement "We will give students multiple opportunities to learn and engage in areas of interest to them, play to their strengths, and provide myriad supports for success" is consistent with a mission that states "All students will learn at high levels, in accordance with state standards." If teachers were failing half of the students in their classrooms year after year, that behavior would not be in line with the school's values or mission, and would need to be quickly addressed in a data-driven conversation that refers back to the school's mission and values.

The values of a school articulate what "we will" *do* and how "we will" *behave* (i.e., "We will model," "We will support," "We will provide")—not what "we *believe*." Although a statement of beliefs might be useful in some circumstances, it lacks the critical element of prescribing action—of telling us what we need to *do* to make our vision a reality.

Effective values are

- few in number;
- direct and simply stated;
- focused on behaviors, not beliefs; and
- linked to the vision statement.

Implementation Guidelines

Some view the establishment of a set of values as the most challenging component of a school's foundation because it requires a commitment to changing behaviors. It can be difficult to convey the full significance of values to staff members and get them to truly grapple with their beliefs and their perceived roles in the teaching and learning process. We must all "live into" our values by evaluating our behaviors over time.

For serious discussions among stakeholders to be successful, schools must invest time. As with developing mission and vision, it is best to start the process by breaking up into small groups. This helps engage participants and fosters honest, genuine dialogue. One easy approach is simply to review the school's vision statement with participants and then ask, "How do we need to behave to make this happen?" Allow time to discuss and draft answers to such questions. Then continue to consolidate lists using the snowball technique described earlier, or have a task force collect the responses and use them to draft a statement of values.

Another approach is to have participants divide into pairs. Have the pairs ask each other, "What are some of the behaviors that we [some, or all of us] engage in that are not consistent with our mission and vision?" After they have identified what they would like to see changed, have them ask each other, "What will you commit to doing, starting today, to change that?" Have participants write down their list of commitments. The facilitator can then ask each person to report out, and consolidate the comments onto one sheet of paper. Or the facilitator might collect the lists and consolidate them into a master list. In either case, it is best to go back to the staff to ask for a collective commitment to the final list.

Whatever process you use, be sure participants know that it is not trivial. Although it may be easy to get a list of values that everyone says they agree to, it is far more difficult to arrive at a list of values everyone will actually be willing to *live* by. One way to partially safeguard against abuses of the collective values is to go down the list and pose scenarios that might lead to someone bypassing a given value. Discuss the scenario and then ask participants to propose alternatives to behaving counter to the values.

The more energy and time you put into the process, the more effective your values will be at guiding day-to-day decision making.

THE GOALS

The three components of a successful school's foundation discussed thus far are meant for long-range planning. A school's vision, for example, may take five years or longer to reach. Values are also ongoing; we commit to them for as long as we are part of the organization.

But we also need short-term successes to help us stay focused and motivated. In fact, little will energize and motivate staff more than success itself. Goals should be structured, therefore, to ensure quick wins as the team builds capacity for more complex action. And feedback loops that are self-sustaining and easy for teachers to regularly access—"feedback on demand"—are far better than hearing "good job" at the monthly meeting from the building or district leader.

It is very difficult to commit to and work toward something that has no definite "success point" or pre-identified benchmark that will allow us to take a deep breath, pat ourselves on the back, and look with pride at a job well done. Most of us need to feel that we are making progress and getting things done. It is through the judicious use of well-written goals—the fourth component of our foundation—that this need can be met.

Strong goals are particularly important in school cultures with little previous record of success. The process of setting, committing to, and accomplishing short-term goals builds credibility and trust. It can also serve as the beginning of positive momentum toward change.

What Are Goals?

If our vision is the grand target—a distant ideal that we are striving for—then our goals are the short-term mini-targets that we aim for along the way. They break our long, winding journey toward school improvement into manageable, measurable steps. Goals provide intermittent reinforcement for our efforts and provide us with feedback on our progress toward the larger vision.

Goals also serve a more pragmatic purpose. They provide a detailed, short-term orientation for us in relation to our vision. They identify priorities and establish a timeline for our process of change. Equally important, goals establish accountability for stakeholders, ensuring that what needs to happen actually *does* happen.

What Good Looks Like

Goals, like the other foundational components we've discussed, are often too vague. A goal that is too vague to be measured is, essentially, worthless. After all, how will you ever know if you reach it? How will you know when to set a new goal?

Effective goals are both specific and measurable. They clearly identify the evidence that must be monitored to assess progress. They also set a time frame for completion. For example, "We will work to increase the participation of our students of color in Advanced Placement (AP) classes by 30 percent this academic year" is a good, specific goal. "We will help all kids become lifelong learners," on the other hand, is too vague to be useful.

Goals should also focus on the results rather than on the process or the task. It's not uncommon for a school to have task-oriented goals, such as "We will adopt a new curriculum" or "We will have team meetings weekly." Although these are perfectly legitimate *inputs*, a SMARTER goal specifies the desired *results* of these actions in terms that are aligned with the school's mission and vision. To be SMARTER goals (defined in Table 5.3), these subgoals must go a step further, to answer the "so that" question: "We will adopt a new curriculum *so that we* . . ." Ultimately, answering this additional question should get us to the *real* goal for student learning.

TABLE 5.3 SMARTER Goals

SMARTER goals are . . .

Specific and strategic	In this sense, *specific* relates to clarity. *Strategic* relates to alignment with our mission and vision.
Measurable	In most cases, this means quantifiable.
Attainable	People must believe, based on past data and current capabilities, that success is realistic.
Results oriented	This means focusing on the outcome, not the process for getting there. This refers to our desired end result, versus inputs to the process.
Time bound	When will the goal be accomplished?
Equitable	How will the goal affect students traditionally marginalized?
Renewing	It is of particular importance during stressful and uncertain times that caregivers' needs are also tended to. Otherwise professionals can meet the goal at their own personal or professional expense. Building in downtime, processing, team support, trauma relief, fun, and celebration is often required in setting goals.

Implementation Guidelines

Developing goals for a school requires asking, "What steps do we need to take, in what order, to create our ideal school?" After identifying these steps, the school must set a time frame or deadline for completion. To be most effective, all stakeholders in the school or district should help to set the goals for which they will be responsible. For example, third-grade teachers should set goals for the third-grade team.

How do you choose a goal? How do you decide what will make it measurable, attainable, results oriented, and time bound? An earlier vision statement example cited a 6 percent increase in reading scores. One might ask, "Why 6 percent? Why not 10 percent or 20 percent? Are folks lazy? Are they overly ambitious?"

There are different ways to begin goal setting, and each should take into consideration the idea of breaking goals up into those that will produce quick wins initially.

- A school will want to determine what will be needed to achieve equitable outcomes for all students, and plan accordingly. The Abington School District in Pennsylvania, for example, decided to ensure access to AP classes as a lever to enhance overall student success *and* allocated the resources necessary to support them (Blankstein et al., 2016).

- Envisioning what is possible, using external benchmarks from similar or different industries, can be a starting point.

- A school may be in academic trouble and have a bottom line that must be achieved.

- A school may look at last year's outcomes and then estimate how much better the school or district can do this year, based on improved processes, technology, or pedagogy.

- A school may start with the long-term vision and determine what needs to be accomplished each year to reach it, and then dedicate the resources necessary for the annual improvements.

Regardless of where you begin in the process, it is essential to look at past data, new circumstances, and processes that can be modified to improve results. What will you do *differently* this year than last? How and when will you evaluate whether you are on target? Heed the warning implied in the statement "If you do what you've always done, you'll get what you've always got!"

After SMARTER goals are defined and implemented, they should be monitored continuously and evaluated over time. If clear evidence emerges revealing that the goal or means of achieving it is not bringing about the desired results, then one or both of these should be amended or abandoned. If goals are well chosen, and the means of achieving them are effective, then a careful analysis of the outcome should be made to determine how to continue and maintain the improvement over a longer period of time.

Celebrating Successes

Many schools are reluctant to avail themselves of one of the best strategies for building positive school culture: celebrating success. In addition to concerns about lacking time, some school leaders are reluctant to single out individual achievements. Indeed, some school cultures are committed to mediocrity or egalitarianism to the point of hiding or ignoring successes!

But regular celebrations have the power to make the school's overall values increasingly positive. Moreover, celebrations help mark milestones and build motivation in the long journey of school improvement.

Here are some guidelines for celebrating staff success:

- Take steps that help ensure the celebrations are deemed fair. This involves clarifying in advance exactly what constitutes success for all involved. (See the SMARTER goals in Table 5.3 for additional guidelines.)

- Tie celebrations explicitly to organizational vision, values, and goals. This provides an opportunity to reinforce these organizational pillars while providing more clarity, credibility, and rationale for the celebrations.

- Design celebrations that are attainable by all staff members. Having only one celebration with one winner per year can alienate a majority of your staff.

- For formal celebrations, communicate in advance the likely outcomes for success. This affirms the fairness of the approach.

- Make the celebration widely accessible. Involving more people heightens the impact of your school's values and goals for everybody.

- Arrange for both formal and informal celebrations. For example, simply using a staff meeting to congratulate a teacher on an excellent job in researching and recommending a new teaching methodology will go a long way toward encouraging others to do the same. Sometimes informal celebrations are needed to provide *timely* encouragement of people's efforts.

- Do not use celebrations to make direct or indirect comparisons between high- and low-achieving staff members. Focus on the positive results you are celebrating.

- Be specific about the nature of the success. "Eleanor actually took the time to visit the home of her most improved student, James," is far better than "Eleanor always helps her students."

- Use stories and be human.

- Build sustainability and community into the celebratory process by allowing staff and students to eventually take it over. Schools can begin early on by involving others in selection committees.

This chapter has outlined specific processes for building the foundation of an equitable learning community. That foundation rests on four pillars: mission, vision, values, and goals. Creating a "product" for each of these pillars is technically simple. But the real gains in doing this come from the *process* and the *relationships* that are shaped along the way. Thus, creating common MVVG is an ideal way to effectively use data, build a collaborative team, and develop sustainable leadership capacity (see principles 4, 3, and 6, respectively, outlined at the end of the previous chapter). Much of this chapter was adapted from *Failure Is Not an Option™: Six Principles That Guide Student Achievement in High-Performing Schools* (Blankstein, 2012), which can be accessed for a "deeper dive" into processes for implementation. The next chapter deals with the critical question: "What will we do when students *don't* learn?"

REFERENCES

American University School of Education. (2020, April 21). *5 effective principal leadership styles*. https://soeonline.american.edu/blog/principal-leadership-styles

Ash, R. C., & Hodge, P. H. (2016). *Five critical leadership practices: The secret to high-performing schools*. Routledge.

Blankstein, A. M. (2012). *Failure is not an option: 6 principles that advance student achievement in highly effective schools* (3rd ed.). Corwin.

Blankstein, A. M., Noguera, P., & Kelly, L. (2016). *Excellence through equity: Five principles of courageous leadership to guide achievement for every student*. ASCD.

Burns, M. K., Riley-Tillman, T. C., & Rathvon, N. (2017). *Effective school interventions: Evidence-based strategies for improving student outcomes*. Guilford Press.

Cardichon, J., & Darling-Hammond, L. (2017, February). *Advancing educational equity for underserved youth: How new state accountability systems can support school inclusion and student success*. Learning Policy Institute. https://learningpolicyinstitute.org/sites/default/files/product-files/Advancing_Educational_Equity_Underserved_Youth_REPORT.pdf

Cardona, G. (2020). *Achievement gap: Changing the educational system into a business model to improve accountability and student success* [Unpublished doctoral dissertation]. California State University, Northridge.

Carter, R. (2017). *A case study of the relationship between professional learning communities and teacher efficacy* [Unpublished doctoral dissertation]. Concordia University.

Carter Andrews, D. J., Castro, E., Cho, C. L., Petchauer, E., Richmond, G., & Floden, R. (2019). Changing the narrative on diversifying the teaching workforce: A look at historical and contemporary factors that inform recruitment and retention of teachers of color. *Journal of Teacher Education*, 70(1), 6–12. https://doi.org/10.1177/0022487118812418

Choyce, T. (2019). *Schoolwide structures, systems, and practices that are closing the achievement gap at a Southern California high-performing, high-poverty urban public elementary school: A case study* [Unpublished doctoral dissertation]. University of Southern California.

Cotter, V. F. (2019). *Igniting school performance: A pathway from academic paralysis to excellence*. Rowman & Littlefield.

Darling-Hammond, L., Burns, D., Campbell, C., Goodwin, A. L., Hammerness, K., Low, E. L., McIntyre, A., Sato, M., & Zeichner, K. (2017). *Empowered educators: How high-performing systems shape teaching quality around the world*. John Wiley & Sons.

Donohoo, J., Hattie, J., & Eells, R. (2018). The power of collective efficacy. *Educational Leadership*, 75(6), 40–44. http://www.ascd.org/publications/educational-leadership/mar18/vol75/num06/The-Power-of-Collective-Efficacy.aspx

Fullan, M. (2018). *The principal: Three keys to maximizing impact*. John Wiley & Sons.

Gregory, A., & Skiba, R. J. (2019). Reducing suspension and increasing equity through supportive and engaging schools. In J. A. Fredricks, A. L. Reschly, & S. L. Christenson (Eds.), *Handbook of student engagement interventions* (pp. 121–134). Academic Press.

Hargreaves, A. (2001). *Changing teachers, changing times: Teachers' work and culture in the postmodern age*. A&C Black.

Hargreaves, A., & Fullan, M. (2012). *Professional capital: Transforming teaching in every school*. Teachers College Press.

HOPE Foundation, Fullan, M., Schmoker, M., Eason-Watkins, B., & McTighe, J. (Eds.). (2002). *Failure is not an option: How high-achieving schools succeed with all students* [Video kit]. Corwin.

Ijei, C., & Harrison, J. (2010). The long and winding road to social justice: Missouri district uses culturally responsive instruction to close the achievement gap (EJ914959). *Journal of Staff Development, 31*(4), 30–33. ERIC. https://eric.ed.gov/?id=EJ914959

Kohli, R., Lin, Y. C., Ha, N., Jose, A., & Shini, C. (2019). A way of being: Women of color educators and their ongoing commitments to critical consciousness. *Teaching and Teacher Education, 82*, 24–32.

Kouzes, J. M., & Posner, B. Z. (2010). *The truth about leadership: The no-fads, heart-of-the-matter facts you need to know*. Jossey-Bass.

Kouzes, J. M., & Posner, B. Z. (2014). *Extraordinary leadership in Australia and New Zealand: The five practices that create great workplaces*. John Wiley & Sons.

Leithwood, K. (2018). *Leadership development on a large scale: Lessons for long-term success*. Corwin.

Leithwood, K., & Azah, V. N. (2017). Characteristics of high-performing school districts. *Leadership and Policy in Schools, 16*(1), 27–53. https://doi.org/10.1080/15700763.2016.1197282

Leithwood, K., Harris, A., & Hopkins, D. (2020). Seven strong claims about successful school leadership revisited. *School Leadership & Management, 40*(1), 5–22. doi: 10.1080/13632434.2019.1596077

Louis, K. S. (2015). Linking leadership to learning: State, district and local effects. *Nordic Journal of Studies in Educational Policy, 2015*(3), 30321. https://doi.org/10.3402/nstep.v1.30321

Louis, K. S., Leithwood, K., Wahlstrom, K. K., & Anderson, S. E. (2010). *Investigating the links to improved student learning: Final report of research findings*. University of Minnesota, Ontario Institute for Studies in Education, Wallace Foundation. https://www.wallacefoundation.org/knowledge-center/Documents/Investigating-the-Links-to-Improved-Student-Learning.pdf

Mintzberg, H. (2004). *Managers not MBAs: A hard look at the soft practice of managing and management development*. Berrett-Koehler.

Mombourquette, C. (2017). The role of vision in effective school leadership. *International Studies in Educational Administration, 45*(1), 19–36.

Murphy, J. F., & Louis, K. S. (2018). *Positive school leadership: Building capacity and strengthening relationships*. Teachers College Press.

Penner, E. K., Rochmes, J., Liu, J., Solanki, S. M., & Loeb, S. (2019). Differing views of equity: How prospective educators perceive their role in closing achievement gaps. *RSF: The Russell Sage Foundation Journal of the Social Sciences, 5*(3), 103–127. doi: 10.7758/RSF.2019.5.3.06

Porter, A. C., Murphy, J., Goldring, E., Elliott, S. N., Polikoff, M. S., & May, H. (2008). *Vanderbilt assessment of leadership in education: Technical manual, Version 1.0*. Vanderbilt University.

Portin, B. S., Knapp, M. S., Dareff, S., Feldman, S., Russell, F. A., Samuelson, C., & Yeh, T. L. (2009). *Leadership for learning improvement in urban schools*. Center for the Study of Teaching and Policy.

Rosenfield, S., Newell, M., Zwolski, S., Jr., & Benishek, L. E. (2018). Evaluating problem-solving teams in K–12 schools: Do they work? *American Psychologist, 73*(4), 407–419. doi: 10.1037/amp0000254

Senge, P., Roberts, C., Ross, R., Smith, B., & Kleiner, A. (1994). *The fifth discipline fieldbook*. Currency Doubleday.

Stanford, K. B. (2017). *Evaluating equity in student discipline: A program evaluation of positive behavior intervention and support in an elementary school setting* [Unpublished doctoral dissertation]. East Carolina University.

Taylor, K. A. (2018). *Leadership practices that affect student achievement: The role of mission and vision in achieving equity* [Unpublished doctoral dissertation]. Boston College.

Wallace Foundation. (2013). *The school principal as leader: Guiding schools to better teaching and learning* (Expanded ed.). https://www.wallacefoundation .org/knowledge-center/Documents/The-School-Principal-as-Leader-Guiding-Schools-to-Better-Teaching-and-Learning-2nd-Ed.pdf

CHAPTER 6

Principle 2—Ensuring Achievement for All Students

Comprehensive Systems for Prevention and Intervention

Not all of us are a mess, you know. . . . People often associate anyone who's been abused with "There's no hope for that child." . . . Tell people we can do it. That you can survive all that and be a fully functioning member of the community. Don't give up on that kid at age 7 and say, "Oh, he's been through so much; he's never going to amount to anything." . . . The abused are labeled. But you can change somebody around. (Gina O'Connell Higgins, 1996, p. 318)

What we want to achieve in our work with young people is to find and strengthen the positive and healthy elements, no matter how deeply they are hidden. (Karl Wilker, 1921)

The opening quote from Karl Wilker was provided a century ago and is equally relevant today. This is reminiscent of the movie *Groundhog Day* in which the comedic star, Bill Murray, is destined to repeat the same day over and over until he finally changes his behavior and his disposition from angry and cynical to loving and open-hearted. The lesson we are often presented is that we are unable to punish students into learning or cajole colleagues into greatness. Gaining people's compliance is quicker and easier than gaining their commitment, but it's unsustainable and less rewarding for all involved.

There is always at least one practitioner within any school to whom students flock and who in turn finds greatness in each student. Now, post-COVID-19, those with the interpersonal skills to reach and motivate their students are becoming the true "master teachers," and the definition itself is due an update.

By rethinking the professional roles of "teaching" and "leading," professionals can reach students using the *best of what we know works*, and have an opportunity to reshape the entire profession while also succeeding with virtually every student. This should ultimately be the destiny that is courageously claimed by educators worldwide at this vital moment . . . when anything is possible.

KNOWING OUR STUDENTS IS KEY

The first lesson we have collectively learned is that we must teach the way students learn, instead of expecting them to learn the way we teach. In order to do this, we need to know our students. *Assuming* who they are based only on their appearance, their past performance, stories that follow them into the classroom, or their deficits will not facilitate their success, as the following case illustrates.

CASE STORY 6.1

Alicia

Alicia's mom had been under great stress even before the pandemic hit, at which point it looked certain she would also soon lose her job. Things hadn't been going well for some time between her and Alicia either, who was an alternatively withdrawn and outspoken teenager. Alicia's world, which once included swimming and animals she loved—like horses, and the dog she hadn't seen for a week—had narrowed considerably since she stopped seeing her father. She was now taken up with incessant use of her cell phone, a string of dramatic boyfriend relations, "chill" time, shoplifting, and drug use. This was especially true when schools closed and her major reason for getting up and out of bed each day ended.

Yet Alicia was excited to celebrate Mother's Day together with her mom on May 10, 2020, as she waited at her aunt's house. She was anxiously awaiting her mother's arrival, but the police greeted her at the door instead. The news was that her mother would not be arriving. She had instead taken her life that day.

Alicia was devastated. She wept hysterically as she was transported by family friends to her father's home. How would she fill this deep hole in her heart? How would she ever trust again?

The drugs she had been taking—both legal and illicit—seemed her only solace. The professionals who quickly surfaced shared with her father that day that Alicia was at extremely high risk of self-harm and should be checked into a twenty-four-hour care unit.

Think About It

Do you and/or your colleagues know of any students at risk of great trauma? What have been some interventions used to support them? What *preventions* have been used to preempt the crisis? Only 29 percent of teachers surveyed feel they've received appropriate support and training for meeting students' social and emotional needs (Will, 2020). How can your team bridge this for students?

What plans are in place to work collaboratively with outside health professionals?

Who do you imagine Alicia to be in your mind's eye? What is your immediate, visceral reaction to Alicia? To her father in this story?

What would you recommend the father do? How would you support him, Alicia, and/or others in this situation?

Who is Alicia, and what actually happened to her?

In reality, Alicia's mother was a high-ranking private college professor and a presidential scholar in the Office of the Provost. After a decade of attempts, she had finally taken full custody of Alicia from her father and was with her almost full-time for more than a year before Alicia began demonstrating major antisocial behaviors. Alicia is a blond, blue-eyed, educated, and financially middle- or upper-middle-class thirteen-year-old who turned fourteen years old ten days after the incident.

Alicia's father was advised by most to double down on her antidepressants and psychotherapy, consider placing her in a safe twenty-four-hour facility, reduce any stressors or obligations including schoolwork, search her baggage for drugs, and take her cell phone away.

Her father decided instead to use strength-based interventions. He had taken her to ride horses from age two to ten regularly before she had left his care, and Alicia loved being around these animals more than anything. He contacted her previous riding coach, who was more than empathetic, and Alicia began working there daily and thereby paying for her weekly lessons. She gained physical activity, routine, agency, confidence, and joy from this. Her prior psychologist was replaced with one who specialized in grief among teens, focused on Alicia's strengths, and committed to Alicia's long-term struggle. Along with other such interventions, like being reunited with her dog, who required walking daily and gave Alicia a *natural* schedule to follow, horses replaced negative behaviors, screen time, and isolation.

How well do you know your students? What and whom do they love? What are their strengths? Their passions? Knowing our students well allows professionals to build on their interests and abilities. Remember the mission statement of Highline Public Schools in Chapter 5?

> OUR PROMISE: *To know every student by name, strength, and need, and graduate all students prepared for the future* they *choose.*

Using Equity to Reach *All* Students

As described in Chapter 4, we define *equity* as providing all students what they need to succeed (Blankstein & Noguera, 2016; Center for Public Education [CPE], 2016). This definition of equity is contrasted with that of equality, in which "students are all treated the same and have access to similar resources" (CPE, 2016, p. 1). Giving homework as a way to *equally* "teach" students, for example, fails to take into account those who don't even have a home, and it grows the disparity between them and those returning to one with two PhD parents at the ready to assist in that homework. Special support and provisions instead must be undertaken.

As discussed in Chapter 4, since everyone is different, professionals must be ready to reach and teach students differently as well. As parents, we do this naturally—each child doesn't get the same clothes, food, and drink at the same time. This is because they all have different interests and needs, *and because we know them.*

We often *categorize* students in lieu of *knowing* them, and are surprised when they don't fit the category (Staats, 2016). More ominously, students often *do* eventually fit the category assigned them because what we believe about students shapes our behaviors toward them and theirs in response (Okonofua & Eberhardt, 2015). These expectations, or implicit biases (Staats, 2016), are why students of color have higher rates of graduation and academic success when taught by teachers of color (Anderson et al., 2020; Kokka & Chao, 2020; Mootoo, 2020; Partee, 2014; Rosen, 2018). If we minimize implicit bias and realize, instead, that *all* students have challenges and that *equity* means ensuring differentiated supports for each student, we can work together toward a culture of win-win rather than one that pits students, staff, and entire schools against one another for limited resources. As demonstrated in previous chapters, when Advanced Placement (AP) classes were accessed by virtually all students in the Abington, Pennsylvania, school district and when the lives of homeless students were stabilized in Tacoma, Washington, the beneficiaries included all the *other* students and the overall school cultures as well (Blankstein & Noguera, 2016).

Dispelling Myths About Your Students

Agreeing as a school community to meet students where they are based on a systematic approach to knowing them and their needs is the starting point for ensuring their success. This includes dispelling preconceived ideas, stereotypes, or implicit biases we hold as individuals and sometimes embrace as a school culture.

In Case Story 6.1, Alicia didn't fall into a commonly considered "risk" category. Yet she, like some 40 percent of her peers (Nord & West, 2001), was living mainly with her mother. Wealthy, White school girls are statistically at risk of anxiety-related conditions like obesity and depression (Luthar, 2013), and almost 40 percent of all children grow up fatherless by twelfth grade. This combination placed Alicia at risk of failing and even dropping out of school (seven of ten dropouts are fatherless) (National Center for Education Statistics, 2020; Nord & West, 2001; Sanchez, 2017; see also Figure 6.1).

FIGURE 6.1   Risk Factors of Fatherless Students Compared With Their Peers

- 4 × the poverty rate
- 2 × as likely to drop out
- Girls 2 × more likely to suffer obesity
- Girls also 4 × more likely to become pregnant teens

SOURCE: National Center for Education Statistics (2020).

Another widely held stereotype is that students with darker skin are more violent (Kohli et al., 2017) and deserving of harsher punishment then their White peers (George, 2015; Kupchik & Ellis, 2008). Perceiving students with darker skin as more violent and ultimately administering harsher punishments has been found to be a result of unresolved implicit biases (Nance, 2016; Staats, 2016). We see such biases played out systemically in the wasting of millions of school dollars spent on law enforcement and metal detectors in schools where the populations are majority Black versus those that are not, even though all mass shootings in the United States took place in majority-White districts (Florida & Boone, 2018). Some districts thankfully are beginning to reallocate these resources (Beckett, 2019), with Minneapolis, Denver, and Toronto public schools among the first.

Case Story 6.1, and the statistics that follow it, isn't meant to provide yet another means of deficit characterization of students such as Alicia. Rather, this chapter has thus far focused on challenging existing sweeping assumptions of people and encourages instead a more individualized, strengths-based approach to knowing our students, becoming "talent scouts," and supporting students in not just *surviving*, but *thriving* (Osher et al., 2020; Osher et al., 2018).

The breakthrough thinking needed here is to change the misperceptions by the school community such that we

1. review who our students are through a strengths-based versus deficit lens and build on those strengths (see, for example, the Emerging Scholars program in Case Story 2.4 in Chapter 2);

2. create the mission, vision, values, goals, and school culture based on positive assumptions and beliefs about all members in the equitable learning community (ELC);

3. develop a unifying philosophy for the school(s); and

4. build a comprehensive system for prevention and intervention for students needing additional support. As part of the system, ensure at least one adult is systematically paired with each student to provide support, encouragement, and advocacy as needed.

WHAT DOES THE SCHOOL COMMUNITY BELIEVE?

In most schools, the answer to this question is, "It depends." Beliefs about low-performing students often vary among teachers. A small number of classroom teachers often account for the majority of those students who are referred to the principal's office. At the same time, other teachers are able to succeed with those same students. This is generally not a case of the students becoming more intelligent or better people once they reach the classroom of the successful teacher. It has more to do with the varying belief systems in operation within the school.

Three Scenarios to Tackle Tardiness

1. Lock the Doors

The first school created a new policy of locking the school doors after the 8 a.m. late bell rings. A few more students wound up coming on time, while many others became truant. The second school, however, chose a much more successful path.

2. Creative Scheduling

The principal at this school has found an effective way to both reduce tardiness and provide students with a "decompression" period between home and school. Every day, the school starts with a designated period in which faculty advisers work with small groups of students to teach life skills, such as cooperation and collaboration, through hands-on activities and exercises. Every student is involved, including those in special education, and students are grouped heterogeneously, with no segregation of any sort. The program has become an invaluable part of the day for both students and teachers, shares the principal:

> We feel like it's almost a sacred time. It's a time when those kids who bring baggage to school are able to get rid of that baggage so that when they go to their academic classes, they're ready to learn—and teachers are able to teach.

A side benefit is that this program has virtually eliminated tardiness to academic classes. Because of its experiential and active nature, students come early to ensure they can participate.

3. Shift Start Times

There's yet a third option a growing number of districts are taking to address school tardiness: starting middle and high school later (Edwards, 2012; Wheaton et al., 2017). The research indicates that students' unsupervised after-school time is when they are most vulnerable to antisocial behaviors, that their biorhythms are conducive to needing more sleep in the morning, and that their concentration and test scores go up when they take on academics later in the day (Edwards, 2012; Wheaton et al., 2017). In fact, as Alyson Klein (2020) reported in *Education Week*, "starting high school later has been shown to reduce teenage depression and car accidents, and contribute to higher test scores." That's partly because teenagers get their most productive, rapid-eye-movement sleep in the early-morning hours (Klein, 2020).

While much of this research has been available for years—and any practitioner could tell you how awake or not their teenage students were at 7:45 a.m.—the bus schedules and parents' work schedules trumped students' needs. Now, post-COVID-19, this is all up for conversation and new adaptive actions (see "slaying sacred cows" in Chapter 2).

Think About It

What are the assumptions about students that are driving each of the three options? What does each one tell you about the sense of agency the school leadership has in making decisions? Which approach systematically addresses students' needs? What are the costs of making such a decision in favor of students? What are the costs of *not* doing so? How could your ELC come to hard decisions and actions that favor your students?

Consider how three different belief systems resulted in widely varying solutions to the same challenge faced by two schools: tardiness.

Changing Belief Systems

Changing the belief systems of people is an extremely difficult and complex process. Most texts don't address this issue, focusing instead on changing behavior. In Chapter 5, we endorsed this approach as a practical way of addressing behaviors that are inconsistent with organizational values. In fact, changing individuals' beliefs more often than not begins with changes in behavior, leading to new and better outcomes.

Ultimately, it is imperative that a school's entire staff hold high expectations for students, and this chapter addresses some of the practical complexities in this effort. Gaining staff *compliance* alone is not enough. It takes total staff *commitment* to succeed in the thorny work of reaching low-achieving and underserved students.

Addressing the core *beliefs* of the entire school community is a lengthy process. Along the way, it is essential to be sure to hold the line on *behaviors* and *language* that may conflict with organizational values and mission. Doing otherwise creates an environment in which "anything goes." Without at *least* commitment to *behavior* that supports the school's values and mission, the fundamental aspect of almost any school's mission—that "*all* students will learn"—will become invalid. It is essential that the mission really means that *all* students—not *some* students—will learn.

A system-wide example of confronting inappropriate behavior in Toronto public schools was provided in the "Mission" section of Chapter 5. Now let's take a quick look at how a school principal confronts a science teacher whose behavior does not support the school's values and mission.

Confronting Behaviors

▶ After numerous discussions with Bob regarding the poor grades his students consistently receive, the school principal meets with him again:

Principal: Hi, Bob. Did you get those grade distributions I sent you?

Bob: Yes, I did.

Principal: Great, let's just go over them. It's obvious from these numbers, Bob, that students in your class consistently underperform, semester after semester. Something is clearly happening in your class to cause this discrepancy, and I'd welcome any explanations you might have.

Bob: This is the way I teach, Mr. Martin. It's the way I've always taught. I teach responsibility. I'm very tough on them. I'm not going to enable them like these other teachers do.

Principal: It's not our mission to make courses difficult for students, Bob. It's our mission to help them succeed. We need assessments that accurately reflect what they know, and we need approaches that are consistent with our value statement—which you helped create. I'm going to ask you to work with the two other teachers in your division, and with your director, to develop some new assessments that are more in keeping with what we're trying to accomplish. If, at the end of the next grading period, your students' scores aren't in line with those of the other classes, I'll work with you directly to ensure the necessary improvements.

WHAT IS THE SCHOOL COMMUNITY'S UNIFYING PHILOSOPHY?

One of the biggest challenges school leaders face is the tendency toward fragmentation of efforts and focus. Many demands are placed on educators, and those demands come from all directions. Often, the demands from the state, district, parents, staff, unions, and students are at odds with one another. Good leaders, therefore, are called on to make organizational meaning out of apparent chaos. In this section, we provide a framework and philosophy for how the entire school community can deal with one of the most difficult challenges: when our instruction fails to guide students to meet high academic standards.

Traditionally, when students did not comply with school policies, they were punished. If this punishment didn't work, the students were suspended or expelled. Whether or not the students succeeded academically or grew from the experience was not generally thought to be the school's concern.

The traditional philosophy regarding student behavior has led to a mismatch between how some schools deal with students who don't comply and what those students actually need to improve their behaviors. The behaviors worsen in such cases. This leads to frustration on the part of many teachers and administrators as they sense that "what we are doing isn't working!" Without an alternative to traditional approaches, there is a tendency to see the inefficacy of the "treatment" as the fault of the "patient."

Banishment becomes a popular response to the problem, and Black and Brown students are disproportionately suspended in comparison with their White and Asian peers (Fergus, 2017). Some schools in which we work have literally hundreds of suspensions each year. The line to the principal's office looks like one for a rock concert! Labeling, then referring students to remedial programs, special education, and even alternative schools, seems to be the only answer for some beleaguered teachers. This has become so widespread that entire mini-industries, as well as billion-dollar pharmaceutical treatments, have sprung up to treat the latest "disorders." So many of these diagnoses for children happen to begin with the letter *D* that the ten *D*s of deviance were created to depict the label used and actions prescribed for each (see Table 6.1).

Once there is a diagnosis for the disorder, the "treatment" becomes clear. Unfortunately, far less time has been spent creating diagnoses for young people's strengths.

A Better Way

Over the past hundred years, a growing number of leading child psychologists and youth professionals have developed a strengths-based approach to viewing and "treating" young people. They have been surprisingly consistent, in fact, in defining the basic needs that drive behavior (see Table 6.2).

The Community Circle of Caring synthesizes this body of research to provide a common framework and core philosophy of action (see Figure 6.2).

TABLE 6.1 The Ten *D*s of Deviance in Approaches to "Difficult" Youth

PERSPECTIVE	PROBLEM LABEL	TYPICAL RESPONSES
Primitive	Deviant	Blame, attack, ostracize
Folk Religion	Demonic	Chastise, exorcise, banish
Biophysical	Diseased	Diagnose, drug, hospitalize
Psychoanalytical	Disturbed	Analyze, treat, seclude
Behavioral	Disordered	Assess, condition, time out
Correctional	Delinquent	Adjudicate, punish, incarcerate
Sociological	Deprived	Study, resocialize, assimilate
Social Work	Dysfunctional	Intake, case manage, discharge
Educational	Disobedient	Reprimand, correct, expel
Special Education	Disabled	Label, remediate, segregate

TABLE 6.2 The Basic Needs That Drive Behavior

SOURCE	BASIC NEEDS
William Glasser, MD *Control Theory in the Classroom* (1986)	1. Survival and reproduction 2. Belonging and love 3. Power 4. Freedom 5. Fun
Circle of Courage (based on Sioux tradition) Larry K. Brendtro, Martin Brokenleg, and Steve Van Bockern *Reclaiming Youth at Risk* (1990)	1. Belonging 2. Mastery 3. Independence 4. Generosity
Boys and Girls Clubs of America *Youth Development Strategy*	1. Belonging 2. Usefulness 3. Competence 4. Influence
Daniel Pink *Drive: The Surprising Truth About What Motivates Us* (2009)	1. Autonomy 2. Mastery 3. Purpose
Alan M. Blankstein *Failure Is Not an Option* (2010)	1. Contribution 2. Connection 3. Competence 4. Self-control

FIGURE 6.2 Community Circle of Caring

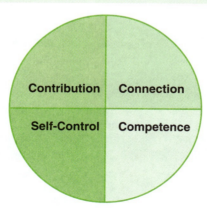

SOURCE: Van Brendtro, L., Brokenleg, M., & Bockern, S. (2002). *Reclaiming youth at risk: Our hope for the future*. Solution Tree.

Young people will naturally attempt to meet each of these four basic needs in either a pro-social or antisocial manner. One of the gangs we studied, the Latin Kings, uses a very similar framework, for example, to recruit and retain youth whose needs for connection are not being met pro-socially. Young people whose need for competence is not being met in a positive manner may turn to auto theft, for example, to gain a sense of competence. The ultimate goal of the school, then, becomes one of creating an environment and culture that meets students' basic needs. Table 6.3 shows examples of practices in such an environment, as well as contrary practices. These school practices either enhance or impede development of each of the four Cs: *connection, competence, control*, and *contribution*.

TABLE 6.3   The Four *Cs*: Practices That Promote Connection Versus Disconnection

CONNECTION OCCURS	DISCONNECTION OCCURS
Welcoming students even when they are late	Sending students to the principal's office, regardless of circumstances of late arrival
Greeting students warmly at classroom door	Working on paper at desk until all students are seated and the start bell rings
Systematically ensuring every student is positively connected to an adult	Leaving personal connections to chance
Using extracurricular engagement data of all students as a measure of school success	Assuming most students are involved in extracurricular activities
Competence Develops	Incompetence Builds
Allowing makeup work	Having "one chance" policies
Demanding mastery of material	Averaging zeros into semester grades
Testing what is taught	"Surprise" tests and pop quizzes
Finding and emphasizing strengths	Focusing on weaknesses
(Self-) **Control** Is Encouraged	Compliance and Obedience Are Demanded
Allowing students to help create class rules	Telling students what the rules are
Eliciting input on class projects and readings	Recycling the prior year's projects
Teaching empathy, self-awareness, and other emotional intelligences	Keeping emotional learning apart from academics
Contribution Results	Self-Centeredness Results
Allowing older students to teach younger ones	Not allowing for student-led mentoring
Creating community service and project-based learning opportunities	Holding learning within the school
Encouraging cooperative learning	Teacher directing all learning

It is often the case that several of these Cs can be addressed at once. They provide a framework for rethinking and coordinating the actions of the entire school community. Once the beliefs and philosophy are agreed on, it is far easier to create a unifying system for action. The next section gives very specific examples of how two schools have done just that, as well as guidelines and steps to proceed on your own.

WHAT IS THE COMPREHENSIVE SYSTEM FOR ENSURING SUCCESS?

Ensuring achievement for *all* students means having an overarching strategy that encompasses the majority of learners—and then having specific strategies aimed at those who need extra support. Essential components of a plan for all students' success include

- ensuring engaging and relevant pedagogy (see Chapter 5, "The Mission");
- having an improvement plan for all students;
- having systems for quickly identifying those in need;
- providing a continuum of support and targeted strategies for low achievers;
- publishing results on closing the achievement gap; and
- using data-based decision making for continuous improvement.

The following sections discuss each of these components in detail. Then, an additional section provides examples of intervention systems and guidelines for their implementation.

Ensuring That Pedagogy Is Engaging and Relevant

Engaging students around activities based on their own passions, interests, culture, thoughts, and beliefs can lead to large gains in student achievement as well as reduce achievement gaps (Yeager & Walton, 2011). The curriculum and instruction should include voices of those being taught and reflect positive views of students' race, ethnicity, and gender.

Engaging the Whole Child

On January 15, 2020, the Chan Zuckerberg Initiative (CZI) released a series of ten profiles highlighting schools expanding the definition of student success beyond academics to more fully consider the developmental needs of the whole child. You can find information about each of the ten schools at the CZI website: https://chanzuckerberg.com/newsroom/whole-child-case-studies/.

The models for these CZI schools begin from the inside out—with the students and their interests. Little will yield greater success and more motivation than unleashing the power of combining one's interests and passions with an opportunity to learn and create something of significance. This approach also works exceptionally well with adults in the building. Keeping one's focus on these intrinsic drivers in the midst of torrential downpour from external distractions and mandates is part of what this book—and acting from one's core and in concert with the lead team's defined interests—is about. Rooting in and keeping true to our core while adapting to significant changes externally is the challenge.

Having an Improvement Plan for All Students

The most effective schools provide a ladder of opportunities for struggling students, ranging from identification of students needing extra support before the school year begins to mandatory enrolment in remedial and/or skills classes. The effect of this range of interventions is to make clear to students that they may *not* fail. It tells students that the only choice is to learn and succeed.

As prescribed in multi-tiered systems of support (MTSS), an effective improvement plan for all students includes components of both prevention and intervention. Some prevention strategies are targeted; others apply to the entire student population. The latter include

- building relationships with students;
- systematically identifying and building on students' strengths;
- meeting with students each day;
- having staff be visible and available;
- involving students in the decision-making process; and
- matching school structures to the real needs of students.

Often, school policies, schedules, and structures simply don't accommodate the young people they're supposed to serve. Earlier in this chapter, for example, we discussed how changing school start times influenced student attendance, behavior, and academic success.

Targeted Interventions

Intervention strategies target students who are not demonstrating learning at the level of expected performance. To be most effective, these strategies are graduated in their intensity. These types of graduated prevention and intervention systems take a pyramidal form; the prevention strategies at the bottom apply to all students, and the high-intensity interventions at the top apply to only a few.

The best and most equitable MTSS begins similarly to the courageous leadership model: with *you* and *why* you are doing this work. It continues by asking, "What if we had a system that truly met the needs of all students? What if we could learn from others, organize our instructional supports, and bring them together in a way that creates a place where students, staff, and families thrive?" (McCart & Miller, 2020).

Having Systems for Quickly Identifying Students in Need

Effective schools do not follow the sink-or-swim approach. Nor do they wade in to rescue students only when they have proven that they can't swim. Schools that are committed to success for all students systematically identify struggling students. They identify problems as early as possible—well before students have a chance to fail. The timely identification of problems is what distinguishes intervention strategies from remediation strategies.

When prevention systems are already in place for all students, it becomes easy to identify those who are at risk for academic difficulties. Mechanisms for identifying struggling students should ideally be built on the programs already in place for supporting all students. For example, a high school that monitors all incoming freshmen by having staff members submit frequent progress reports automatically has a net in place for catching struggling students. Here's an example of how an elementary school set up a similar net.

Identifying Students in Need

▶ At Pelham Road Elementary School in Greenville, South Carolina, a special kindergarten class comes under the umbrella of the school's special education department. The children in the class are completely unaware that they are in a special program. The object of the class is to give children who have been identified as lacking necessary social or academic skills the boost they need before starting first grade without saddling them with the "special ed" label. The school chooses these students based on interviews with Head Start participants and places the identified students in a smaller-than-average class. The program's goal is to prepare participants for immediate mainstreaming into first-grade classrooms. In the great majority of cases, the program accomplishes that goal.

Providing a Continuum of Support and Targeted Strategies for Students Who Aren't Meeting Their Potential

Students who are moving from one level of schooling to another—from elementary to middle school or from middle school to high school—need a continuum of support that sees them smoothly through the transition. Schools provide the resources necessary to ensure that new students can hit the ground running.

Schools use various mechanisms to facilitate a seamless transition for incoming students. One is collaboration between counselors in the feeder schools and in the receiving school. This allows counselors at the receiving school to become familiar with new students' needs and with what approaches have been successful at meeting those needs in the past. Another is "red-flagging" incoming students with the greatest needs and putting them in a "good buddy" program in which an adult at the incoming school is assigned, unbeknownst to the student, to be a friend and advocate of that student serendipitously.

Other projects and programs include the following:

- Programs to prepare for the next school level (e.g., "Survival Skills for High School"). Such "skills" will now need to be inclusive of handling emotions and loss brought on by COVID-19, as well as ways to broach sensitive topics around race.

- Reviews of student records before school starts in order to provide extra supports for children in need. As noted in the Brockton High School cases in Chapters 2 and 3, staying systematically connected to students at this juncture is more important than ever.

- Faculty mentor programs, in which every incoming student is closely monitored by an adult overseeing upperclassmen who gets to know the new student well. Faculty will also need support and assistance in dealing with new levels of crisis, grief, and learning loss post-COVID-19.

Once high-performing schools have identified those students who are at risk of failure, they find ways to bolster their weak areas to ensure success. The types of strategies used vary depending on the grade levels served by the school and the needs of the students.

Publishing Results

Making the opportunity gaps an agenda item and publishing them for the stakeholder community to review adds focus to the staff's efforts. The schools in San Diego, California, used this strategy to help close their achievement gap. With so much media and public attention now on school and teacher "results," it's increasingly important to actually educate external stakeholders as to the *meaning* of grades and other data.

Using Data-Based Decision Making for Continuous Improvement

What Good Looks Like

Effective systems of prevention and intervention ensure that no student slips through the cracks. They are designed so that the majority of students benefit from careful, continuous monitoring and low-level support strategies. They have mechanisms in place to ensure the early identification of struggling students. And they follow a prescribed order so that higher-level strategies are implemented only after lower-level ones have failed to produce results.

1. At the base of the school's common mission and vision is "all students can and will learn." There are no excuses or exceptions.

2. All staff members are responsible for every student's success, both academically and behaviorally.

3. There is a clear, articulated MTSS or pyramid of support for students needing additional assistance or for those already exceeding the standards. (This answers the question, "What strategies should we use to support our learners?")

4. There is a comprehensive plan for the implementation of strategies, tracking of data, and design for whole-staff discussion and involvement in supporting students through vertical teams. (This answers the question, "How do we ensure that we are meeting the specific needs of individual students based on data?")

5. The focus is on equity in meeting students' needs, not on curriculum, although best practices and strategies for high-quality instruction are integrated into the discussion.

6. Staff unfailingly revisit the pyramid and process for implementation two times per year in order to refine and improve strategies and teamwork. This is focused on data and results of student achievement, as well as on the keys to effective teaming.

Implementation Guidelines

Developing an MTSS or system of prevention and intervention is a major task. The approach you take will depend on both the culture of your school or district and the extent to which such strategies are already in place. As the previous examples indicate, a successful approach includes all of the following:

1. *Rooting the work in the school's mission.*

2. *Getting engagement from the leadership team, and ultimately the entire faculty, around defining the goals of the intervention and the integral—versus separate—role it plays in the overall work of the school.* In Chapter 5, for example, the four critical questions around the school's mission include what should students be learning; how will you ensure relevant, engaging pedagogy; how will you know if students are learning; and how will you respond when they don't? All of this relates directly to this chapter.

3. *Putting the emphasis on instruction, which minimizes the need for distracting interventions that take focus away from the core of the educational enterprise.*

4. *Slotting students into programs like special education only as a last resort.* Deeper questioning, built on relational trust (Chapter 4), well-developed protocols (Chapter 5), meticulously developed collective teacher efficacy (Chapters 7, 8, and 10), and rootedness in leadership's core purpose (Chapters 1 and 2), will likely address the needs of 95 percent of the school's students.

5. *Agreeing on criteria for identifying students in need of assistance and ensuring they enter the appropriate programs.* The referral of any student to a prevention or intervention program should depend on data that provide good evidence of the student's strengths, weaknesses, and root causes of learning difficulties (guidelines for the use of data are provided in Chapter 7).

    Selection of these criteria must always be informed by the lens of equity. An increasingly common critique of MTSS is that its implementation assumes a "one size fits all" set of "evidence-based" interventions that fail to meet the needs of increasing numbers of culturally and linguistically diverse students. Dwayne Williams, author of *An RTI Guide to Improving the Performance of African American Students* (2015a), identified the question that should be part of every MTSS team:

    > When I train educators on culturally responsive MTSS, SEL [social-emotional learning], or trauma-informed work, the most common question I get is, "What can I implement in the classroom that will boost engagement among culturally diverse learners?" The answer is, culturally responsive instruction is not simply about "What can I do to engage students of color or culturally diverse learners." No, *culturally responsive instruction*

begins with knowledge about culture and cultural awareness, and it is a process of becoming aware of cultural values, cultural tools, and cultural clashes or tensions that present in the classroom between culturally diverse learners and teachers and students who come from different cultural backgrounds.

When students do not respond in the classroom (i.e., MTSS) or when they disengage, become disruptive, or refuse to establish or maintain relationships with teachers or students (which often leads to special education referrals), it is critical that we consider how cultural tools might play a factor, rather than believing students are unmotivated, oppositional, or defiant. . . .

One question that should be a part of every MTSS or problem solving team meeting, when addressing the performance of culturally diverse learners: Are students able to use their tools to interact, to act upon their environment, to establish relationships, and to express themselves in meaningful ways? If the answer is "no," or if the answer is "I'm not sure . . ." then this question should be the focus of discussion during MTSS meetings and when problem solving to move students through tiers.

Just because a student is disruptive doesn't mean he or she has an emotional disturbance issue, and just because a student underperforms and does not respond to instruction within a specified time period does not mean that he or she has a learning disability. Considering culture within the context of educational practices (i.e., MTSS, SEL, trauma-informed work, PBIS [positive behavior interventions and supports], restorative practices) requires that we understand how culture and cultural tools mediate all that we do as humans—and how cultural tools mediate relationship building among students and teachers. If we do not begin with culture, our MTSS and other educational practices will reflect deficit thinking, and we will continue to misdiagnose and misplace culturally diverse learners in special education programs who really do not have needs that require specialized services.

How do you use the cultural values, interests, and passions of students to boost engagement in the classroom? (Williams, 2015b)

In addition, make decisions in advance regarding what will be used as criteria for inclusion in each support program. Questions to ask include the following:

- What criteria, data, or information will be used to identify students who are eligible for each intervention program?

- Who will help provide the information?
- Who will be responsible for gathering and evaluating the data?

6. *Surfacing objections and addressing resistance.* Techniques for doing so are covered in detail in Chapter 8. Without a plan for this, rolling out MTSS in a major, system-wide effort will be most effective on paper alone.

7. *Piloting aspects of the new program.* Start slowly, with just one easily implemented aspect of the pyramid. This will allow for more complete monitoring of the effectiveness of the programs, allow schools to work out any kinks, and allow for an early success to motivate further reform.

8. *Building a culture of success.* As soon as any strategy is implemented, a system for regularly monitoring its effectiveness should be established. As data come in that indicate a positive outcome, celebrate your success. In addition, be alert to any positive actions by staff or students that lead to better performance and an improved school climate. Be sure to acknowledge and praise these efforts publicly. Such public celebrations and "pats on the back" help to build a culture that believes in, values, and expects success.

9. *Refining and adding to interventions.* As you receive data on the results of your programs, use the information to refine existing strategies and to better develop new ones. Continue to phase in more intervention programs and strategies as outcome and disciplinary data suggest a need.

Getting Started

Work with your colleagues to sketch plans or procedures on separate sheets of paper for (1) identifying students in need of extra support and attention; (2) monitoring these students intensively; (3) providing mentors, "good friends," or other adult support to these students; and (4) establishing intervention programs. List programs that already exist; note whether they need to be modified or expanded and, if so, in what ways. For new programs, state the specific goal and then address questions that arise.

In this chapter, you have seen best practices in meeting the great challenge of providing for students who *don't* initially learn to standards. This has included gaining staff commitment to the task, developing a unifying philosophy, ensuring relevant and engaging approaches to teaching and learning, and creating systems of prevention and intervention. These are among the greatest challenges a school will face. How a school responds to the question, "What do we do when students *don't* learn?" tells more about the values and collective commitment of that school than anything else. Although this chapter has provided a clear picture of and direction for how high-performing schools tackle this challenge, the subsequent chapters will help you develop the *capacity* to use these practices to address success for *all* students in your school.

REFERENCES

Anderson, M. B., Bridges, B. K., Harris, B. A., & Biddle, S. (2020). *Imparting wisdom: HBCU lessons for K–12 education.* Frederick D. Patterson Research Institute, UNCF.

Beckett, L. (2020, June 1). Minneapolis public school board votes to terminate its contract with police. *The Guardian.* https://www.theguardian.com/us-news/2020/jun/01/minneapolis-public-school-end-police-contract

Blankstein, A. M. (2010). *Failure is not an option.* Corwin.

Blankstein, A. M., & Noguera, P. (with Kelly, L.). (2016). *Excellence through equity: Five principles of courageous leadership to guide achievement for every student.* ASCD.

Boys and Girls Club. (n.d.). *Youth development strategy.* https://bgcuv.org/who-we-are/youth-development-strategy/

Brendtro, L., Brokenleg, M., & Van Bockern, S. (1990). *Reclaiming youth at risk: Futures of promise.* Solution Tree.

Center for Public Education. (2016, January). *Educational equity: What does it mean? How do we know when we reach it?* https://cdn-files.nsba.org/s3fs-public/reports/10901-4496-16_CPE_%20Equity%20Symposium_FINAL.pdf?LKIv6zrRE08mxahlArLZ8PdfeQzWahY2

Edwards, F. (2012, Summer). Do schools begin too early? Education*Next, 12*(3). https://www.educationnext.org/do-schools-begin-too-early/

Fergus, E. (2017). *Solving disproportionality and achieving equity: A leader's guide to using data to change hearts and minds.* Corwin.

Florida, R., & Boone, S. (2018). *Where do mass shootings take place?* Bloomberg CityLab. https://www.citylab.com/life/2018/03/where-do-mass-shootings-take-place/554555/

George, J. A. (2015). Stereotype and school pushout: Race, gender and discipline disparities. *Arkansas Law Review, 68,* 101–129.

Glasser, W. (1986). *Control theory in the classroom.* Perennial Library.

Higgins, G. O. (1996). *Resilient adults: Overcoming a cruel past.* Jossey-Bass.

Klein, A. (2020, February 25). Starting high school later shows "big impact." *Education Week.* https://www.edweek.org/ew/articles/2020/02/26/starting-high-school-later-shows-big-impact.html

Kohli, R., Pizarro, M., & Nevárez, A. (2017). The "new racism" of K–12 schools: Centering critical research on racism. *Review of Research in Education, 41*(1), 182–202. https://doi.org/10.3102/0091732X16686949

Kokka, K., & Chao, T. (2020). "How I show up for Brown and Black students": Asian American male mathematics teachers seeking solidarity. *Race Ethnicity and Education, 23*(3), 432–453. https://doi.org/10.1080/13613324.2019.1664002

Kupchik, A., & Ellis, N. (2008). School discipline and security: Fair for all students? *Youth & Society, 39*(4), 549–574. doi: 10.1177/0044118X07301956

Luthar, S. (2013, November 5). The problem with rich kids. *Psychology Today.* https://www.psychologytoday.com/us/articles/201311/the-problem-rich-kids

McCart, A., & Miller, D. (2020). *Leading equity-based MTSS for all students.* Corwin.

Mootoo, A. N. (2020). Students of color and anecdotal pedagogy: A success story. In S. L. Niblett Johnson (Ed.), *Examining Social change and social responsibility in higher education* (pp. 94–106). IGI Global.

Nance, J. P. (2016). Student surveillance, racial inequalities, and implicit racial bias. *Emory Law Journal, 66,* 765. https://law.emory.edu/elj/content/volume-66/issue-4/articles/student-surveillance-racial-inequalities-implicit-bias.html

National Center for Education Statistics. (2020, May). *Characteristics of children's families.* U.S. Department of Education. https://nces.ed.gov/programs/coe/indicator_cce.asp

Nord, C. W., & West, J. (2001). *Fathers' and mothers' involvement in their children's schools by family type and resident status.* National Household Education Survey. Statistical Analysis Report. ED Pubs, PO Box 1398, Jessup, MD 20794-1398.

Okonofua, J. A., & Eberhardt, J. L. (2015). Two strikes: Race and the disciplining of young students. *Psychological Science, 26*(5), 617–624. https://doi.org/10.1177/0956797615570365

Osher, D. (in press). *Thriving, equity, and learning and development.* American Institutes for Research and Forum for Youth Investment.

Osher, D., Cantor, P., Berg, J., Strayer, L., & Rose, T. (2018). *Drivers of human development: How relationships and context shape learning and development.* Applied Developmental Science.

Partee, G. L. (2014, June 28). *Retaining teachers of color in our public schools: A critical need for action.* Center for American Progress. https://www.americanprogress.org/issues/education-k-12/reports/2014/06/28/91962/retaining-teachers-of-color-in-our-public-schools/

Pink, D. (2009). *Drive: The surprising truth about what motivates us.* Riverhead Books.

Rosen, J. (2018, November 12). Black students who have one black teacher are more likely to go to college. *The Hub.* https://hub.jhu.edu/2018/11/12/black-students-black-teachers-college-gap/

Sanchez, C. (2017, June 18). *Poverty, dropouts, pregnancy, suicide: What the numbers say about fatherless kids.* NPR. https://www.npr.org/sections/ed/2017/06/18/533062607/poverty-dropouts-pregnancy-suicide-what-the-numbers-say-about-fatherless-kids

Staats, C. (2016). Understanding implicit bias: What educators should know. *American Educator.* https://www.aft.org/sites/default/files/ae_winter2015staats.pdf

Wheaton, A. G., Chapman, D. P., & Croft, J. B. (2017). School start times, sleep, behavioral, health, and academic outcomes: A review of the literature. *Journal of School Health, 86*(5), 363–381. doi: 10.1111/josh.12388

Wilker, K. (1921). *Der Lindenhof.* Lichtkampf-Verlag.

Will, M. (2020, April 7). The success of social-emotional learning hinges on teachers. *Education Week.* https://www.edweek.org/ew/articles/2020/04/08/the-success-of-social-emotional-learning-hinges-on.html

Williams, D. (2015a). *An RTI guide to improving the performance of African American students.* Corwin.

Williams, D. (2015b, February 11). *The question every teacher should ask in MTSS meetings.* Begin With Their Culture. https://tier1education.com/justice-and-equity

Yeager, D. S., & Walton, G. M. (2011). Social-psychological interventions in education: They're not magic. *Review of Educational Research, 81*(2), 267–301. https://doi.org/10.3102/0034654311405999

CHAPTER 7

Principle 3—Data-Based Decision Making for Continuous Improvement

> *What has been discovered is that first, people will not voluntarily share information–especially if it is unflattering—unless they feel some moral commitment to do so and trust that the data will not be used against them. . . . Data without relationships merely causes more information glut. Put another way, turning information into knowledge is a social process and for that you need good relationships.* (Michael Fullan, 2001, p. 6)

Even in the "hard" area of data, it will be the "soft" skills that determine their successful use. The past decade has seen an explosion of new ways to collect, sort, and distribute every type of data imaginable to schools. Test data alone are now a multibillion-dollar industry. Yet the real challenge in successful use of data toward continuous improvement lies not in the technical side of the equation, but rather in the human side.

Many would argue that the testing regimen for our students has denied them an education (Darling-Hammond, 2014), left educators beleaguered (see PDK Poll [2019] for recent stats on their complaints re: time on testing, as well as stress), and led to mind-deadening "boredom" for students (Fullan, 2001). Even worse, our assessments have more often than not been used as a weapon to call our students failures rather than a tool to support them. This is particularly true for students of color, whose disproportionally cited misbehavior often leads them out of the classroom and away from instruction, such that they fall further behind academically as well. For a more detailed discussion of standardized testing, please refer to the "Rethinking Testing" section in Chapter 8 (page 161).

Consider this all-too-common scenario as well as the alternative presented in Case Story 7.1.

CASE STORY 7.1

The Wounds We Carry: Fractal Challenges, Fractal Possibilities

Picture a typical staff meeting at a contemporary school. Let's call it a "data walk." Imagine it's August, the week before school starts. The principal is presenting standardized test data from the math and English assessments administered the previous spring. A PowerPoint presentation flashes up colorful bar graphs and percentages, displaying the school's flatlined math scores and incrementally increasing English scores. "Our goal this year is to increase math performance by 5 percent and maintain our English language arts growth pattern," asserts the principal. "We are especially concerned that our long-term English learners and African American students are not making adequate yearly progress." Teachers stare blankly at the screen, their expressions flat and body language uninspired.

Freeze this scene. Now imagine you are a teacher in the room.

Do you feel inspired to meet your students the following week? Are you ready to hunker down with your colleagues to plan a dynamic opening unit? If you're feeling deflated, you are not alone. What is wrong with this staff meeting?

- Children's voices and experiences are ghosted. We are talking *about* students without listening *to* students.

- Teachers are situated as passive recipients of student data rather than active co-creators.

- The complex process of learning is reduced to a single metric that tells a single story.

- Students of color are viewed through a deficit lens, as those who *struggle* to succeed.

Here is the central problem that this meeting represents: we have put "children at the center" of the wrong system and thereby stripped them, and their teachers, of agency and humanity.

Now picture a new scene: a classroom in which a student is presenting and defending a piece of academic work to a committee of teachers, peers, and community members. The student makes oral arguments and provides evidence to back them up, using visual graphics to strengthen her case. When she finishes, the committee members ask her tough questions: "What is a counter-perspective to what you've offered? How do you know that . . . ? Can you elaborate on your theory that . . . ? Can you provide us with an exception to the rule you've offered and explain how your position is still legitimate?" The student stands her ground, responding with more evidence, grace under pressure, and professionalism.

This type of performance-based assessment experience should be ground zero in our data collection for equity. There is no way to develop a theory of action that improves macro, "big data" metrics without knowing what our students are doing on the micro, street level. Yet we continue to throw our weight behind test scores and other big data, as if one day those measures will magically rectify centuries of inequality (Safir, Dugan, & Wilson, in press).

Even the concept of the "achievement gap" is built on biases that implicitly fault the student for inability to "achieve" at the same time that the definition of *achievement* itself is based on a narrowly defined set of skills that more often than not are determined in a manner that is inconsistent with the stated educational goals:

> *Are we currently assessing everything that matters, or only those things that are easiest to test and grade? With respect to large-scale standardized assessments, the answer is fairly obvious. For example, virtually all current standards in English language arts include listening and speaking skills . . . yet those are rarely, if ever, assessed on standardized tests.* (McTighe, 2018)

This misalignment between stated goals and means of assessment is more than a technical issue. It is one thing to espouse an agenda of equity, and yet another to realize the many possible disconnects between that agenda and acting in concert with it, like failure to disaggregate data. This is due more often than not to lack of sensitivity and awareness relative to the "norm," which was originally created to *sort and select winners and losers* à la the bell curve (Herrnstein & Murray, 2010), and a society founded on subjugation of entire races of people.

In a post-COVID-19 "restart," it behooves us to reconsider the use of data for continuous improvement in fundamental and equitable ways. This chapter challenges deeper thinking about the purpose of measuring student and school success, while also providing solid and time-tested methods to consider in implementation.

WHAT IS THE PURPOSE OF EDUCATION?

When leading assessment experts share their lists of major issues, often they begin with "purpose" of the data, echoing this same sentiment for individuals in Chapters 1 and 2; leadership around data starts with thinking about the purpose.

At the start of this book, many invoked this question. Sue Szachowicz (personal communication, April 26, 2020) challenged many of the fact-based questions on standardized tests as virtually irrelevant; many interviewed in the creation of this book challenged "seat time" as the primary measurement toward graduation; and Dan Domenech (personal communication, April 6, 2020) asked about the value of tests themselves in a system in which there was no schooling for much of the 2019–2020 academic year and where the vast majority of students would need to be qualified to enter the workforce instead of attend college in any event.

In reconsidering this critical question, consider how you and your school community would respond to these questions:

- Who is determining the answer to the question of the purpose of education in your locality? For many, it is a confluence of policymakers and testing agencies. How do state, provincial, and national tests align with the relevant and salient issues of your school community?

- How does the purpose of education align with the *needs* of your school community, including if not focusing on those who have been traditionally marginalized?

- How will education prepare your students for success in their pursuit of higher levels of academic attainment and/or career?

- How does your school community define "success" or achievement, and how does that align with a holistic view of the needs for social, emotional, physical, and spiritual well-being of the children you serve?

- What specifically and explicitly can your school community do to define the purpose of education in terms that embrace the values and cultures of the stakeholders it affects?

Beyond the traditionally defined purposes of education like development of basic reading and writing skills, knowledge of critical facts about civics or history or another subject, and understanding of general concepts like cause and effect, a growing number of people are seeing transference of students' capacity to do things like think critically, problem-solve, or collaborate as a higher purpose for contemporary education (McTighe, 2018; Jay McTighe, personal communication, May 5, 2020; Zaretta Hammond, personal communication, May 8, 2020).

Developing a Disposition for Breakthrough Thinking and Actions

Another potential purpose for a modern-day education may be preparing students to think and act "out of the box." While some have made distinctions between teaching students to read and creating great literature (Wagner, 2014), others have implored Western leaders and policymakers to consider our differential advantage of creativity in the world stage vis-à-vis other countries far more focused on traditional academic rigor (Zhao, 2009). The thinking is that any number of societies can produce managers or even presidents for Apple, but few can produce a Steve Jobs, let alone a Lin-Manuel Miranda! Now that we are seeing a wholesale reevaluation of our civic society in light of the enormous and glaring inequities before us, this may be a good time to consider how to prepare our young people to take moral leadership in a manner described in Chapter 2.

HOW CAN WE ASSESS WHAT MATTERS MOST?

Once we are clear on our purpose for the overall enterprise of education and our specific goals related to and supporting this, we would devise assessments that inform our work. Yet, as Jay McTighe (2018) describes, "Most standardized tests have limited capacity to assess transfer goals [mentioned earlier], or related complex skills like scientific investigation, historical inquiry, research, argumentation, and creative thinking." He advocates "performance-based measures in which students are asked to: 1) apply their learning to a *new* situation and 2) *explain* their thinking, show their reasoning, or justify their conclusion" (McTighe, 2018; see also Hibbard, 1996). This idea is furthered by deeply engaging students and their families in providing their own personal evidence of creativity, persistence, understanding, and accomplishments. Consider the four Cs of data usage for improvement:

- Creating the climate and culture of trust for effective data use

- Capacity building for analysis of data

- Committing to implementation

- Collecting, sorting, and distributing disaggregated data in the form of reports

While there are still some important things to consider in terms of the fourth C, which are taken up later in this chapter, the major challenges facing schools involve having productive, data-based conversations that lead to consistent implementation. Each of the "soft Cs" is taken up as follows.

Climate and Culture of Trust for Effective Data Use

Peter Hill, whose work led him to the top ranks of educational assessment in Australia and Hong Kong, makes the link between purpose and trust for us: "Openness, transparency, and frank discussion of any accountability program are essential, so that both declared and perceived purposes can be aligned. There needs to be a climate of trust, rather than of misunderstanding and fear" (Hill, 2010, p. 45). Bringing this statement full circle to the four components of relational trust in Chapter 4, clarifying the "purpose" provides the *ethical* alignment between actions and intention; "transparency" addresses the same, as well as builds confidence in leaders' *competence*; and the "openness" and "frank discussions" provide for the *professional respect* that builds trust. Building a climate of trust requires explaining who will be evaluating whom and to what end.

Although data teams and other forums for data analysis have become ubiquitous fixtures of schools, the question that lingers is why so many of these conversations devolve into blame and shame fests and fail to have an impact on student achievement and/or well-being—particularly when the focus of interrogation is on the students who haven't been well served by our inequitable systems. First, keep in mind that such conversations are, in essence, a form of professional learning that, when implemented properly, can facilitate teacher growth. As teachers gain an understanding of the impact of their decisions and actions on specific groups of students—particularly those that elicit *positive* results—they gain a greater sense of mastery, leading to enhanced self- (and ultimately collective) efficacy.

Collaborative professional learning focused on analyzing past experiences is among the most powerful forms of professional learning. With that said, most of the experiences we analyze center on where we went wrong (i.e., our professional failures and disappointments). It isn't that such postmortems are without value; however, we can also grow as professionals by taking a close look at what we *did right*. Author Chen Schechter (2019) has conducted research in Israel on the power of learning from our successes. Similar to the concept of positive deviance, learning from success entails identifying *action principles* that contributed to the successes of the past and can contribute to successes in the future. Schechter's research pinpointed the following as benefits of learning from success:

1. Reduces defensiveness and enhances motivation

2. Generates transformation

3. Enhances reflection on effective practices

4. Creates positive organizational memory

5. Generates commitment to and investment in learning among diverse members of a school community (pp. 19–20)

One of the few "silver linings" of the COVID-19 pandemic has been the rapid elevation of the teaching profession, after years of being devalued and even demonized. Parents who were able to stay home had a rare glimpse into the hard work of engineering positive and productive learning experiences. Just as we are constantly reminded of the importance of applying a growth mindset to the students we teach, now is the time to remember that teachers alike have the capacity for growth across their professional life spans. Innovative professional learning designs like learning from success can do much in the way of restoring a climate of trust in our schools and in our profession at large (Schechter, 2019).

Capacity Building for Analysis of Data

One of the big challenges around effective use of data is the staff's capacity to interpret it. In fact, so often school teams seek easy, off-the-shelf solutions—and there are plenty of corporations ready and willing to sell them! As one big-city school superintendent shared about his experiences with many technology salesmen, "they try to shoehorn in" their products to your situation. Yet these approaches are capacity depleting, not expanding. Externally provided professional development resources "typically represent others' ideas about needed skills and knowledge but seldom reflect teachers' thoughts about what they need to learn or how to learn it" (McLaughlin & Talbert, 2006, p. 2).

The better (and far less expensive) investment is in a highly trained and experienced facilitator of the collaborative change process (Fullan, 2001; McLaughlin & Talbert, 2006). In their extensive school study around building school-based teacher learning communities, McLaughlin and Talbert (2006) noted, "Schools that made significant progress did so with expert guidance . . . they achieved significantly greater student learning gains than schools where this strategy was not well implemented" (p. 46).

Breakthrough leadership frequently necessitates reframing or redefining the problem to solve it. This generally takes a deeper analysis on the part of the learning community, and highly skilled guidance from the leader or leadership team. Consider this:

In communities and schools with incidences of violence among youth, educators may be inclined to identify violence itself as the primary crisis for their students and disciplinary action as the proper response. A further analysis, however, reframes the issue by investigating the root causes of that violence. Several studies in the last two decades have found that children who threaten or commit violence are likely to be victims of violence themselves, either in the form of abuse or in witnessing abuse, and children who are suspended or expelled as a result typically benefit from more adult supervision rather than less (Kernic et al., 2002; Rushton et al., 2002).

In 2013, *Pediatrics*, the official journal of the American Academy of Pediatrics (AAP), reaffirmed its position against zero tolerance practices and urged schools to review their policies with the educational, emotional, and social well-being of their communities in mind. In its review of the literature, the AAP (2013) found that "out-of-school suspension and expulsion often place the child back into the very environment that may have contributed to the antisocial behaviors in the first place, thereby negating the effectiveness of a 'lesson-learned' from out-of-school suspension and expulsion." Early intervention, positive behavior interventions and supports, and the implementation of school-based mental health programs are alternatives that stand to benefit the child and community while improving the learning environment at the same time.

This analysis could, and should, go further. As reported by Anya Kamenetz (2018) for NPR, overall school suspension rates in the United States decreased between 2012 and 2016, but suspension rates disaggregated by race revealed continuing disproportionalities among Black students, who were twice as likely to be suspended as White students at the high school level.

Now our hypothetical question, which began with school violence, has moved from deficit thinking into questions about what schools can do to support their students emotionally and equitably. Instead of punishing the child, we are asking what more we can do as educators to hold our students up and foster their continued education.

Effective analysis of data, therefore, requires several elements:

- *Clarifying accuracy of the data.* This may also require using multi-sourced data and soft, "perceptual" data. The stories that people carry with them, as well as their interpretations and understandings of a given event, have generally not entered the mainstream narrative regarding our history, democracy, what is of value culturally, and what success means. As outlined earlier in this chapter, this is essential to redress to ensure an equitable outcome for all of our students.

- *Understanding what the data are telling you.* If, as described earlier, there is an interpretation linking truancy to violence among teens, the data alone do not provide this interpretation; people do! All of our students— and their voices, perceptions, and streetwise street data—matter!

- *Understanding what the data mean.* For example, how can we make sense of grading disparities across groups in a single school when every teacher is married to a different grading policy? While such variance has existed for many years, our industrial age grading practices must be called into question as they have disproportionately harmed historically marginalized students for over a century (Feldman, 2018).

- *Tapping well-established (see Chapter 5), high-performing teams in open and frank dialogue.* This will normally develop better analysis than will any one individual (though this is not so for teams where trust or well-facilitated exchanges are an issue).

- *Including those who comprise the data in the data design, its collection, and interpretation.*

Commitment to Implementation

If the purpose for data collection is defined by those who will use it, and a trusting, collaborative culture composed of capable staff allows for honest and incisive dialogue about the meaning of the data and actions that should be taken, the chances of consistent implementation are great. And the more depth and breadth of involvement of stakeholders within the learning community, the more widespread the implementation will likely be.

Possible Uses of Data

Good data used appropriately offer a multitude of benefits for schools and their stakeholders:

- To advance student achievement

- To address "whole child" needs

- To provide feedback to students on academic progress

- To support students for special programs

- To inform parents of student performance and inform the larger community of school and district gains

- To inform teacher judgments about improving classroom instruction
- To organize school-wide learning support programs to ensure no student falls through the cracks
- To validate student and teacher efforts to improve
- To guide professional development activities
- To gauge program strengths and identify opportunities for program improvements
- To promote public accountability
- To monitor continuous progress

To successfully use data to drive continuous improvement, schools need to answer two important questions:

- What data should be collected?
- How should data be used?

Each of these points is discussed in the sections that follow.

WHAT DATA SHOULD BE COLLECTED?

Many schools rely on state or provincial and national standardized test scores as the primary indicator of student learning. These scores can provide evidence of system-wide, school-wide, and classroom-level achievement and, when properly disaggregated, can help identify students in need of additional support and intervention (as outlined in Chapter 6). Increasingly, schools are tracking a broader set of data types to more fully assess their progress. For example, the Every Student Succeeds Act, which supplanted No Child Left Behind, calls on states to include at least one nonacademic indicator in their accountability systems. Without question, the most productive data are generally formative (addressed later in this chapter), and that includes data generated by teachers reviewing student work together.

One of the most powerful and effective ways of working with data is for vertical or grade-level teams to analyze student work together based on common assessments or assignments. This process encourages all faculty members to share in the responsibility for success of *all* students.

Results-oriented data analysis should include such questions as these:

- What criteria will be used to determine proficiency?
- Does this piece of work show proficiency?

- In what areas are students doing particularly well?

- What are patterns of weakness?

- What can be done to address the weak areas?

Teachers who are accustomed to using data strictly as an evaluative or summative device—to determine whether students did or did not learn what was required—may need training and encouragement to add formative assessment to their instructional practice. As trust among teachers grows (see Chapter 4) and as team-meeting protocols become well established (see Chapter 5), data sharing among teachers becomes easier. This is always done with the intent of collegial sharing of internal best practices. It is never used to rank or blame individual teachers for poor performance.

Other Data Sources

Academic Outcomes

- Outcomes on nationally normed tests

- Student performance on district- or school-level common assessments

- Grade spread on unit tests or semester exams, compared with previous results

- Course and curriculum analysis to measure alignment with state and national standards

- Graduation rates for high schools

- Disaggregated data on participation in Advanced Placement courses

- Continuing education levels, such as the percentage of graduating students pursuing higher education or the percentage of students entering regular or honors high school classes (after junior high or middle school)

- Outcomes on state or provincial achievement tests compared with previous years and with other schools of similar demographics

Correlates to Student Achievement

- Engagement levels of students in extracurricular activities

- Social and emotional learning

- Attendance numbers, including enrollments and dropouts during the course of a year and hour-by-hour or class-by-class attendance figures

- Referrals to special education, disaggregated by race

- Participation of students in gifted and talented education programs, disaggregated by race
- Discipline actions, such as the number of in- or out-of-school suspensions, the number of repeat cases, and times and places of their occurrence—all disaggregated by race

Descriptive Data

- Census, enrollment, and lunch subsidy applications, to profile the demographics of the whole school
- Observations of daily activities, occurrences, and situations that would not appear in any type of formal record keeping
- Surveys of students, staff, external stakeholders, and parents to gauge satisfaction and attitudes toward the school
- Classroom observations and peer observations
- In-depth interviews and collections of descriptive "stories"

Combining hard demographic and formal assessments with soft data about engagement and behavior—while protecting student confidentiality—is a complex task.

Guidelines for Data Quality

A school's ability to make improvement plans is directly tied to the quality of its data. Without clear, quantifiable information about the school's current status, leaders will find it very difficult to create focused improvement plans. Data from diverse sources guide each step of planning and implementing initiatives for academic improvement. At a minimum, useful data should be disaggregated, multisourced, relevant, timely, and consistent.

Disaggregating Data

All data should be analyzed in terms of the identifiable ethnic and socioeconomic groups in the school. Although district-level enrollment information available from the central office may not reveal an individual child's cultural, ethnic, linguistic, or socioeconomic status, creative improvement teams can utilize this information by correlating test results, grades, and other outcomes with known data sets, like subsidized lunch lists, English learner class enrollments, residential addresses, and other recorded information.

They can also require teachers to correlate the children in their classes with preestablished categories (e.g., limited English proficient, newcomer to the community, and living in public housing), then compare the scores of these groups with those of the school as a whole. Such analysis allows schools to set goals and devote extra attention to the children who need them most.

Multisourced Data

The data collected should be drawn from a variety of sources to give a complete picture of the school's progress. Many of those sources are discussed in the section of this chapter titled "What Data Should Be Collected?" Data should include demographic and socioeconomic information, absentee rates, dropout rates, suspension and disciplinary rates, report card grades, and, of course, scores on state and nationally normed tests.

A school is more than a set of numbers, however, and student, teacher, and parent perceptions of their learning community are an essential part of its achievement. Uncovering and recording these perceptions is a fundamental part of the improvement process. Doing so requires a variety of "soft" data and the use of information-gathering strategies such as surveys, questionnaires, interviews, focus groups, brainstorming, or roundtable discussions (see Case Story 7.1).

Relevant Data

To be useful, data must be relevant to the school's goals. Schools revamping their curriculum to align more closely with new standards, for example, will want to look closely at the results on related assessments. Schools that have adopted a goal of improving writing skills through a program of writing across the curriculum may find that samples of current student work provide the best indicators of progress.

Relevant assessment data

- align with the curriculum and the overarching SMARTER goals of the school (see Chapter 5);

- are sufficiently specific to show achievement and progress of all groups of students and to drive targeted interventions; and

- reveal problem areas and areas of strength to build on.

Timely Data

Since large proportions of student populations turn over annually, outcomes of last year's tests may not reflect the strengths and weaknesses of this year's enrollment. Curricular goals and emphases also change, and they do not always correspond to state test standards. The most useful data for teachers and students, therefore, are the more immediate feedback from formative assessments.

In many schools, the timeliest data are generated by internal assessments and measurements. Teachers cannot rely solely on test results to guide their daily decision making. The data on which they base their day-to-day instructional decisions must be more immediately derived from classroom tests, homework, class work, and observations. At the end of this chapter, we take a closer look at the three major categories of assessment—assessment *as* learning, assessment *for* learning, and assessment *of* learning.

Consistent Data

In order for assessments to indicate trend lines, outcomes from the same assessment instruments are viewed at different points in time. Data from this year—whether test scores, absentee rates, or average numbers of writing exercises completed per student—need to be compared with similarly collected data from previous years to be meaningful. Only a comparison of results from several years will indicate the trend line of the school.

HOW SHOULD DATA BE USED?

Once data have been collected and analyzed, teachers and administrators can find ways to apply the results of their data explorations to their day-to-day efforts with students. Following are some ways in which data can be effectively used.

Using Data to Drive Decisions and Set Goals

The selection of goals, instructional practices, materials, programs, and policies in a school should be directed by good information. If a school's data reveal a strong correlation between discipline problems and a particular time of day or place in the school, for example, staff schedules and assignments can be adjusted accordingly.

Data can be used first to determine where the needs are, what kinds of goals need to be established, and whether a goal is achieved. A measurement (or rubric) must be chosen to indicate whether progress has occurred. For example, a school that is determined to raise students' math performance needs to decide how to measure improved performance: What test or observable performance demonstrates how well students are doing? How will the school know when the goal is attained? The selection of the measure and a target score are best established at the outset and articulated as part of the goal.

Using Data to Target Interventions

The more current the data are, the better they can be used to create on-the-spot interventions for struggling groups of students. Teachers can now get real-time data on student performance using whiteboards and other monitoring devices. It is no longer necessary to wait until the grading period to identify and assist struggling students. Interventions can be immediate.

Using Data Continuously in Collaborative Teams

Classroom assessments offer some of the best inputs for creating new interventions. The information from state or provincial testing is less usable than what is learned from district testing—which is less usable than what comes from classroom assessments. Teachers use data from classroom assessments for instructional planning and also for evaluating whether they should reteach or revisit a concept or skill.

Using Data to Support Change Initiatives

It is in the interest of school leaders to use relevant and credible data to support their calls for change to teachers and other stakeholders. A bar graph showing declining student success over time, for example, can be a powerful motivator for action.

Using Data to Guide Continuous Improvement and Redefine Success

Although it may seem that data can most effectively be used to identify problem areas within a school, data can also be used to discover areas of strength that could be made even stronger.

Continuous improvement can play out at the school level in various ways. One way to improve is through periodic evaluation of teaching plans, lessons, unit designs, and assessments by using a set of design standards. Such an approach compels administrators and teachers to apply these same standards to their own work.

Using Data to Monitor Progress

The value of any instructional practice should be judged according to its results. When implementing a new instructional strategy such as culturally responsive teaching, teachers must use data to monitor outcomes regularly and frequently to determine how well the new practices work.

Using Data to Guide Professional Learning

School and district decisions related to the focus of professional learning should never be made in a vacuum. Rather, they should be informed by a wide range of data related to student achievement and significant nonacademic indicators such as perceptions of inclusiveness and belonging. The current version of Learning Forward's *Standards for Professional Learning* includes the following data standard:

> *Professional learning that increases educator effectiveness and results for all students uses a variety of sources and types of student, educator, and system data to plan, assess, and evaluate professional learning.*

The standards document itemizes an array of data types including formal and informal assessments, achievement data such as grades, and annual, benchmark, end-of-course, and daily classroom work and classroom assessments. In addition, the standard references other forms of data including demographics, engagement, attendance, student perceptions, behavior and discipline, and so on (Learning Forward, 2011).

A Closer Look at Student Assessment: A Call for Equity and Social Justice

by Margo Gottlieb

▶ What if in a post-COVID-19 world we add a more human element to assessment and revisit data through the lens of stakeholders rather than center our attention on district- or school-level comparative statistics and scores generated from testing that leave "gaps" in student performance? With guidelines for data quality and usefulness, the added dimension of stakeholder voice enhances the comprehensiveness and meaning of data sets while simultaneously empowering those persons impacted by the results. A three-pronged approach to assessment—that is, assessment *as, for*, and *of* learning—directly engages students, teachers, and administrators in the process and invites the convergence of multiple perspectives in data-driven decision making.

The triad of assessment *as, for*, and *of* learning is derived from assessment for formative and summative purposes. Rather than focusing on outcomes or time frames, however, this model of inclusion and equity centers on leveraging the roles and experiences of stakeholders. The most important stakeholder in education, the students, are deserving of their own space and identity, thus assessment *as* learning. Assessment *for* learning is a collaborative undertaking that involves teachers, and students in partnership with teachers, in building classroom relationships. Assessment *of* learning fosters relational trust (within a distributive leadership culture) among teachers, coaches, leadership teams, principals, and other administrators.

Assessment *as* Learning

Ownership for assessment *as* learning resides in students. At the heart of assessment *as* learning is student–student interaction, where there is deliberation, discussion, negotiation, making meaning, and sharing of concepts and ideas. There are several additional defining qualities that distinguish student-centered assessment from the other approaches; it entails

- personalizing learning based on student strengths;

- motivating students to actively pursue learning from their own vantage point or perspective;

- student choice in selecting mode(s) of communication (e.g., oral, written, graphic, visual) for processing information and expressing learning; and

- focusing on student growth and reflection on learning.

In learner-centered classrooms, students are expected to assume active roles in designing and enacting assessment practices. For example, in multilingual settings, use of more than one language is increasingly becoming an acceptable classroom instructional and assessment policy (Gottlieb, 2021). Additionally, classroom assessment is becoming more inclusive of student voice where students are co-contributors, facilitated by teachers, in formulating individual goals for learning along with identifying accompanying evidence for reaching them. Ultimately, learners are becoming instructional resources for one another and are activated to be responsible for their own learning (Wiliam & Leahy, 2016).

Assessment *for* Learning

In this approach, assessment is an active social process that serves to promote and instill learning, not used only to describe, monitor, or audit it. Thus, assessment *for* learning encompasses a broad conceptualization of interaction between teachers and students on an ongoing basis to plan, gather, analyze, and share information to improve teaching and learning. Assessment tasks are based on student understanding during learning in which students are critical assessors and teachers are instructional decision makers (Earl, 2013).

A primary attribute of assessment *for* learning is feedback. Black and Wiliam's (1998) groundbreaking research, confirmed by Hattie and Temperley (2007),

(Continued)

(Continued)

unequivocally confirms the value and importance of feedback within the instructional cycle as pivotal in improving student achievement. It is feedback—descriptive information that is goal-oriented, transparent, actionable, user-friendly for students, and timely—not test scores, that helps students move toward reaching their academic goals (Wiggins, 2012). Data collected during assessment *for* learning allow teachers to

- apply criteria for success to give students criterion-referenced feedback rather than relying on or giving grades based on points;

- plan differentiated instruction for student achievement and for language development of multilingual learners;

- respond in real time to individual student performance, interests, and needs;

- document student performance minute by minute, day by day, week by week; and

- examine personal instructional practices and make adjustments.

Assessment *of* Learning

Assessment *of* learning is unique in that it often operates at two levels. Classroom assessment that focuses on what students have accomplished at the culmination of a period of instruction, such as a unit of learning, has been characterized as assessment *of* learning since it documents accumulated student performance. In contrast to what happens in classrooms, assessment *of* learning at a school or district level often refers to commercial interim measures, which often are predictive of large-scale annual testing given for accountability purposes. Unlike performance project-based assessment, testing tends to be an individual activity where students act alone (Moss, 2008).

The educational landscape is changing, and so, too, must traditional testing that is distal to the happenings in classrooms. Shepard and colleagues (2017) suggest that large-scale accountability testing should not be the primary driver of educational reform; rather, change should begin with local decisions about curriculum and instructional practices. Being informed by classroom-centered assessment is consistent with evidence from research about learning and development, motivation, and identity formation. Socially embedded practices that view the students and teachers as change agents should be a motivator for instilling assessment *as, for*, and *of* learning and as a means for promoting equity in schools. Table 7.1 describes specific features of these approaches within a growth mindset.

TABLE 7.1 Assessment *as, for,* and *of* Learning: Highlighting Stakeholder Roles

ASSESSMENT *AS* LEARNING, WHERE STUDENTS:	ASSESSMENT *FOR* LEARNING, WHERE TEACHERS, ALONG WITH STUDENTS:	ASSESSMENT *OF* LEARNING, WHERE SCHOOL AND DISTRICT LEADERS, ALONG WITH TEACHERS:
Partner in brainstorming assessment strategies and selecting modes of communication	Set mutually agreed-on goals for learning	Liaise to help determine school- and district-wide data trends
Help each other in solving instructional and assessment-related issues	Co-construct success criteria based on learning goals	Mentor coaches and teachers on assessment literacy
Serve as agents and advocates of their own learning	Co-create a menu of assessment tasks	Form networks to discuss assessment issues and their impact on curriculum and instruction
Monitor their learning and seek support	Collaborate in forming classroom and school assessment policies	Support teachers in designing and interpreting common performance assessment
Document and show evidence of learning	Determine themes from student and community interests and resources	Offer professional learning opportunities
Engage in self- and peer reflection	Participate in assessment conversations	Strategize with teachers to ensure equitable assessment opportunities for all students
Become autonomous self-regulated learners	Engage in action research on effectiveness of assessment tasks	Design and enact a comprehensive assessment plan
Legitimize their funds of identity	Agree on evidence of learning	Ensure psychometric properties (validity and reliability) of school-wide and district measures
Gain metacognitive and metalinguistic awareness	Share data during student-led conferences	Meet compliance with state and federal mandates/ guidelines
Interact with each other in one or more languages	Help scaffold learning for individual students	

SOURCE: Adapted from Gottlieb (2016).

REFERENCES

American Academy of Pediatrics. (2013). Out-of-school suspension and expulsion. *Pediatrics*, *112*(5). doi: https://doi.org/10.1542/peds.2012-3932

Black, P., & Wiliam, D. (1998). *Assessment for learning: Beyond the black box*. University of Cambridge.

Darling-Hammond, L. (2014). *Want to close the achievement gap? Close the teaching gap*. https://www.aft.org/ae/winter2014-2015/darling-hammond

Earl, L. (2013). *Assessment as learning: Using classroom assessment to maximize student learning* (2nd ed.). Corwin.

Feldman, J. (2018). *Grading for equity: What it is, why it matters, and how it can transform schools and classrooms*. Corwin.

Fullan, M. (2001). *Leading in a culture of change*. Jossey-Bass.

Gottlieb, M. (2021). *Classroom assessment in multiple languages: Engaging educators, English learners, and other multilingual learners*. Corwin.

Gottlieb, M. (2016). *Assessing English language learners: Bridges to educational equity: Connecting academic language proficiency to student achievement* (2nd ed.). Corwin.

Hattie, J., & Temperley, H. (2007). The power of feedback. *Review of Educational Research*, *77*, 81–112.

Herrnstein, R. J., & Murray, C. (2010). *The bell curve: Intelligence and class structure in American life*. Simon & Schuster.

Hibbard, K. (1996). *Teacher's guide to performance-based learning and assessment*. ASCD.

Hill, P. W. (2010). Using assessment data to lead teaching and learning. In A. M. Blankstein, P. D. Houston, & R. W. Cole (Eds.), *Data-enhanced leadership* (pp. 31–50). Corwin.

Kamenetz, A. (2018, December 17). *Suspensions are down in U.S. schools but large racial gaps remain*. NPR. https://www.npr.org/2018/12/17/677508707/suspensions-are-down-in-u-s-schools-but-large-racial-gaps-remain

Kernic, M., Holt, V. L., Wolf, M. E., McKnight, B., Huebner, C. E., & Rivara, F. P. (2002). Academic and school health issues among children exposed to maternal intimate partner abuse. *Archives of Pediatrics & Adolescent Medicine*, *156*(6), 549–555. https://doi.org/10.1001/archpedi.156.6.549

Learning Forward. (2011). *Standards for professional learning*. https://learning forward.org/standards-for-professional-learning/

McLaughlin, M. W., & Talbert, J. E. (2006). *Building school-based teacher learning communities: Professional strategies to improve student achievement*. Teachers College Press.

McTighe, J. (2018). Three key questions on measuring learning. *Educational Leadership*, *75*(5), 14–20. http://www.ascd.org/publications/educational-leadership/feb18/vol75/num05/Three-Key-Questions-on-Measuring-Learning.aspx

Moss, P. (2008). Sociocultural implications for assessment I: Classroom assessment. In P. Moss, D. C. Pullin, J. P. Gee, E. H. Haertel, & L. J. Young (Eds.), *Assessment, equity, and opportunity to learn* (pp. 222–258). Cambridge University Press.

PDK Poll. (2019, September). *Frustration in the schools: Teachers speak out on pay, funding, and feeling valued*. The 51st Annual PDK Poll of the Public's Attitudes Toward the Public Schools. https://pdkpoll.org/wp-content/uploads/2020/05/pdkpoll51-2019.pdf

Rushton, J., Focrier, M., & Schectman, R. (2002). Epidemiology of depressive symptoms in the National Longitudinal Study of Adolescent Health. *The Journal of the American Academy of Child & Adolescent Psychiatry, 41*(2), 199–205. https://doi.org/10.1097/00004583-200202000-00014

Safir, S., Dugan, J., & Wilson, C. (in press). *Street data; How the information we need will lead us to equity.* Corwin.

Schechter, C. (2019). *The collective wisdom of practice: Leading our professional learning from success.* Corwin.

Shepard, L. A., Penuel, W. R., & Davidson, K. L. (2017, January 23). Design principles for new systems of assessment. *Phi Delta Kappan.* http://www.kappanonline.org/design-principles-new-systems-assessment/

Wagner, T. (2014). *The global achievement gap: Why even our best schools don't teach the new survival skills our children need—and what we can do about it.* Hachette UK.

Wiggins, G. (2012). Seven keys to effective feedback. *Feedback, 70*(1), 10–16. http://www.ascd.org/publications/educational-leadership/sept12/vol70/num01/Seven-Keys-to-Effective-Feedback.aspx

Wiliam, D., & Leahy, S. (2016). *Embedding formative assessment.* Hawker Brownlow Education.

Zhao, Y. (2009). *Catching up or leading the way: American education in the age of globalization.* ASCD.

CHAPTER 8

Principle 4— Collaborative Teaming Focused on Curriculum, Instruction, and Assessments

The greatest challenge to school transformation is resistance to change. According to the World Future Society (n.d.), "Covid-19 is the first time in our species' existence where we at a global scale are experiencing a potential systems collapse of our civilization. . . . While the outcome of the Covid-19 [pandemic] is uncertain . . . there will be many more future threats likely of greater intensity that will ultimately bring down our systems if we maintain our status quo operations." We should have paid closer attention to the threats early on.

A question asked by Bill Hite (personal communication, April 18, 2020), superintendent of Philadelphia schools, is, "Why did we need a crisis to force us to do what we should have been doing for kids all along?" Hite argues that a crisis can create the birth of new opportunities, further stating, "We are actually in a better place today than we were before the crisis. We have been able to accomplish in a few weeks what it would have taken years to achieve before this crisis." The cry for change should make it easier for education leaders to make teaching and learning more relevant for students.

At the end of each day when educators reflect on their work, they ask themselves, "Did we make a difference for our students? Did we focus on what matters most for their future success?" During and immediately following the pandemic, instructional leadership took a back seat to more immediate needs (e.g., feeding children, providing access to technology, and attending to safety and psychosocial needs). Yet, access to quality curriculum, instruction, and assessment remains an enduring priority for educational leaders at all levels of the education system.

In this chapter, we will discuss National Policy Board for Educational Administration (NPBEA) Standard 4: Curriculum, Instruction, and Assessment. "Effective educational leaders develop and support intellectually rigorous and coherent systems of curriculum, instruction, and assessment to promote each student's academic success and well-being" (NPBEA, 2015). While it is beyond the scope of this book to provide a comprehensive examination of *all* best practices for curriculum, instruction, and assessment, we encourage instructional leaders to consider the following promising strategies that support individual needs of students in a pandemic and post-pandemic learning environment:

1. Culturally responsive teaching

2. Blended learning

3. Trauma-informed care

But first, let's begin with a general introduction to the urgent need for access to high-quality, rigorous, and culturally responsive curriculum and instruction—a need that was present long before the onset of COVID-19.

ACCESS TO RIGOROUS CURRICULUM AND INSTRUCTION

For far too long, curriculum, instruction, and assessments have ignored educational inequities. Children of color, English learners, students living in poverty, and students with disabilities are commonly denied opportunities to participate in rigorous academic programs. Yet, we know these students want to be challenged. According to the Education Trust (2020), in thirty-six of thirty-seven states, Black students are underrepresented in gifted and talented programs. One-third of these states would need to at least double the enrollment of Black students in gifted and talented programs in order for Black students to be properly represented (Education Trust, 2020). The professional standards for school leaders articulate a responsibility to ensure that each student has equitable access to effective teachers, learning opportunities, academic and social support, and other resources necessary for success (NPBEA, 2015).

Case Story 8.1 illustrates how breakthrough leadership can be applied to disrupt inequitable practices.

CASE STORY 8.1

Algebra for All

When I (Marcus) first arrived in Chesterfield County (Virginia) Public Schools as superintendent on October 1, 2006, one of several inequities caught my attention—student enrollment in eighth-grade algebra. For decades, algebra has been a gatekeeper course to higher-level mathematics and a requirement for college. Students who had not enrolled in eighth-grade algebra were frequently placed at a disadvantage when applying for more rigorous programs such as honors, Advanced Placement, dual enrollment, or International Baccalaureate. They were altogether eliminated from several other prominent programs in the school district and the region. Multiple studies indicate that students who take more high-quality math courses are more likely to declare science, technology, engineering, or mathematics for college majors (Bottia et al., 2015; Sahin et al., 2017).

The analysis revealed that district-wide, 35 percent of all eighth-grade students were enrolled in algebra. A deeper dive revealed that among these 35 percent, 16 percent were Hispanic/Latinx, 15 percent were Black, and 4.5 percent were identified as economically disadvantaged. This meant a disproportionate number of students were eliminated from high school academic rigor before they had a chance to even get in the game.

I asked the community, "Why are 95 percent of the students identified as economically disadvantaged unable to enroll in eighth-grade algebra? Is there something different in their DNA?" Not only were the questions met with silence; it became clear that there were some in various communities who did not want to entertain the problem. However, there were others who were hopeful for a better solution. Thus, we began a process led by Dale Kalkofen, district assistant superintendent for curriculum and instruction, and Michael Bowling, supervisor for mathematics, of creating a plan to ensure that every eighth-grade student in the district was enrolled and successfully completing eighth-grade algebra prior to entering high school. The plan included opportunities for accelerated math beginning in the fourth grade, and doubling the math periods in the sixth and seventh grades.

The strategy allowed students to receive the equivalent of four math courses in the sixth and seventh grades combined—a foundation that would better prepare them for success in eighth-grade algebra. Within two years, the plan was fully implemented district-wide. What some people thought was impossible is just routine today. It was not easy, but it was the right thing to do. We had to provide compelling evidence to the community that it was in the best interest of all students.

GENERAL PRINCIPLES OF CURRICULUM, INSTRUCTION, AND ASSESSMENT DEVELOPMENT

Effective breakthrough leaders will implement coherent systems of curriculum, instruction, and assessment that promote the realizations brought about by COVID-19 and a growing awareness of institutional racism through a vibrant mission, vision, values, and goals that embody high expectations for all students' learning, align with academic standards, and are culturally responsive. They align and focus systems of curriculum, instruction, and assessment within and across grade levels to promote student academic success, love of learning, and a healthy sense of self (NPBEA, 2015). To ensure buy-in, breakthrough leaders will organize teams to update their vision and processes for implementing relevant curriculum, instruction, and assessments, as illustrated in Table 8.1.

TABLE 8.1 Team Process for Developing Engaging and Relevant Curriculum, Instruction, and Assessments

Action Plan	Define and clarify problems and desired outcomes
	Allocate funding to organize curriculum, instruction, and assessment content development aligned to professional standards
	Develop curriculum and instructional goals, strategies, and actions based on empirical research and best practices
	Develop a fair and open process for selecting and compensating team/work group members
	Collect and analyze relevant data
	Organize use of time, space, and human and material resources
	Implement solutions for effective teaching and learning • Demonstrate knowledge of content • Demonstrate knowledge of students • Demonstrate knowledge of digital resources • Implement engaging and relevant instructional strategic goals • Align age-appropriate and adaptive assessments to the written and taught curriculum
	Ensure equity and culturally responsive practices
	Institutionalize the change
	Plan for new and unforeseen challenges and threats to curriculum, instruction, and assessments

CHALLENGES TO DISTANCE LEARNING HOME INSTRUCTION

Clearly, most schools were not prepared for promoting teaching and learning while practicing social distancing. According to Cyndee Blount, principal of Acquinton Elementary Schools in rural King William, Virginia, students and families experienced several challenges to home instruction, as illustrated in Table 8.2. As they return to school buildings, educators need to take inventory of the inequities experienced during school closings.

TABLE 8.2 Impact of Distance Learning on a Rural School District

Challenges for Students	
	75% of the community does not have cable or fiber lines
	Students and families lack access to Wi-Fi connectivity
	Schools experienced logistical difficulties in delivering learning packets to students
	Students struggled to work independently to complete learning packets, as many parents were still working
	Students lacked motivation without the direct daily support and reinforcement of the teacher
	Students experienced the need for direct instruction from the teacher
	• Long spans between when students do the work and when they receive feedback on the work—4 weeks in between starting the first page of a learning packet and receiving the feedback
	• Work is not graded, further minimizing motivation
	Lack of social interaction with peers
	Students have struggled with an abrupt end to the school year
	Inadequate systems to provide food to students in need
	Fear of the unknown—"Will I see my teacher again? When can I get my supplies? What will school look like next year? When will I get my yearbook? We missed field day."
Challenges for Teachers	Asked to change the face of education overnight
	Spending lengthy hours creating learning packets to send out every 2 weeks due to lack of adequate technology
	Long hours offering feedback on each packet as it is returned
	Feeling defeated by spending hours to make packets with an 80%+ pickup rate, yet only a 67% return rate
	Days are consumed by hosting office hours to accommodate families
	Lack of social interaction with peers
	Teachers are struggling with abrupt end to the school year

(Continued)

TABLE 8.2 (Continued)

Concern for neediest students receiving little to no educational support from home
Asked to shift the report card cycle and change grading practices late in the school year
Lack of accurate and consistent information—when students and staff pick up items, and what is going to happen when school buildings reopen
Changing expectations without consistent guidance

Despite such formidable hurdles and obstacles, breakthrough leadership created results-oriented solutions to similar pre-COVID-19 challenges, as Case Story 8.2 demonstrates.

CASE STORY 8.2

Anywhere, Anytime Learning

The fallout of the 2008 economic recession forced institutions to find new solutions to new problems. Due to draconian decreases in federal, state, and local funding, Chesterfield County Public Schools in Virginia was forced to cut more than $100 million in operating costs and more than 550 positions. These cuts resulted in the loss of personnel, textbooks, supplies, and equipment funding. Many of the gains achieved through funding for additional academic intervention specialists, class size reductions, and safety net resources to close achievement gaps were gutted. Business and higher education leaders advised school officials that classrooms must look different. In response to these challenges, the district developed a new strategic plan called *Design for Excellence 2020*. It shifted its traditional budget allocations to provide students with daily access to technology, intended to increase "anywhere, anytime learning" and strengthen its focus on college and career readiness.

The "anywhere, anytime learning" initiative began after the Great Recession, in the fall of 2014, when the school system implemented the largest Chromebook initiative in the United States. After all, the cost of a Chromebook and access to *open education resources* could replace traditional textbooks and supplies for just a fraction of the cost. These devices were powerful tools that directly contributed to the achievement results outlined in the strategic plan.

Teachers were employed during the summer to build the digital curriculum that significantly accelerated learning opportunities for students. Technology staff were able to track students' use of their new mobile devices, which revealed student logins to education sites peaked during the hours of 6 p.m. on Fridays through 11 p.m. on Sundays. The digital divide was practically eliminated, and test scores increased.

During the pandemic, most students were quarantined at home where they received instruction through distance learning, provided they had adequate internet access and digital devices. Teachers and administrators made valiant efforts to provide students with quality instruction through distance learning technology, learning packets, and worksheets. Nonetheless, many students experienced what we call a *corona slide*, similar to the summer slide, where students lose academic gains made during the traditional school year. One of the lessons learned is that distance learning, even at its best, is not a viable replacement for face-to-face instruction. Moreover, the learning loss has been especially profound for low-income, Black, and Hispanic students (Dorn et al., 2020). In all likelihood, students in the United States will be facing continued instability in the 2020–2021 school year, in which at least some of their schooling will be enacted at home. Consequently, educators will be well served with knowledge of best practices for blended learning.

BLENDED LEARNING, EQUITY, AND CULTURAL RESPONSIVENESS

The effective leader promotes the use of technology in the service of teaching and learning (NPBEA, 2015). When implemented effectively, blended learning provides the best of face-to-face instruction integrated with the best of digital educational resources and opportunities.

Unlike distance learning, blended learning requires the physical presence of both teacher and student, and promotes student independence by offering a fair amount of control over their space, time, and path. However, as previously stated, one of the lessons of COVID-19 is that distance learning is more effective for some student groups than others. For this reason, we advocate blended learning designs that incorporate culturally and linguistically responsive teaching and learning—practices that affirm students' cultural identities and leverage their funds of knowledge.

Blended learning provides an opportunity to enrich learning with more equitable and culturally responsive experiences. Zaretta Hammond describes three key areas when engaged in equity work:

1. Multicultural education—celebrating diversity, creating positive social interactions across differences, and exposing privileged students to multiple perspectives and other cultures

2. Social justice education—exposing the social political context that students experience, raising students' consciousness about inequity in everyday situations, and creating a lens to recognize and interrupt inequitable patterns

3. Culturally responsive education—improving the learning capacity of diverse students who have been marginalized educationally; affective and cognitive aspects of teaching, learning, and accelerating learning; and building cognitive capacity and academic mindset by pushing back on dominant narratives about people of color (quoted in Major, 2020)

According to Hammond, one of the primary goals of culturally responsive instruction is to promote the growth from dependent to independent learners. Dependent learners rely on teachers to carry most of the cognitive load of academic tasks. Frequently, the least experienced teachers are assigned to teach the neediest students, and they lack the knowledge or skills to engage these students in productive struggle—the very thing that expands our intellective capacity. Far too often, students of color, English learners, and students from low-income households aren't supported in facilitating their cognitive growth. Hammond (2015) states that culturally responsive teaching is one of the most powerful tools for fighting the "epidemic of dependent learners" (p. 15). Additionally, Hammond (quoted in Major, 2020) recommends three culturally responsive strategies that can be utilized in the context of distance or blended learning to help students gain independence:

1. Deepen background knowledge—help students connect new things they are learning to their brain's existing schema or background knowledge

2. Cultivate cognitive routines—essential to building growing brain-power connecting the known to the unknown

3. Build word wealth—through word games like Scrabble, Heads Up, or simple word searches

Such strategies can be implemented in a distance learning environment as well as in brick-and-mortar classrooms.

What Are the Advantages of Blended Learning?

When implemented effectively, blended learning can provide differentiated and individualized learning opportunities to close opportunity gaps. A 2019 study reported that in blended classrooms, participants deemed in-person teachers necessary for supporting students. Across subjects, students felt that teachers as tech supporters were key to making the course function at specific moments. Monitoring of the learning experience by teachers helps daily and weekly pacing so students might finish in a shorter amount of time. Face-to-face teachings helped improve outcomes for dependent learners such as low-income students. The study also indicated that teacher support helped improve student use of the computer, and comprehension improved with the support of a teacher (Pollock et al., 2019).

CASE STORY 8.3

How Do We Learn Best?

The COVID-19 quarantine inspired millions of children and adults to learn a new skill or hobby during their time in isolation. T. J. Randall is a millennial husband and father of two sons who lives in a suburb of Washington, DC. He works in information technology for a federal contractor on weekdays, and his evening and weekend hobby is arranging digital music. He had always wanted to learn to play the guitar, so just days before a state-wide quarantine was enforced, he purchased one. His dilemma: "How do I learn to play the guitar without taking a class or hiring a tutor?"

Let's assume you wanted to learn something new—perhaps playing the piano, coding, speaking a new language, playing chess, or practicing yoga. In the past, you may have picked up an encyclopedia or hired a teacher. In the twenty-first century, online sources like YouTube and Wikipedia are the new encyclopedia. You can view and study relevant processes and applications of desired skills and knowledge you expect to learn. You can chunk, isolate tasks, replicate, practice, critique, and assess your progress. You would not move to the next task until you had mastered the prerequisite knowledge and skills. This is the approach used by T. J. YouTube videos served as his model, and within a few weeks he had learned to play the basic chords to several songs. His five-year-old son, Jordan, wanted to learn also, so T. J. began to teach him to play using the same methodology. Jordan's mother had always wanted him to play the piano, but the guitar was Jordan's choice. The goal was to play an instrument. Too frequently, parents and educators do not allow children to choose their own path to achieve an identified goal.

A motivated and engaged Jordan's blended learning experience was facilitated through face-to-face instruction from his father, and digital support from videos. Within one week he had learned to play "Mary Had a Little Lamb." His immediate success prompted an enormous jump in his confidence and self-esteem. Soon Jordan was playing his guitar for family and friends on Zoom gatherings. Both T. J. and Jordan understood they were still beginners, but they would continue to learn by doing.

When five-year-old Jordan, our budding musician, began kindergarten in September 2019, he was filled with excitement and the wonderment of learning. Like most young children, he was like a sponge and always curious about learning new things. He could barely wait for that big yellow bus to arrive in front of his house every morning, to take him to his school that had just been recognized as a National Blue Ribbon School. He was fortunate to attend an excellent school with great teachers. Even so, several months into the school year, his excitement began to diminish with each

(Continued)

passing day. The excitement for learning was not quite the same within the structure of the six-and-a-half-hour school day. Long stretches sitting at a desk for an energetic five-year-old is not the optimal learning experience. It was nothing like his online blended experiences with the authentic guidance of his father in learning to play the guitar. We can only hope when Jordan and children everywhere return to school following the pandemic, they will all receive a more engaging and relevant learning experience than before the pandemic.

CHILDHOOD TRAUMA–INFORMED CARE AND SOCIAL-EMOTIONAL LEARNING

Trauma-Informed Care

With the increase of consumption of alcohol and other mind-altering substances during the pandemic quarantine, there has also been a corresponding increase in child abuse and neglect. Case Story 2.2 in Chapter 2, which detailed Ms. Lewis's Zoom call to her student, Sam, focuses on a teacher's firsthand glimpse into a student's chaotic home life during the pandemic. The pandemic has illuminated the plight of children who have been impacted by adverse childhood experiences (ACEs) that not only impact their ability to learn but, in many instances, have long-term negative effects on their physical and mental health. Students who have experienced trauma are prone to lapse into what Hammond (2015) calls the "amygdala highjack," a physiological response to stress that elicits an overload of cortisol and a resultant "fight or flight" response (p. 40).

In 2018, nearly 1,770 children died of abuse and neglect in the United States. According to the Substance Abuse and Mental Health Services Administration's National Center for Trauma-Informed Care, "traumatic experiences can be dehumanizing, . . . singular or multiple compounding events over time, and often include betrayal of a trusted person or institution and a loss of safety. . . . Trauma includes physical, sexual and institutional abuse, neglect, intergenerational trauma, and disasters that induce powerlessness, fear, recurrent hopelessness, and a constant state of alert" (National Association of State Directors of Developmental Disabilities Services, 2020).

In the United States, the total lifetime economic burden associated with child abuse and neglect was approximately $428 billion in 2015, rivaling the cost of other high-profile public health problems, such as type 2 diabetes and stroke (Centers for Disease Control and Prevention [CDC], 2020).

We know child abuse and neglect are preventable. The CDC (2020) has developed a technical package that includes five strategies to impact individual, family, community, and societal behaviors that influence risk and protective factors for child abuse and neglect:

1. Strengthen economic supports to families—strengthening household financial security and family-friendly work policies

2. Change social norms to support parents and positive parenting

3. Provide quality care and education early in life

4. Enhance parenting skills to promote healthy child development

5. Intervene to lessen harms and prevent future risk

We also know schools that promote climates of safety and fear reduction through cognitive behavioral interventions, positive behavior interventions and supports, and social-emotional learning that is trauma-informed, which can help counteract the damage caused by ACEs. In a 2018 Twitter chat hosted by Alex Shevrin Venet, educators discussed building trauma-informed social-emotional learning environments. They agreed teachers need to (1) focus on the individual student and strong one-to-one relationships and (2) create bonds requiring a broader cultural adjustment and reprioritization, where the whole community works together to cultivate a space in which students and educators thrive (Venet, 2018).

Social-Emotional Learning

Joshua Starr, CEO of Phi Delta Kappa International, recently said, "I worry that there's a sense that the most important thing to do right now is to focus on academics and get kids learning, and we're not dealing with this collective punch to the gut. We have multiple punches to the gut coming our way. Our most important job is to attend to kids' emotional needs, their confusion and concern. We've got to give space for that, and schools have to balance that" (quoted in Krueger, 2020). School systems like Baltimore County Public Schools have assembled entire teams dedicated to addressing students' psychosocial and emotional needs during the school shutdown (Krueger, 2020).

Social-emotional learning can serve to promote equity but only if the harmful effects of institutional racism and other injustices are openly addressed in its implementation. Approaching this work with implicit biases or a deficit mindset can cause more harm than good. In a statement prepared by the National Equity Project (n.d.), we are reminded that *all learning is social and emotional*:

> *Social emotional learning offers the possibility of acknowledging, addressing, and healing from the ways we have all been impacted by racism and systemic oppression and to create inclusive, liberatory learning environments in which students of color and students living in poverty experience a sense of belonging, agency to shape the content and process of their learning, and thrive.*

CASE STORY 8.4
"All the Children Who Will Come Behind Me Deserve Better"

Adverse childhood experiences were impacting students in Petersburg, Virginia, schools at a disproportionate percentage. When the new leadership team arrived in 2016, the city ranked at or near the bottom of the state in almost every measurable indicator associated with community health: morbid obesity, mortality rate, teen pregnancy, and crime. Students across the district were also tormented with the negative news reports about their city that seemed to bombard their television screens daily. They struggled to avoid the self-fulfilling prophecy that they would likely experience the same struggles as those who had come before them. In spite of the conditions, the students craved the love and support of their teachers, and wanted to make them proud.

I (Marcus) was the superintendent at the time. I reflected on two different conversations with students that would crystalize the need for breakthrough leadership to meet the social-emotional learning needs of students. The staff had written a grant called *Windows to the World*, which included a Chromebook for every student in Grades 5–12. In speaking with a group of eighth-grade students, I asked, "How do you think your education would be different if we gave every student a computer?" A student named Jamal responded, "Petersburg is broke. You can't afford to give us computers." Her response seemed to be a reaction to the negative daily news reports she had heard about the financial struggles of the city. It was also a reflection of a mindset, that "things will never get any better for students."

In another conversation that I had with high school student leaders, I asked them to share their desires for a quality education. They mentioned things like more honors and Advanced Placement courses, the need for repairs to failing facilities, internships, and more licensed and experienced teachers in the classroom. As they began to brainstorm solutions, a student named Kris (leader and captain of the soccer team), with tears in his eyes, became very emotional. He said emphatically, "The adults in this city don't care about us, because if they did, they would do better! I'm a senior, so I won't benefit from these changes.

But all the children who will come behind me deserve better." Kris and I worked together with other students to advocate for the needs of all students. The attitudes expressed by Jamal and Kris were representative of most of the city's children. These conversations contributed to the district's leadership development of its social-emotional learning strategies to be reflected in the written, taught, and tested curriculum. Five strategies we suggest for integrating social-emotional learning in the classroom appear in Table 8.3.

TABLE 8.3 Five Strategies for Integrating Trauma-Informed Social-Emotional Learning (SEL) in the Classroom

	WHAT	HOW
1. *Take care of yourself*	We entered this profession because we wanted to help others. The key to effectively implementing SEL in any classroom starts with you! It is difficult if not impossible to help others if you are experiencing instability in your personal or professional life, or struggling with the impact of COVID-19. Before you try to assist others, your first responsibility is to put your oxygen mask on (air travel metaphor). Make your own psychosocial health a priority by organizing your time to include activities you enjoy and making connections with friends and family.	• Begin each day with something that inspires you—a quote, an affirmation, a routine, a prayer • Practice mindfulness—stay in touch with your thoughts and feelings, and stay in the moment • Stay socially connected • Talk to relatives or trusted friends at least 20 minutes a day • Take brief stretch or exercise breaks every 30 minutes • Seek win-win solutions • Avoid stressors that can result in burnout
2. *Establish structures for trusting relationships*	An essential feature of trauma-informed SEL is trusting relationships among students, teachers, and classmates. Following prolonged school closings, students are craving structures that reinforce predictable routines and safety.	• Strengthen relationships by providing students with an environment with clearly understood classroom procedures • Promote culturally responsive practices that support each individual student's academic needs and well-being and leverage students' assets • Provide opportunities to practice identifying and regulating emotions • Establish high expectations immediately upon the return to school • Minimize unstructured time, and plan engaging learning activities that motivate and inspire students

(Continued)

TABLE 8.3 (Continued)

	WHAT	HOW
3. *Communicate enthusiasm and optimism*	"Nothing great was ever achieved without enthusiasm" (Ralph Waldo Emerson). Enthusiasm and optimism are contagious. Students need it now perhaps more than ever.	• Set the emotional thermostat every day when you enter the school or classroom • Introduce new content with enthusiasm • Be innovative and creative in everything you do • Be proactive and initiate your priorities
4. *Treat students with respect*	You must give respect to receive respect from your students. Embarrassment and humiliation often lead to defiance and classroom disruptions. Fairness and consistent treatment are important to students.	• Demonstrate your concern and appreciation for your students • Do not raise your voice, single students out, or attempt to embarrass them • Teach nonviolent conflict resolution skills and address discipline problems individually in a professional and caring, yet confident, manner • It is unavoidable to prevent students from feeling embarrassed when they get something wrong, so offer students nonpublic (digital) ways to respond to questions • Observe body language to guarantee your students the message they are receiving is the same one that you are sending • Give students the right to pass when called upon • Remain consistent with praise: don't praise a student for simple tasks because it sends a message of low expectations for them • Don't take misbehavior personally • Be consistently the same yesterday, today, and tomorrow
5. *Go beyond expectations; go the extra mile*	School closings have revealed troubling inequities in the lives of your students. They need teachers who will do whatever it takes to ensure their success. Students need tiered instructional support and social-emotional support.	• Provide students with frequent and consistent feedback • Schedule extra time for tutoring, either before or after school • Organize tiered systems of interventions • Organize extra work packets

WHAT	HOW
	• Frequently communicate with students and parents • Donate food or clothing • Refer students who have needs beyond your scope to other school resources, government agencies, and civic or faith-based charities • Invest significant time in planning meaningful and engaging lessons

RETHINKING TESTING

In Chapter 7, we explored Gottlieb's three-part framework built around assessment *as, for,* and *of* learning. For decades, public school educators have been directed to make critical decisions based on a single metric—the results of high-stakes, norm-referenced, standardized test scores. More recently, the wisdom of relying on this single measure has been called into question by a variety of stakeholders including researchers, policymakers, and parents. Consider the following:

It was a typical spring morning at Chillum Elementary School in Chillum, Maryland. Students were feeling anxious about participating in an annual ritual—the end-of-school-year state tests. For the past month, they had endured the typical "drill and kill" test prep with large portions of their school day spent completing practice tests. Parents and families participated in the daily countdown to the big day. On the eve prior to testing, there was a school-wide pep rally, with a display of bicycles and other prizes advertising the rewards students would receive if they did well on their tests. Even the youngest students were aware the school had performed poorly for the past several years, and there would be harsh consequences if scores did not improve.

As students entered the school on the day of the big test, a parent ran into the main office to inform the staff of a car accident near the school. By the time the principal and several staff members had rushed outside to the scene, an ambulance had already arrived to examine the passengers in the two-car accident. Fortunately, there were no serious injuries. However, the paramedics wanted to transport ten-year-old Elisa to the hospital for observations. She pleaded with them, "Please let me go to school. I have to take my MSPAP [Maryland School Performance Assessment Program] test. Please don't make me miss my test." Since the emergence of the accountability era launched by the report *A Nation at Risk* in 1983, and reinforced by the No Child Left Behind Act of 2002, Elisa and millions of other students have become engulfed in out-of-control testing anxiety.

Pedro Noguera has stated that "instead of using assessment to tell us what children really need to learn, we use it as a weapon, to tell a child, you're low or you're high" (quoted in WSU News, 2012). In recent years, parents and communities have begun to rebel, with some pulling their children out of school during spring testing. In *The Testing Charade: Pretending to Make Schools Better*, Harvard's Daniel Koretz makes a persuasive argument on the failure of the standardized test accountability system and how so many of our educational and political leaders still blindly believe that high-stakes, punitive testing can improve students' educational achievement (Ed. Magazine, 2018). Some policymakers even call for more testing of "soft" skills, such as grit and social-emotional learning (Stevenson, 2018). Testing and assessments certainly have their place in the education ecosystem. It is important to measure student progress and growth to adapt and modify instruction. But tests should not only align with meaningful content; they should be integrated into the lessons through formative assessments that reinforce inquiry-based teaching and learning, student engagement, and critical thinking, creative problem solving, communication, collaboration, and citizenship. Some have also argued that formative assessments shouldn't be linked to grades.

A Historic "Breakthrough" Opportunity to Change Our Assessment System

A headline in a May 2020 edition of *Education Week* read, "Coronavirus Throws Spring Testing in Disarray" (Gewertz, 2020). Federal law requires states to administer annual assessments in math and English language arts, and periodic testing in science during the spring of each year. The Individuals with Disabilities Education Act also requires that all students with disabilities be included in all general state and district-wide assessment programs, including assessments required under the Elementary and Secondary Education Act (ESEA).

Section 8401 of ESEA (20 U.S.C. § 7861) permits the secretary of education to grant waivers of certain ESEA requirements, thus allowing the United States Department of Education to provide some flexibility to schools, districts, and states that may be necessary due to the impact of COVID-19 on the provision of educational services. In the face of opposing evidence, traditional assessments are still the instrument by which schools are judged and resources—staffing assignments and funding, not to mention community support—are allocated. Table 8.4 contains our five recommendations for assessments.

TABLE 8.4 Five Assessment Recommendations

1. *Educators need data to measure student growth*	Assessments, data collection, and analysis are important elements of teaching and learning. They help teachers and school leaders understand the degree to which their methods and strategies are promoting student learning.
2. *Students need data to measure their own growth*	Students at all levels need measurable and concrete information to assess their own progress. Quick and immediate feedback helps students make timely adjustments to their short- and long-term goals. Rubrics, letter grades, smiley faces, written or verbal feedback—all serve as a yardstick to inform students of their progress. Educators should go a step further to teach metacognitive skills to enable students to regulate their thinking and to become self-directed learners.
3. *Use multiple methods of assessment*	The traditional method of using test scores alone cannot adequately measure what a student knows or is able to do. The best way to measure a student's growth or understanding is to merge data with teacher observations, authentic projects, conversations, and discussions.
4. *Give students a voice in the assessment process*	There is a direct correlation between student learning and student engagement, including in the assessment process. Teachers can allow students to select from a menu of assessment options for which they wish to measure their learning. Students can also participate in peer performance evaluation using an agreed-on rubric. This strategy is frequently used in music and art classes. Giving students a voice encourages them to reflect on their own learning, which can lead to improved student performance.
5. *Select from a variety of open education resources (OERs) and assessments*	OERs are freely accessible licensed digital resources for teaching, learning, and assessments. In 2013, Prime Minister David Cameron announced that more UK universities were joining *Futurelearn*, the United Kingdom's first provider of free, open online courses (with the British Library). In both the United Kingdom and the United States, there are hundreds or thousands of free, open online courses being used; increasingly, we are seeing other countries, like Brazil and India, become prominent users of OERs (Hollands & Tirthali, 2014).

Benefits of Adaptive Testing in Assessment

Computerized adaptive testing (CAT) is a digital testing system created by psychometricians, content specialists, web designers, and programmers. CATs typically contain large test-item banks that can attain high discriminating power through constant calibration or adaptation (Burns, n.d.). The testing system continues to reestimate the student's ability and adjust the difficulty of the questions based on the student's answers.

When the Delaware Department of Education switched to CAT for its state assessments, officials found the results were available more quickly, the amount of time students spent taking tests decreased, and the tests provided more reliable information about what students knew—especially those at the very low and high ends of the spectrum (Davis, 2012).

Adaptive testing in assessment is also more efficient than traditional testing. It allows high-achieving students to move quickly through lower-difficulty levels and on to the questions that more accurately reflect their current achievement levels. Struggling students avoid wasting time on questions that are beyond their current reach. Instead, each student spends time answering questions centered around their current ability and comprehension level.

FINAL THOUGHTS ABOUT CURRICULUM, INSTRUCTION, AND ASSESSMENTS

Schools will never achieve their goals for student academic success if they do not have a comprehensive alignment of excellent curriculum, instruction, and assessments. At a juncture in history in which all of our policies, practices, and assumptions have been called into question, educators and policymakers have a unique opportunity to right the mistakes of the past by building new and better systems. Our collective breakthroughs around a deeper understanding of inequities call on leadership to disrupt a status quo that perpetuates them.

REFERENCES

Bottia, M. C., Stearns, E., Mickelson, R. A., Moller, S., & Parker, A. D. (2015). The relationships among high school STEM learning experiences and students' intent to declare and declaration of a STEM major in college. *Teachers College Record, 117*(3), n3.

Burns, D., Darling-Hammond, L., & Scott, C. (2019). *Closing the opportunity gap: How positive outlier districts in California are pursuing equitable access.* Learning Policy Institute. https://learningpolicyinstitute.org/product/positive-outliers-closing-opportunity-gap-brief

Burns, M. (n.d.). *eLearning authors: Latest articles by Mary Burns.* Education Development Center. https://elearningindustry.com/elearning-authors/mary-burns

Centers for Disease Control and Prevention. (2020). *Preventing child abuse and neglect.* https://www.cdc.gov/violenceprevention/childabuseandneglect/fastfact.html

Davis, M. (2012, October 17). Adaptive testing evolves to assess common-core skills. *Education Week.* https://www.edweek.org/dd/articles/2012/10/17/01adaptive.h06.html

Dorn, E., Hancock, B., Sarakatsannis, J., & Viruleg, E. (2020, June 1). *COVID-19 and student learning in the United States: The hurt could last a lifetime.* McKinsey & Company. https://www.mckinsey.com/industries/public-sector/our-insights/covid-19-and-student-learning-in-the-united-states-the-hurt-could-last-a-lifetime

Ed. Magazine. (2018, Winter). *The testing charade.* https://www.gse.harvard.edu/news/ed/18/01/testing-charade

Education Trust. (2020, January 9). *Advanced coursework in your state.* https://edtrust.org/resource/advanced-coursework-tool/

Gewertz, C. (2020, March 16). Coronavirus throws spring testing into disarray. *Education Week.* https://www.edweek.org/ew/articles/2020/03/16/coronavirus-throws-spring-testing-into-disarray.html

Hammond, Z. (2015). *Culturally responsive teaching and the brain.* Corwin.

Hollands, F. & Tirthali, D. (2014). Why do institutions offer MOOCs? *Online Learning,* 18(3). https://olj.onlinelearningconsortium.org/index.php/olj/article/view/464

Krueger, N. (2020, April 7). *Meeting students' social-emotional needs during a COVID-19 lockdown.* International Society for Technology in Education. https://www.iste.org/explore/meeting-students-social-emotional-needs-during-covid-19-lockdown

Major, A. (2020, May 20). *How to develop culturally responsive teaching for distance learning.* MindShift. https://www.kqed.org/mindshift/55941/how-to-develop-culturally-responsive-teaching-for-distance-learning

Mayo, L. (2013). *Essential elements of project based learning.* Sam Houston State University. https://www.shsu.edu/centers/project-based-learning/k-12.html

National Association of State Directors of Developmental Disabilities Services. (2020). *National Center for Trauma Informed Care.* https://www.nasddds.org/resource-library/co-occurring-conditions/mental-health-treatment/trauma-informed-care/national-center-for-trauma-informed-care/

National Equity Project. (n.d.). *Social emotional learning and equity.* https://nationalequityproject.org/about/social-emotional-learning-equity

National Policy Board for Educational Administration. (2015). *Professional standards for educational leaders.* https://www.npbea.org/wp-content/uploads/2017/06/Professional-Standards-for-Educational-Leaders_2015.pdf

Pollock, M., Yonezawa, S., Gay, H., & Rodriguez, L. (2019). Pursuing deep equity in "blended" classrooms: Exploring the in-person teacher role in supporting low-income youth through computer-based learning. *Teachers College Record.* https://www.tcrecord.org/Content.asp?ContentId=22628

Sahin, A., Ekmekci, A., & Waxman, H. C. (2017). The relationships among high school STEM learning experiences, expectations, and mathematics and science efficacy and the likelihood of majoring in STEM in college. *International Journal of Science Education,* 39(11), 1549–1572.

Stevenson, S. (2018, January 10). *Review of* The Testing Charade: *Pretending to make schools better. Knowledge Quest.* https://knowledgequest.aasl.org/review-testing-charade-pretending-make-schools-better/

Venet, A. S. (2018, August 3). *The how and why of trauma-informed teaching.* Edutopia. https://www.edutopia.org/article/how-and-why-trauma-informed-teaching

World Future Society. (n.d.). https://www.worldfuture.org/

WSU News. (2012, October 24). *Pedro Noguera says we're using assessments as a "weapon."* https://news.worcester.edu/pedro-noguera-says-were-using-assessments-as-a-weapon/

CHAPTER 9

Principle 5—Meaningful Engagement With Families and Community

What is the most accurate predictor of academic achievement? It is not socioeconomic status, or how prestigious the school is that a child attends. Research has shown that the effect of parents and what they do at home to support learning can account for 80 percent of a child's academic success (Atieno, 2018). Every student has unlimited potential. But there are contributing factors that can affect whether one eventually lives up to that potential. Experts believe that a parent's role in a child's life has a far-reaching impact. Parental involvement is extremely important for a child to do well in school (Atieno, 2018). What can the school do to facilitate family engagement in students' lives?

CASE STORY 9.1
Going the Extra Mile for Aishia

Aishia was polite and happy, yet very unorganized, and struggled academically as a first-grade student attending Chisholm Elementary School in Maryland. Her mother, Ms. Horne, was a single parent who worked as a freelance writer for a small community newspaper. Ms. Horne and Aishia enjoyed breakfast and conversations together every morning. It was a beautiful relationship. However, because of their morning bonding time, Aishia's mom dropped her off at school at least an hour late every day. Aishia's

(Continued)

absence from meaningful morning routines and instruction with her peers, as well as her lack of organization skills, made it difficult for her to focus and meet identified academic learning targets.

Even though the school was located in a financially distressed community, and family and community support for some students was less than desired, the faculty and staff had set a goal for 100 percent of the first-grade students to be able to read on grade level by the end of the school year. Aishia's teacher, Ms. Rustin, and the school principal had politely encouraged Ms. Horne to bring Aishia to school on time every day. And if she came to school on time, they could guarantee that Aishia would be reading on grade level by the end of the year. Ms. Horne responded, "My morning time with Aishia is important. I never had quality time with my mother. So, I will not be bringing her to school any earlier, and you better make sure Aishia is reading on grade level by the end of this school year."

Sometimes your strategy may not succeed. In Ms. Horne's case, parent, teacher, and principal conferences failed. So, what do you do? You try a new strategy, and keep trying until you succeed, because failure is not an option. The Chisholm team put in place a tiered individualized instructional plan for Aishia and every other student reading below grade level, which included targeted reading support. The team also realized that quality morning time with Aishia was her mother's top priority. Recognizing her flexible work schedule, they encouraged Ms. Horne to have breakfast with Aishia every morning in her classroom, and they would designate her as a classroom volunteer. It was a brilliant compromise. As a writer, Ms. Horne loved to read, and became excited about assisting Aishia, and her classmates as well. She was also better positioned to assist her at home. Aishia began to grow in confidence and became more organized, and by the end of the school year, she and all 118 other first-grade students at Chisholm Elementary School were reading on grade level, as documented by the school district's grade-level reading assessment.

Think About It

How would Aishia have initially been viewed in your school? What would have been the initial reactions to her mother's unwillingness to meet school policy? How could you and your team use this case to create systems that accommodate variations in home life for your students?

MEANINGFUL ENGAGEMENT WITH FAMILY

Meaningful engagement within the family has been seen as a crucial component to successful schools (Cook et al., 2017; National PTA, 2007), yet there is no consensus on where the responsibility rests for ensuring parental involvement in schools (Harris & Goodall, 2008). In 2019, a survey of over nine hundred parents, four hundred teachers, and four hundred school leaders revealed that 92 percent of parents indicated that they were involved in their children's learning, though teachers and administrators estimated far lower parental involvement, with 64 percent of teachers and 84 percent of school leaders viewing parents as actively engaged (Benner & Quirk, 2020).

Parents across the board care about their children and attempt to help them with school. Yet they are not always seen in this light by teachers or administrators. "Those parents" statements can sometimes be heard in disparaging certain groups of parents, without knowing their circumstances. Often even hardworking parents who attempt to assist their children regularly with their homework don't fare as well as better-organized and economically successful parents. A pilot study in New Mexico, for example, indicates that economically struggling parents can gain and leverage social capital through supports that network them and focus their efforts on goal setting for their child and managing their own finances in a manner that brings stability to the family and academic gains for their children (Family Independence Initiative, 2018; Sparks & Harwin, 2017). The challenge that these families experienced wasn't lack of interest in their children, nor was it valuing education and doing homework with them. It was understanding the *system* in the way middle-class parents do. How can *your* school level the playing field for all students?

The point is that families are important for student success. Schools and other community partners, in turn, can support families to play a vital role in their children's academic lives.

Parent and Family Engagement

The family is the most intimate and first teacher of a child. Therefore, it is reasonable to initiate engagement with the family, then extend engagement into the community. Parental involvement in the form of meaningful engagement has been described as regular, purposeful communication involving student academics and other school-related activities (U.S. Department of Education, 2007). COVID-19 has provided an even greater sense of urgency for parental involvement, as children are engaging in classwork from home (Seale, 2020). The National Association for Family, School, and Community Engagement (2020) has provided suggestions and resources in response to the COVID-19 pandemic, in an effort to increase parental involvement and in turn ensure students' success. Schools can and should convert these new opportunities for partnering with families into sustainable relationships and new systems of and approaches to communication.

At a time when the pressures on parents are greater than ever, what can schools do to create welcoming and supportive environments so that parents want and are able to be involved, particularly in so-called failing schools where poverty is often concentrated? Parents of children in such schools often develop distrust and even hostility toward educators they may believe are not serving their children well. Disaffection often results in low levels of parental involvement and hostile relations between parents and teachers. In turn, this creates a cycle of negative reinforcement, blame, and distrust. In some cultures, parents are very deferential to school officials and may trust them to the point of seeming "uninvolved" to those who don't understand the culture.

One thing educators have intimately experienced during COVID-19 is the diversity that exists among families. There is no one size to fit all families any more than there is one to fit all children. Creating "support networks" among families based on their areas of interest and need is among the constructs that will be most successful for all involved.

Schools that have become true learning communities have addressed the gap between parents and schools by employing three key principles to build positive family relationships:

1. Mutual understanding based on empathy and recognition of shared interests

2. Meaningful involvement of family and community in a variety of school activities

3. Regular outreach and communication to family and community

Mutual Understanding and Empathy

The first step toward building or repairing home–school relationships is to gain a common understanding and empathy for students' families. This means that the school staff become aware of the specific challenges that affect many families and thus make it difficult for them to support their children's learning. This includes the recognition that many parents have had negative experiences with school and are afraid to become involved. Parents may be intimidated by feelings of ignorance and uncertainty, and they may assume that their children will experience the same kinds of difficulties that they encountered while in schools. Additionally, many parents are struggling to make ends meet. Some are working more than one job and have little time to supervise homework. Others are grappling with layoffs, housing uncertainty, foreclosures, and lack of health benefits. Instead of penalizing children and criticizing their parents for lapses and failures in attendance or preparation, teachers in high-performing schools work with families to help them overcome problems and barriers.

Schools that are committed to student success devise creative ways to respond to the difficulties that students face. Some areas in which schools can extend understanding and support include

- closing the digital divide by providing technology access to all students, fostering better communication between home and school;

- creating after-school homework centers so that children who don't have someone at home to help them are not penalized because they have not completed assignments;

- creating schedules, policies, and programs that take into account students' home-life challenges;

- providing translators who can communicate with non-English-speaking families and produce versions of important school announcements and communications in the languages spoken by the families that are served;

- creating welcoming areas at school for parents while waiting to speak to a member of the staff;

- arranging for transportation of students to after-school activities, and for families to school events;

- holding meetings for parents at public libraries and community centers where transportation to school is a problem; and

- meeting the needs of *families*, as well as their children.

Family Engagement Specialists

More schools, especially those in communities with high percentages of poverty, are using federal funds to hire family engagement specialists. Parental involvement has been a component of federal funding since the Elementary and Secondary Education Act of 1965 (ESEA). ESEA was reauthorized as the No Child Left Behind Act in 2002 and, most recently, as the Every Student Succeeds Act (ESSA) in 2015. Each act recognized parental involvement as a key element of student learning and has attempted to focus on engaging parents in the learning process. Schools identified as Title I were provided guidance and expectations regarding parental involvement and held accountable for measures being implemented to ensure parents, families, and the community were involved as decision-making stakeholders in schools. ESSA is especially clear on the critical role of parents as equal partners. It includes requirements for outreach to all parents and meaningful involvement with parents (U.S. Department of Education, n.d.).

Gaining Active Engagement From Family and Community

The Global Family Research Project (2018) defines family engagement as "moving from where we are now—a scattered, marginal, and unaligned set of programs and policies—to more strategic and systemic approaches to family and community engagement in and out of school and from birth through young adulthood" (p. 4).

Regardless of the circumstances, it is clear that the proper support and involvement of students' families and the community at large is fundamental to student achievement in schools. Joyce Epstein at Johns Hopkins University, James Comer and the late Edward Zigler at Yale (one of the creators of the federal Head Start program), and Maurice Elias at Rutgers University all have spoken eloquently on the topic of parent/guardian involvement in schools (see, e.g., Comer, 1996; Comer et al., 2004; Elias & Arnold, 2006; Elias et al., 2003; Epstein et al., 2018; Zigler & Muenchow, 1992). Their research concludes that greater parental involvement leads to higher levels of student achievement and improved student behavior, irrespective of such factors as socioeconomic status or ethnic background. That same research shows that the most accurate predictor of student academic achievement is the ability of the student's family to create a home environment that encourages learning; to communicate high, yet reasonable, expectations for achievement; and to stay involved in the student's education in meaningful ways (Comer et al., 2004; Elias & Arnold, 2006; Epstein et al., 2018; Griffin & Steen, 2010; Hampden-Thompson & Galindo, 2017).

Moreover, most educators show that their highest-performing students come from families where the parents are involved. This doesn't necessarily mean that they are present at the school for meetings and events. Rather, it means they play an active role in the home reinforcing the importance of learning and the value of education for their child. Given the clear importance of this kind of involvement to child development and student achievement, how do we get more parents to play an active and supportive role in the education of their children?

A 2016 report, *The Importance of Parent Engagement*, highlights the research of several thought leaders: Susan Auerbach, James Comer, Joyce Epstein, Nancy Hill, William Jeynes, and Karen Mapp (Families & Schools Together, 2016). Epstein is perhaps most famous for her heavily cited framework on the six types of parent involvement (Epstein et al., 2018):

1. *Parenting* aims to strengthen the school climate and provide a forum for parents of students to meet and speak with other parents and school counselors.

2. *Communicating* enables students and parents to meet new teachers, gather information, see their classroom, and learn about the curriculum. It also engages parents on goals for all students and allows parents to observe learning activities.

3. *Volunteering* encourages parents and others to share their time and talents in support of the school, teachers, and activities both inside and outside the school.

4. *Learning at home* provides families with information about academic work in the classroom and how to help their children with homework. It may also guide parents to help children practice specific skills, choose extracurricular programs, and plan for college.

5. *Decision making* increases parents' input and enables families to make decisions concerning policy, programs, and practices that directly affect their children.

6. *Collaborating with community* encourages cooperation between schools, families, community groups, and other entities and fosters enrichment through mutually beneficial relationships.

Effective Involvement of Families in the School

The best way to ensure parental and community involvement in a school is to welcome people into the school. Although this may seem obvious, it is actually a common stumbling block in community–school relationships. In some cases, this is based on biases against any number of groups: parents of color, single fathers, LGBTQIA+ parents, parents with low socioeconomic status, and so on. In other cases, it is simply an unwelcoming school culture that may be further codified by an elaborate metal detection system or "security protocol" or just a "receptionist" who'd rather not be receiving people.

As previously stated, such feelings of being unwelcome and shut out may alternatively stem from parents' own experiences in school. Those parents who struggled during their own academic careers may feel distrust or even anxiety about interacting with school authorities.

In other cases, language and cultural differences create a barrier to parental involvement in schools. Parents who do not speak English may be hesitant to contact schools or unsure of how to best communicate their students' needs. For undocumented immigrants, the barriers may be even more significant. Family involvement in schools is not something that occurs naturally or easily when cultural, economic, political, or racial barriers are not addressed. Partnerships with parents must be purposely cultivated and planned. Professional learning communities can cultivate such involvement by bringing parents and other adults in to share their expertise and talents in meaningful ways and by creating parent-to-parent support networks.

Ways of encouraging meaningful parent involvement include

- establishing a parent-to-parent outreach that contacts all parents to see what they can contribute to student learning;

- inviting parents and community members to provide lessons in the language and/or culture of ethnic groups that are represented in the school community;

- inviting parents and community members to provide leadership for extracurricular clubs based on special interest; and

- training teachers and the school receptionist in how to greet parents and conduct productive parent–teacher conferences.

A middle school in Boston, for example, uses the quarterly report card as a time to celebrate students' achievement by inviting parents to come in and meet teachers while the band plays music in the auditorium, food is served in the cafeteria, and friendly basketball games between teachers and students take place in the gymnasium.

Parents or community members can serve as translators to facilitate communication between the school and non-English-speaking families. They can also make presentations—talks, slide shows, or videos relevant to current events, areas, or subjects being studied.

Reaching Out to Family and Community

In effective schools, teachers and administrators go the extra mile to reach those children and families whose problems stand in the way of their full involvement in schooling. Part of reaching out is simply making staff members visible in the neighborhood, at fast-food restaurants, malls, and other places students and families are likely to visit. In the digital age, educators are enhancing their connections through social media: Facebook, Twitter, and Instagram. For example, tweets can be designed to engage parents and volunteers:

One of the most festive moments in the lives of students and their family is graduation day. As superintendent, at every graduation ceremony, as students prepared to receive their diploma, I (Marcus) always tweeted pictures of them in real time. The first time I tweeted, I received over six thousand responses. It provided an incredible opportunity to generate a large following for the school district with expanded opportunities for outreach.

During pandemic school closures, teachers in school districts across the country paraded through neighborhoods to congratulate their students. Students stood outside of their homes and apartments with signs waving at their teachers. Families agreed that this was a great way to see the teachers again and thank them for their work.

CASE STORY 9.2

A Day in the Life of a Student

James River High School, located in Midlothian, Virginia, was a two-time recipient of the National Blue Ribbon Schools award. As the demographics of the community began to change with an increase of lower-income families, many teachers and community members were surprised by the impact on the school's academic performance. Some were unaware of the many personal challenges facing students. So, the school administration initiated an experiment called *A Day in the Life* of a James River student. Twelve students were randomly selected to participate in the experiment, with the permission of their parents. The group ranged from students who were struggling to pass, to students in Advanced Placement (AP) courses with 4.0 grade point averages.

Each student was given a camera (this was prior to the emergence of smartphones) and asked to record every aspect of their day from the time they got out of bed in the morning until they went to bed at night for one week. At the end of the week, the school administrative team edited the video into a forty-five-minute documentary. The film was shown to the entire faculty and staff during a professional development teacher workday. It was an eye opener for every faculty member. The lives of these students were filled with stress beyond the school day. The staff were surprised to learn that most of the students worked part-time jobs after school and on weekends. Two students were cheerleaders and enrolled in three to five AP classes. One worked a part-time job after cheerleading practices. After arriving home between 9 and 10 p.m., she ate dinner and then worked on homework until 1 or 2 a.m. She got up at 5:30 every morning in time to get ready for school and board her bus at 6:10 a.m. The routine was repeated daily. The other AP student had a similar schedule, although she spent much of her time volunteering after school.

Another student worked as a janitor in a hotel until midnight every evening to help pay the rent and buy groceries for his mother and two younger sisters. Getting transportation home after midnight was always an adventure for him. Homework was not high on his list of priorities. And, finally, one of the twelve students was homeless, moving from one family member to another

(Continued)

(Continued)

and often staying with friends. To protect his privacy, the details of his homeless situation were not included in the documentary. Nonetheless, the faculty and staff gained a new understanding and appreciation for their students. They realized the time their students spent in school was often less important than surviving and thriving outside of school. They placed a new focus on school–home relationships. They worked with organizations within the community to provide wraparound supports for students. For example, one community citizen offered to pay college tuition for the homeless student.

CASE STORY 9.3

A Day in the Life of a Family

During one of their professional development days, all Chesterfield County school assistant principals, principals, and administrators participated in a simulation sponsored by the Virginia Department of Social Services (DSS) called *A Day in the Life of a Family (With School-Age Children)* designed to help them better understand the challenges faced by families living in poverty. In the simulated role play, each participant was assigned to a hypothetical family living in poverty. Participants received a list of monthly bills (housing, utilities, food, transportation, etc.) and a monthly income based on their status (job, unemployed, public assistance, etc.). Their family assignment may have been a single mother with four living children, ages three to seventeen, working two jobs; a grandmother living on a fixed income taking care of a disabled veteran and her three young children; or an unemployed single father taking care of his two children. The goal was to survive two months without getting evicted from their home.

Community volunteers recruited by DSS were assigned to stations around a large room representing the various agencies and businesses families interacted with—public schools, rental office management, utility companies, employment commission, grocery stores, bus/Uber transportation, and so on. During the course of the ninety-minute simulation exercise, several participants were reduced to tears as they had never personally experienced the frustrations and trauma associated with poverty. As a profession, educators typically live in a middle-class community, and some have never acquired the skills necessary to survive poverty. We were informed by the director of DSS that it is common for educators to experience a high percentage of evictions during the simulation, which was the case with the Chesterfield County group. Everyone left the simulation understanding that many of the actions of children living in poverty are the result not of defiance or apathy, but of skills necessary to survive in an impoverished community. These children failed middle-class norms, just as educators failed poverty norms.

MEANINGFUL ENGAGEMENT WITH COMMUNITY

Collective Impact

"Too many organizations are working in isolation from one another. Collective impact brings people together in a structured way to achieve social change" (National Veterans Intermediary, 2019). The notion of collective impact was first formalized in 2011 by the *Stanford Social Innovation Review* in an effort to define the work in Cincinnati, which led to the creation of the StriveTogether™ Cradle to Career Network. Rather than work apart, Cincinnati and northern Kentucky leaders came together around a set of common goals and shared data to solve complex community challenges that limited opportunities for young people. To date, more than seventy communities across thirty states and Washington, DC, have used the StriveTogether model to achieve a vision of success for every child from cradle to career (StriveTogether, 2020a, 2020b).

CASE STORY 9.4

Collective Impact: Petersburg City and Schools Partnership

The Petersburg City and Schools Partnership (2020a, 2020b), a collaboration between Petersburg City Public Schools, the city of Petersburg, and multiple state, local, and nonprofit partners, was founded through the Governor's Children's Cabinet of the Commonwealth of Virginia in 2015 and utilizes a collective impact framework to bring about change through a group of important actors from different agencies, different levels of government, and different sectors tied by a common agenda for solving a specific problem. It was the first time such a group came together to support Petersburg schools, and the partnership has become the largest, most powerful, and most successful of its kind in Virginia.

This work led to transformation systems for the benefit of the children, youth, and families of the city of Petersburg. It is arduous work and requires commitment and dedication by all parties. The mission of the consortium is to create the climate and conditions for every child to succeed by providing a sustainable, coordinated system of support and access. The collective vision is to support Petersburg schools in providing a quality education that ensures every child is college ready, career ready, and life ready with marketable skills and industry certification. The three impact areas chosen are to (1) eliminate chronic absenteeism, (2) foster a trauma-responsive environment where students and families thrive, and (3) bridge the gap between high school and the workforce.

(Continued)

(Continued)

In 2016, a steering committee was formed, and the school superintendent and city manager were selected as the co-chairpersons. To increase the credibility and stability of the partnership, the group decided it needed an anchor institution to serve as its backbone. United Way of Greater Richmond and Petersburg (UWGRP) agreed to fill the role, and immediately began the process of funding and hiring a full-time director to manage the day-to-day operations of the partnership, which has grown from approximately thirty-five organizations and individuals to over two hundred active and engaged members.

Unfortunately, in many urban districts too many students are chronically absent, meaning they miss a significant amount of school days during the school year. This leads to academic struggles and eventually school dropout. The wraparound support provided through the Petersburg City and Schools Partnership, UWGRP, and Attendance Works produced promising results. During the 2017–2018 school year, the chronic absentee rate was 22.4 percent. Just one year later during the 2018–2019 school year, the rate had decreased to 6.2 percent.

One of the signature initiatives of the partnership is the opening of the school-based health center, housed at Petersburg High School. "A school-based health center (SBHC) is a shared commitment between a community's schools and health care organizations to support the health, well-being, and academic success of its students" by providing preventative, early intervention, and treatment services where students are: in school (School-Based Health Alliance, 2020).

In 2019, the United Way presented the partnership with its highest award—the *Steps to Success* Award, "given to an outstanding group that shows their commitment to create lasting change across the *Steps to Success* framework and best exemplifies our mission to empower individuals and drive systemic change" (United Way, 2019). During the same year, Keurig Dr Pepper and the national nonprofit KABOOM! (2020) awarded the partnership with a Let's Play Community Construction grant.

Think About It

What partners does your school district currently have, and what are they working on together? Is their agenda a high-impact one? For example, ensuring 100 percent attendance for the Petersburg district meant all partners had a role—transportation, food, trauma relief, great instruction, welcoming and equitable school climate, and much more had to be addressed. What *new* COVID-19 contacts could now be engaged in your partnership? What personnel and infrastructure is needed to sustain a meaningful agenda for collective impact to occur?

The Current Importance of Meaningful Engagement

Meaningful engagement within the community is a crucial part to the success of all students (Henderson & Mapp, 2016; International Survey Associates, 2016).

Meaningful engagement is clearly an essential part of schools operating optimally, while considering what can be done to positively impact all students' comfortability, inclusion, opportunities, and academic success. This concept is *crucial* in the face of current challenges. The reopening of schools in an effective manner will require well-thought-out engagement of families and partners (Domenech et al., 2020). Let's think through this in a practical, realistic manner:

COVID-19, School Closures, and Meaningful Family and Community Engagement

The closure of schools in the midst of a worldwide pandemic not only stripped educational systems of direct student and community contact, but also posed a challenge for incorporating family engagement in a purposeful and strategic manner once schools begin to reopen. Reopening schools effectively will focus not solely on academics, but rather on the student as a whole, in consideration of the effects from COVID-19. This will require active engagement of the entire learning community. This is true of decision making to yield both coherent planning and support from the community (Bailey & Hess, 2020). Meaningful engagement will be especially important within the community to "allocate resources to provide an integrated focus on academics, health and social services, youth and community development, and community engagement" (Domenech et al., 2020). Engaging the department of health will also be essential when considering an overall plan for opening schools (Department of Education and Skills, 2020).

Racial Injustice

Racial injustice has been observed throughout the school system, although the most recent occurrences have spotlighted this. Inequities in the health care system can often have a profound effect on family involvement, which we have noted is an essential part of equitable schools. Another issue that has become prevalent is the rising rate of unemployment and poverty, due to the COVID-19 pandemic. This affects schooling for the children not only directly, but also indirectly. Indirect issues that can arise from this include childhood hunger, homelessness, poor mental health, poor physical health, and family conflicts. Finally, community-based agencies that effectively serve persons of color are currently in dire financial straits. All of these are contributing factors that are placing equity in jeopardy, necessitating the need for meaningful engagement.

Implementation

Getting Started

As you begin preparing to open the lines of communication with parents and other community members, first take a moment to evaluate where your school currently stands with regard to community and parental involvement.

- How many and *which* community members participate as members of teams for various improvement activities in your school?

- How many parent volunteers does your school have?

- In what capacities are those volunteers used?

- Of the ethnic and cultural groups forming significant parts of the school population, how many are represented on school teams? As parent volunteers?

- What is the racial and demographic makeup of your parent volunteers? Are they reflective of your student demographics?

- What outreach initiatives have been undertaken to ensure diversity and equity?

- What forums or meetings have been organized to explain school-related issues and answer families' questions?

Challenges and Solutions

Teachers and administrators face numerous post-pandemic challenges as they work to strengthen school and community ties. The following are some of those challenges—and some of our suggestions for resolving them. Note that when the challenge is framed in deficit language such as the first one that follows, it is important to reframe it in a manner that challenges implicit biases.

Challenge: "I've tried to reach out to the parents of my students . . . but most of them, especially the parents of the kids who are struggling, don't seem to care, and some are downright hostile. The ones who do care are generally parents of kids who are doing well, and some are so overly involved that they second-guess my every move."

In many schools, the parents of students who do least well academically are also least likely to be involved. However, don't fall into the trap of assuming that this a function of parental neglect. Particularly at times like the present, families are under great duress, and many of the COVID-19 frontline workers represent the very populations that have been underserved by our schools. With that said, there is an abundance of evidence that reaching out to these parents can serve as an important step in improving the performance of struggling students.

> *Solution*: Parents and administrators, and designated parent coordinators, need to actively reach out to parents and families not connected to the school. It is very important that the first communication not be a call home about bad behavior or poor academic performance. Make contact before problems occur. Demonstrate empathy and understanding to parents who may be struggling to make ends meet. Let them know that you value their support and that you truly believe their children can succeed if you work together. Meeting them in places where they feel comfortable facilitates the communication and the school professionals' empathy.

> *Challenge*: "Our school has no problem communicating with parents! We post weekly updates, announcements, and calendar updates on our social Facebook and Twitter pages. Every teacher maintains a current 'web page' of students' assignments, grades, and announcements, so parents can check their children's assignments."

Many schools mistakenly believe that communication flows in only one direction—that as long as they're getting information to the parents, they're doing their part. Meaningful communication, however, must be two-way, constantly alternating among information, listing, and feedback.

> *Solution*: Ensure your communication is interactive—including but not limited to voicemail, email, web pages, and assignment logs. Also make sure school communication is interactive with the entire community, such as parent surveys, key communicators, robocalls (but don't overdo them), community meetings, and education fairs. If there are language barriers in communicating with families, engage translators as needed.

> *Challenge*: "We have some great parents, and I know they want to be involved in their kids' education—but they just don't seem to have a clue."

> *Solution*: Again, this is a deficit-laden statement. Clearly, achievement is enhanced when students receive help with schoolwork at home. However, not all parents know how to help, and they may not feel qualified to offer guidance on subject matter that is unfamiliar to them. Nonetheless, even if families may not hold the academic knowledge to support their

children, when educators are able to draw from a family's vast funds of knowledge (home language, family traditions, family occupations, etc.), levels of engagement can dramatically increase (González et al., 2005; Moll et al., 1992).

Encourage educators to engage in home visits in the interest of enhancing communication with families and integrating students' funds of knowledge into classroom practice (see the companion website, https://resources.corwin .com/BreakthroughLeadership, for links to critical resources on home visits and funds of knowledge). Set up community-based homework support. Use students in the National Honor Society, students earning community service credit, and other peer tutors. Pay transportation costs for tutoring after school and on the weekends. Organize videos or social media chats. Invite parents in or communicate with them virtually to help them help their children with academics and social issues.

REFERENCES

Atieno, L. (2018, August 21). Why a parent's role is essential to student success. *The New Times*. https://www.newtimes.co.rw/lifestyle/parent-student-success

Bailey, J., & Hess, F. (2020, May 4). Blueprint for back to school. Education*Next*. https://www.educationnext.org/a-blueprint-for-back-to-school-what-will-it-take-get-schools-ready-coronavirus-covid-19/

Benner, M., & Quirk, A. (2020, February 20). *One size does not fit all: Analyzing different approaches to family-school communication*. Center for American Progress. https://www.americanprogress.org/issues/education-k-12/reports/2020/02/20/480254/one-size-not-fit/

Comer, J. P. (Ed.). (1996). *Rallying the whole village: The Comer process for reforming education*. Teachers College Press.

Comer, J. P., Joyner, E. T., & Ben-Avie, M. (Eds.). (2004). *Six pathways to healthy child development and academic success: The field guide to Comer schools in action*. Corwin.

Cook, A. L., Shah, A., Brodsky, L., & Morizio, L. J. (2017). Strengthening school-family-community engagement through community dialogues. *Journal for Social Action in Counseling & Psychology*, *9*(1), 9–37. doi: https://doi.org/10.33043/JSACP.9.1.9-37

Department of Education and Skills [Ireland]. (2020, June 12). *Planning for reopening schools in line with the Roadmap for reopening society and business: Report to government*. https://www.education.ie/en/covid-19/planning-for-reopening-schools.pdf

Domenech, D., Hansen, M., Hough, H., & Vegas, E. (2020, June 3). *Reopening schools amid the COVID-19 pandemic: Your questions, our answers*. Brookings Institution. https://www.brookings.edu/blog/brown-center-chalkboard/2020/06/03/reopening-schools-amid-the-covid-19-pandemic-your-questions-our-answers/

Elias, M. J., & Arnold, H. (2006). *The educator's guide to emotional intelligence and academic achievement: Social-emotional learning in the classroom*. Corwin.

Elias, M. J., Bryan, K., Patrikakouo, E. N., & Weissberg, R. P. (2003). Challenges in creating effective home-school partnerships in adolescence: Promising paths for collaboration (EJ666071). *School Community Journal, 13*(1), 133–153. https://eric.ed.gov/?id=EJ666071

Epstein, J. L., Sanders, M. G., Sheldon, S. B., Simon, B. S., Salinas, K. C., Jansorn, N. R., Van Voorhis, F. L., Martin, C. S., Thomas, B. G., Greenfield, M. D., Hutchins, D. J., & Williams, K. J. (2018). *School, family, and community partnerships: Your handbook for action* (4th ed.). Corwin.

Families & Schools Together. (2016, August 25). *The importance of parent engagement: A list of research and thought leadership.* https://www.familiesandschools.org/blog/the-importance-of-parent-engagement/

Family Independence Initiative. (2018). *Annual report: A summary of our work, findings, and engagement with families who are on a path to mobility across the United States.* http://2018.fii.org/

Global Family Research Project. (2018, October). *Joining together to create a bold vision for next generation family engagement: Engaging families to transform education.* https://globalfrp.org/content/download/419/3823/file/GFRP_Family%20Engagement%20Carnegie%20Report.pdf

González, N., Moll, L., & Amanti, C. (Eds.). (2005). *Funds of knowledge: Theorizing practices in households, communities and classrooms.* Lawrence Erlbaum.

Griffin, D., & Steen, S. (2010). School-family-community partnerships: Applying Epstein's theory of the six types of involvement to school counselor practice. *Professional School Counseling, 13*(4). https://doi.org/10.1177/2156759X1001300402

Hampden-Thompson, G., & Galindo, C. (2017). School–family relationships, school satisfaction and the academic achievement of young people. *Educational Review, 69*(2), 248–265. https://doi.org/10.1080/00131911.2016.1207613

Harris, A., & Goodall, J. (2008). Do parents know they matter? Engaging all parents in learning. *Educational Research, 50*(3), 277–289. https://doi.org/10.1080/00131880802309424

Henderson, A. T., & Mapp, K. L. (2002). *A new wave of evidence: The impact of school, family, and community connections on student achievement.* SEDL. https://www.sedl.org/connections/resources/evidence.pdf

International Survey Associates. (2016, May 6). *Why community involvement in schools is important.* Pride Surveys. https://www.pridesurveys.com/index.php/blog/community-involvement-in-schools/

KABOOM! (2020). *Let's Play Community Construction grants.* https://kaboom.org/grants/lets-play-community-construction

Moll, L. C., Amanti, C., Neff, D., & González, N. (1992). Funds of knowledge for teaching: Using a qualitative approach to connect homes and classrooms. *Theory Into Practice, 31*(2), 132–141. https://www.jstor.org/stable/1476399

National Association for Family, School, and Community Engagement. (2020). *NAFSCE's response to the COVID-19 pandemic.* https://nafsce.org/general/custom.asp?page=coronavirus

National PTA. (2007). *National standards for family-school partnerships: What parents, schools, and communities can do together to support student success.* https://www.pta.org/docs/default-source/files/programs/national-standards-for-family-school-partnerships/national_standards.pdf

National Veterans Intermediary. (2019). *CIF webinar series: Backbone roles.* https://www.nvi.org/calendar/backbone-roles

Petersburg City Public Schools. (2020a). *Family Engagement Action Plan.* https://www.petersburg.k12.va.us/site/handlers/filedownload.ashx?moduleinstanceid=2509&dataid=7947&FileName=Family%20Engagement%20Action%20Plan.pdf

Petersburg City Public Schools. (2020b). *Petersburg City and Schools Partnership: About the partnership*. https://www.petersburg.k12.va.us/domain/2266

School-Based Health Alliance. (2020). *Core competencies*. http://www.sbh4all.org/resources/core-competencies/

Seale, C. (2020, May 19). Parent involvement has always mattered. Will the COVID-19 pandemic finally make this the new normal in K–12 education? *Forbes*. https://www.forbes.com/sites/colinseale/2020/05/19/parent-involvement-has-always-mattered-will-the-covid-19-pandemic-finally-make-this-the-new-normal-in-k-12-education/#37d974695e46

Sparks, S., & Harwin, H. (2017, April 19). How parents widen—or shrink—academic gaps. *Education Week*. https://www.edweek.org/ew/articles/2017/04/19/how-parents-widen--or-shrink--academic-gaps.html

StriveTogether. (2020a). *Collective impact: Stronger together*. https://www.strivetogether.org/what-we-do/collective-impact/

StriveTogether. (2020b). *Where we work*. Retrieved from https://www.strivetogether.org/where-we-work/

United Way. (2019). *2019 Steps to Success Award winners*. https://www.yourunitedway.org/steps-awards/2019-award-information/

U.S. Department of Education. (n.d.). *Every Student Succeeds Act (ESSA)*. https://www.ed.gov/essa?src=rn

U.S. Department of Education, Office of Innovation and Improvement. (2007, June). *Engaging parents in education: Lessons from five parental information and resource centers*. https://www2.ed.gov/admins/comm/parents/parentinvolve/engagingparents.pdf

Zigler, E., & Muenchow, S. (1992). *Head Start: The inside story of America's most successful educational experiment* (ED357887). https://eric.ed.gov/?id=ED357887

CHAPTER 10

Principle 6—Building Sustainable Leadership Capacity

> *The reality of life post-COVID-19 has not fully sunk in yet, and its consequences for our businesses, organizations, economy, and society will play out over the rest of 2020 and beyond. Right now, we really need sober, smart, values-driven, and focused leadership. Remember the old adage, "Crisis does not build character, it reveals it."* (Mark Nevins, 2020)

Just as we began writing this book, COVID-19 led to the closing of businesses and borders throughout North America. This was followed months later by a long-overdue and, for many, long-awaited global demand for racial justice catalyzed by the execution of George Floyd and Rayshard Brooks, among others. (As pointed out in Chapter 2, this was presaged by many, including Archbishop Desmond Tutu, who stated: "America may be reaching a breaking point" [Blankstein & Noguera, 2015; Tutu, 2015, p. vii]).

Throughout this book, we have shared examples of courageous and breakthrough leadership underway throughout North America toward equitable outcomes for every student. We have demonstrated the best methods and guiding principles to date for creating equitable learning communities (Chapters 4–9), while pushing the envelope toward courageously acting on and leveraging our collective breakthrough: the system is slanted heavily against people of color, and isn't working for a growing number of our students and families, and must be uprooted.

Many school districts, like corporations across the nation, have issued statements and made declarations that they support Black Lives Matter, they will do more in the fight for racial justice, and be more reflective about how to best support Black students.

These declarations are encouraging and can offer guarded optimism, but let's be clear, a healthy dose of skepticism is in order when schools come out and make such statements when it is safe to do so when chanting "Black Lives Matter" has gone mainstream, and when the entire world is saying that anti-Black racism is a problem. (Howard, 2020)

As we have emphasized throughout this book, we inhabit a rare moment in time in which institutionalized racism has been publicly "outed" and has inspired a call to action. But we need to be prepared to sustain this momentum well beyond the summer of 2020. After all, the systems of oppression that we aim to uproot have been built over the course of centuries. Inspired breakthrough and courageous leadership rooted in a "core" community commitment to *act long-term* on a vision for ensuring equity will be necessary, but insufficient for the task at hand. Our plans must also address *sustainability* since the work of disrupting the status quo of inequity may need to extend well beyond our own tenure. We need to develop sustainable leadership capacity that enables school cultures to thrive despite challenges, including transition of the leadership. In this chapter, we will connect concepts developed in earlier chapters, share additional examples of breakthrough leadership, and describe best practices underway in bringing about equity via sustainable leadership capacity.

We have evoked great men and women—young and old and throughout the centuries—who have used breakthrough leadership to change the world. From Aristotle to Malala Yousafzai, we have called upon leaders from virtually every continent who have taken the struggle and strife of their time to advance the greater good of humankind. At the same time, in speaking with scores of frontline educators, we have documented how leaders at every level—from the classroom to the boardroom—are breaking new ground and adding to the social and spiritual velocity of an emerging movement of true equity for all of our young people. In the final analysis, the soul of the United States and the world will be determined by you, and the collective will you and your colleagues muster. As Martin Luther King Jr. once expressed, it was not the few "bad people" that most concerned him; it was that we not "become a nation of onlookers," claiming what Michael Eric Dyson (2017) referred to as "white innocence."

We have all seen firsthand the stark reality of the existing inequities upon which many nations have been built and discussed the urgency of real action necessary for this unprecedented moment of history. Your morally rooted breakthrough actions will beget more of the same from colleagues around you. This in turn builds collective capacity for more courageous action. Interviews with scores of noted thought leaders and practitioners coping with and leading through crisis and uncertain times indicate that this capacity building was underway prior to COVID-19, but the pace has since quickened.

COVID-19 has been devastating to millions of lives around the world. However, we have also witnessed incredible examples of the human spirit to overcome challenges. World reactions on the six continents infected by the pandemic were initially slow. However, once the devastating reality of the disease was understood, leaders sprang into action. The world learned lessons from Hong Kong—with a population of 7.5 million, it had reported just four deaths as of May 2020, due to its approach to quarantine and social-distancing measures. The World Central Kitchen organization began distributing over 240,000 meals daily in United States cities. Protests and riots aimed at eliminating racism and police brutality resulted in police reform bills by the United States Senate and House of Representatives, and a signed executive order by President Donald Trump. According to the World Health Organization, there are more than one hundred possible vaccines in various stages of development around the world.

While these encouraging actions demonstrate the power of the human will, it will be up to local leaders to sustain themselves, their communities, and the march forward toward an equitable society. "Knowledge is power. Information is liberating. Education is the premise of progress, in every society, in every family. And quality education starts with leadership" (Kofi Annan, quoted in Helsley, 2014).

LEADERS TO LEARN FROM

Breakthrough leaders are not just people who garner the national and international spotlight, or who influence world events. "Our Leaders see the big picture. They know that the educators who interact with students every day will succeed when they feel supported to face challenges, just as students will learn best when they can depend on warm meals and safe places to live. They confront head-on the quotidian, under-recognized, and sensitive needs that impact students' lives. And they won't stop until they've found solutions" (Sawchuk & Superville, 2020).

Case Stories 10.1 and 10.2 provide examples of breakthrough leadership from two of *Education Week's* Leaders to Learn From.

CASE STORY 10.1

Angela Ward

Angela Ward is the supervisor of race and equity programs in the Austin (Texas) Independent School District. She also oversees the district's restorative practices, an alternative to traditional forms of discipline that teaches students to talk through their problems and experiences. Under her leadership, the program recently won a $3.5 million federal grant, which allows researchers to evaluate its effects. Three lessons can be learned from Ward:

- *Race Matters: Understand the socio-political impacts of institutional racism on your ability to shift the outcomes of marginalized students. Awareness is consciousness and a critical consciousness creates opportunity for reflective dialogue.*

- *Listen to Students: Acknowledge the authenticity of youth and value their perspective on their schooling experiences. Create opportunities for them to use their voice to inform school and district-level decision making.*

- *Collaboration Is Key: Recognize the wealth of knowledge through collaborative networks. Collaborative planning and problem solving creates the opportunity for rich dialogue and opens each person to new perspectives and growth opportunities. (Blad, 2019)*

CASE STORY 10.2

Bryan Johnson

Bryan Johnson points to Waltkia Clay, a tenth-grade student in the health sciences "Future Ready Institute" he created at The Howard School in Chattanooga, Tennessee, one of twenty-eight career-oriented programs in the district. The program allows Waltkia to study core subjects through a health care lens and get real-world opportunities to practice what she's learning. She says, "In 8th grade, my thinking [about a career] was all over the place. Coming here gave me a clear vision, a straight shot, of what I wanted to do." Johnson had hoped to create a sense of direction for students when he spearheaded the Future Ready Institutes after he was appointed superintendent in 2017. Three lessons can also be learned from his work:

- *Don't be afraid to jump off the ledge: You don't have to have it all figured out. Of course you try to mitigate as many things that could go wrong as you can. But if you've built deep ownership in the idea, and the community sees it as their thing, it's good to move ahead.*

- *Ask what your community needs—and mean it:* You've got to be extremely genuine. When we involve partners in our work, we often say, "I need your help with X." But when you ask a business leader what they need from us, it shifts the conversation. It becomes: "How do I, as a school system, help you fill that need?"

- *Seek—but don't demand—the support of school-level leaders:* We involved our school leaders in conversation early on. That was really important. It was also important that we didn't demand that they be part of it. This wasn't top-down; it was bottom-up. (Gewertz, 2020)

The program works. In the 2017–2018 school year, there were only 61 students who earned industry certifications. The next year, 224 students earned them, and the number of students taking Advanced Placement and dual-enrollment courses increased from 1,951 to 2,867 during that same period. The district also earned the state's top rating, a 5, for growth in student achievement in the last school year, a dramatic improvement from two years ago when it received the state's lowest rating.

Think About It

What do these two cases have in common? What role did students play in each? What resources did these leaders begin with to effect change? What would ensure the leadership capacity and ability to sustain these efforts?

These examples demonstrate that breakthrough leaders can excel in any position and lead teams from any position in the school district.

Lessons From Leaders Achieving Equitable Outcomes

The Council of the Great City Schools (in press) has undertaken an exhaustive study of large city school districts that have sustained equitable outcomes vis-à-vis other districts as measured by the National Assessment of Educational Progress. These align closely with our courageous leadership paradigm and conversations with thought leaders and practitioners throughout North America. Collectively, this research is summarized as follows.

1. *Develop strong and stable leadership focused on instruction.* There are many distractions within education to teaching and learning for our students. Courageous leadership calls for constancy and consistency of focus (Blankstein & Noguera, 2015), and everything from political squabbles, to angry community members, to the latest off-the-shelf solution *du jour* can distract us from the core of our work: student learning.

   Effective leaders help staff keep focus by talking about children and about what good teaching looks like. They talk about the schools they've visited and the inspiring lessons they've observed. We need more focus on high-quality instruction, and this begins with passionate, engaged leadership. Having consistent leadership is also correlated with success over time:

> *The relative stability of leadership was cited as a key factor in the progress made by several of the site-visit districts. At a time of increasing leadership turnover in districts throughout the country, the relatively long tenures of superintendents in districts such as Miami, where Alberto Carvalho has been superintendent since 2008, and San Diego, where Cindy Marten has been superintendent since 2013, has enabled these districts to pursue a consistent and sustained reform agenda over the years.* (Council of the Great City Schools, in press)

One must also organize the work around what is most important. Given fast-paced changes and new challenges facing schools, it is easy to get sidetracked. What is most important? COVID-19 has produced a popular phrase for educators: "Maslow's before Bloom's," meaning you should focus your initial attention on the essential health and safety needs of students and adults before you focus on academic needs. For students still receiving virtual learning from home, determine how you can provide equitable support and opportunities. Yet, as pointed out throughout this book, we must resist the urge to sympathize (versus empathize) and to create false dichotomies between supporting children's well-being and developing their sense of self-efficacy based on academic mastery.

2. *Build strong leadership teams.* Build your team. Surround yourself with competent people who know how to get things done. Do not be so arrogant that you feel you have to be the smartest person in the room. Find smart people to work with who will give you the advice you need to hear (Noguera, AASA Urban Institute, 2018).

As indicated in Chapter 5, the leadership team is the engine for school success. "The strength of teachers and principals was another defining feature across the six districts [Editor's note: Miami-Dade, Chicago, Dallas, Boston, San Diego, and District of Columbia Public Schools], and the result of intentional district human capital strategies on the part of district leaders to boost the capacity of schools to make instructional improvements" (Council of the Great City Schools, in press).

Teamwork is also an antidote to burnout. The job was always too much for one person, and it's lonely at the top! This was never truer than it is now. Moreover, the initiatives will be sustained if they are "embedded in the hearts and minds of the many and not rest[ing] on the shoulders of a heroic few" (Blankstein, 2013, p. 230).

Your team will also need you to thrive. Consider the leader's role in helping the leadership team flourish:

- *Empower your team.* Effective leaders do not try to be the superhero; they understand that they are not in it alone. They unite their team to ensure clear communication and alignment of the mission, vision, values, and goals of the organization. They engage them on the front end of the planning and decision-making process. They model the behaviors they wish from their team and frequently check in on the well-being of every team member—personally and professionally.

- *Overcommunicate.* You will never be criticized for over-communicating. Be honest, transparent, optimistic, realistic, and positive. Frequently self-assess your communication approach and tone. Clarity and repetition of major details and themes are important. Be prudent, judicious, and succinct when communicating to large groups. Toastmasters International (2020) is an excellent resource for tips on public speaking. Use digital resources wisely and effectively to communicate to a variety of audiences. Quick and immediate responses are important. When you have a concern about an individual, do not communicate the concern to the team; instead, address the individual.

- *Build connections.* Make sure you are accessible to your team and members of the organization. Also, when invited to attend events, no matter how large or insignificant, show up when possible: showing up is 90 percent of the battle. Often people feel validated just by your attendance to an invited event. In the pandemic era, Skype, WhatsApp, Zoom, Microsoft, and Google offer free videoconferencing communication tools. CNN Business offers videoconferencing tips (Vasel, 2020).

- *Be authentic.* Don't forget the things that have made you successful thus far, and why people trust and follow you. The person with the title is not always the leader. The person to whom people gravitate during a time of crisis is their leader. Get comfortable in your own skin; do not try to change who you are or your leadership style, especially in times of crisis. Honesty and transparency always prevail in the long term. No one has all the answers to every situation, but effective leaders try to understand the questions and a process to solve the problem (Nevins, 2020).

3. *Expand capacity building for equity work.* The state of New Jersey has the highest ratio of municipality to population, meaning that there are more towns, suburbs, and cities per person than any other state. Like students in much of the country, students in New Jersey are likely to attend racially segregated schools. Black and Latinx families are primarily concentrated in cities while their White and Asian counterparts live in rural and suburban municipalities. The New Jersey Network of Superintendents (NJNS) is a unique leadership development vehicle for New Jersey–based district leaders. The network, which has been in existence for over a decade, initially adopted the approach used by Richard Elmore (2016) with the Connecticut Superintendents' Network, focusing on the instructional core and using Instructional Rounds (IR) as its primary design for professional learning. Over time, it became apparent that many of the problems of practice that surfaced in their work were actually problems of inequity. With this growing awareness, the network modified the IR protocol to become *Equity Visits*. Equity Visits are hosted by superintendents or principals who invite participants to observe their schools and classrooms. They serve two key purposes: (1) supporting the host leadership team in deepening its understanding of the identified inequity in order to effectively address it and (2) developing the observers' understanding of equity and instruction in order to support their own equity-focused practice. The NJNS fuses its commitment to equity with a focus on the instructional core, integrating these within an equitable learning community in which educational leaders identify key levers for change: school and district structures (e.g., policies, curriculum), culture and beliefs, and practices related to academic, discipline, and social-emotional outcomes. By focusing on instruction through an equity lens, educational leaders bring sustained attention to development and implementing strategies that address specific challenges in their schools and districts. These include students' access to rigorous educational opportunities, disproportionality in disciplinary actions, and identification for and placement in special education (Roegman, Allen, Leverett, & Hatch, 2020).

   Consider also

   - building capacity by requiring as a condition for employment the participation in a learning team that meets at regularly scheduled times within school hours and outside of them;

- developing a system where successful turnaround school teams take on a second or third school in a "paired school" model;

- strategic staffing like that undertaken by Charlotte-Mecklenburg Schools, in which high-performing teams move to a lower-performing school and receive the support and respect necessary to make the transition work for both schools (see Clark, 2015); and

- coaching teachers who appear to have little leadership capacity to expand the pool and break the mythology that "leaders are born!"

All of these actions not only enhance capacity; they help to ensure sustainability of current leaders, and the future of emerging initiatives, as well.

4. *Build an ambitious reform agenda and scale it.* At a recent AASA Urban Leadership Institute, this advice was provided:

- Have a proactive agenda. Too many leaders are consistently in reaction mode. They don't have an agenda.

- Make it an ambitious reform agenda. You need to have an agenda to win the confidence of your community. That agenda can't be based on low standards and low expectations.

- Inspire your staff. Create an environment where people want to work for you. Create an environment where people want to come to your district.

Having a compelling vision is galvanizing. Approaches to turning it into a reality vary.

Acting at Scale

Another similarity we observed across the case study districts was a shared belief that system-wide results could only come from system-wide change. Rollouts of reform initiatives, curricular materials, and programming (including implementation of college- and career-readiness standards) were therefore undertaken at scale in many—if not all—of these districts.

In Miami-Dade County, for instance, Superintendent Alberto Carvalho explained that he doesn't believe in pilots. His strategy for districtwide reform instead involved spending a lot of time planning, but then acting at scale in order to remove all vestiges of past practice. "If you want improvement at scale, act at scale (with deep planning)," he told the

Council team. *"The only way to overcome the gravitational pull of the status quo is to execute forcefully."* (Council of the Great City Schools, in press)

5. *Practice systems thinking.* "Systems thinking is a sensitivity to the circular nature of the world we live in; an awareness of the role of structure in creating the conditions we face. Systems thinking is also a diagnostic tool. As in the medical field, effective treatment follows thorough diagnosis. In this sense, systems thinking is a disciplined approach for examining problems more completely and accurately before acting. It allows us to ask better questions before jumping to conclusions" (Goodman, 2018).

You do not need to incorporate every possible variable from an issue. There are frequently external elements whose changes are irrelevant, slowly change, or do not change at all. Do not complicate things by including such details, especially those over which you have little or no control.

CASE STORY 10.3
The Thirty-Day Challenge

Frequently, organizations get intimidated and paralyzed by a leader's challenge to fix enormous problems. Some leaders respond to situations rather than create a system that addresses the root cause of the problem. Teachers and staff also need to possess self-efficacy to believe that they have the power to make positive change. Leaders in Petersburg, Virginia, involved the district staff and high school faculty in a thirty-day challenge to build their self-efficacy to identify a problem and work as a cohesive team to plan, and solve, it.

Petersburg High School teachers expressed frustration over students' inappropriate use of cell phones in classrooms and throughout the school. The policy was clear: "The non-instructional approved use of cell phones in class is prohibited." Cell phone use had become an escalating distraction. The inconsistent enforcement of the policy had led to numerous disciplinary issues.

Following a book study on systems thinking, the leadership team realized they needed a systems approach to the problem. Typically, it takes thirty days to form habits that produce change. For teams, the time allows everyone to feel that they are an essential part of the change process. In schools, the more united the team, the less opportunity there is for students to receive mixed messages and to pit one staff member against another. For the next thirty days, students who had previously enjoyed exploiting different expectations found the gaps narrowing.

Every person in the school district—from the superintendent, to central office administrators and school administrators, to support staff (food service, transportation, clerical, custodial, etc.), to teachers—committed to the exact same comment when they saw a student with a cell phone: "Good morning/afternoon. Thank you for making Petersburg High a great school. You can help make it better by putting your cell phone away. Thank you. Have a wonderful day." Adults did not allow students to bait them into an argument or get upset when a student did not comply. Everyone was brought into the system, and the outcome was remarkable. Discipline referrals generated by cell phone issues decreased by almost 90 percent in the first thirty days. Everyone was asked to recommit to the system for the next thirty days, and so on. This may seem like a small thing, but if an organization can master the small things, it will build capacity to achieve greater heights as well.

6. *Actively engage community investment.* In prior chapters, we have highlighted the importance and some methods for ensuring community engagement in support of schools and students. Chapter 9 takes this on writ large as one of our guiding principles for equitable learning communities, and both Case Stories 10.1 and 10.2 reiterate this essential ingredient. Likewise, the Council of the Great City Schools (in press) validates this:

    Another notable feature of many of the school districts we visited was the active engagement and investment of community organizations, educational groups, foundations, businesses, and local colleges and universities—particularly in Boston, Chicago, and Miami.

    Boston Public Schools, in particular, benefits from having a high concentration of educational institutions located in the city. School and district staff alike cited investments made in after-school and summer enrichment opportunities for area students as an important factor in students' progress and sustained achievement. One district leader estimated that some 80 percent of Boston students have benefitted from some sort of outside investment. This high concentration of colleges and universities also means a plethora of training programs and residencies for teacher candidates.

7. *Succession planning at all levels.* What we have seen in many countries in the world, but particularly in the United States, is well captured by Charles Payne (2008): "So much reform, so little change." This has largely been due to factors such as uneven implementation of new initiatives, leading to their abandonment, and prurient profit interests that too often guide policy, research agendas, and decision making about use of public funds for educating students.

Rotating leadership is also a challenge in sustaining successful initiatives. Stability can be achieved, however, both through the continuity of the leader and, more importantly, through plans to sustain the leader*ship* and worthwhile initiatives. Here are some tips:

- Insist that all school improvement plans contain leadership succession plans. This does not mean naming successors, but it means having continuing conversations and plans, shared by the community, about the future leadership needs of the school or the district.

- Write your own professional obituary. It makes you think hard about the legacy you want to leave, and how, deliberately, you can bring that into being.

- Ensure your personal well-being. Leaders often connect with students for renewal and grounding in their moral purpose. Meditation, working out, and spiritual practices are also all common (Blankstein, 2017). Make time for you!

CONCLUSION

The human spirit holds strength beyond measure, the kind that will break down the walls of all the blocks that come our way. (Nikki Rowe)

Chapter 1 of this book reminds us that the educators spotlighted exemplify what has been named throughout recorded history, and even prior among Indigenous Americans, as the virtue above all others: courage (Lassiter, 2017). Born to two pandemic survivors, Maurice Hilleman drew his dedication from deep within his own life experiences. Like Hilleman's, our passion for fairness, equity, and success is fueled by a desire to improve the human condition through education.

The educators whose experience we have featured are morally rooted in ensuring success for each of their students. Their deep connection to the importance of the work allows leaders from the classroom to the boardroom to overcome enormous obstacles to meet the needs of the young people they serve. As leaders, especially in times of crisis, we encourage you to consider the undefeatable power of the human spirit.

There seems to be a certain sadness in the world today. The pandemic and protests are certainly contributors. But it goes deeper. The lack of civility is all around us. One needs only to attend a school board meeting when school boundary changes or budget cuts are on the agenda. Just the mention of these and similar topics seems to bring out the worst in our communities.

Verbal or physical attacks, rudeness, religious intolerance, political intolerance, racism, discrimination, cyberbullying, and name-calling are all too prevalent. As the world is becoming increasingly flatter and more interactive, incivility is a global issue.

The antidote for incivility is mankind's most powerful emotion: love. If our decisions were based on love, compassion, empathy, charity, and generosity, what would the world, and our schools for that matter, look like? It may be idealistic to hope the world changes, but it is not unrealistic for all who read this book to be a catalyst for change in their classrooms, schools, districts, and communities. You can use lessons learned from the examples of breakthrough, courageous, and adaptive leaders; case stories; and detailed strategies outlined in this book. *Breakthrough leadership where inequity is not an option* should be used in your professional development training from the classroom to the boardroom.

If we really loved our students, we would provide every one of them with a loving, caring, qualified, and well-paid teacher in every classroom; breakthrough leaders in every school and district; research-based curriculum, tiered instruction, and authentic assessments; individualized learning and nurturing learning environments; student voice and choice; and equity in access, opportunities, and high expectations.

At the end of today, ask yourself again, "Did I help make a difference for our students? Did I focus on what matters most for their futures?"

REFERENCES

Blad, E. (2019, February 20). Confronting and combatting bias in schools. *Education Week*. https://leaders.edweek.org/profile/angela-ward-supervisor-race-equity-programs-cultural-proficiency

Blankstein, A. M. (2013). *Failure is not an option: Six principles that advance student achievement in highly effective schools*. Corwin.

Blankstein, A. M. (2017, June). Courageous and uplifting leadership. *School Administrator*. http://my.aasa.org/AASA/Resources/SAMag/2017/Jun17/Blankstein.aspx

Blankstein, A. M., & Noguera, P. (2016). *Excellence through equity: Five principles of courageous leadership to guide achievement for every student*. ASCD.

Clark, A. B. (2016). Human capital as a lever for districtwide change. In A. Blankstein & P. Noguera (Eds.), *Excellence through equity: Five principles of courageous leadership to guide achievement for every student* (pp. 127–134). ASCD.

Collins, J. (2020). *Level 5 leadership*. https://www.jimcollins.com/concepts/level-five-leadership.html

Council of the Great City Schools. (in press). *Mirrors or windows: How well do large city public schools overcome the effects of poverty and other barriers?* https://www.cgcs.org/cgcs

Dyson, M. E. (2017). *Tears we cannot stop: A sermon to white America*. St. Martin's Press.

Elmore, R. F. (2016). "Getting to scale . . ." it seemed like a good idea at the time. *Journal of Educational Change, 17*(4), 529–537.

Gewertz, C. (2020, February 19). A superintendent's commitment to getting students "future ready." *Education Week*. https://leaders.edweek.org/profile/bryan-johnson-superintendent-career-and-technical-education/

Goodman, M. (2018). Systems thinking: What, why, when, where, and how? *The Systems Thinker*. https://thesystemsthinker.com/systems-thinking-what-why-when-where-and-how/

Helsley, R. (2014, September 14). Leadership lesson from Kofi Annan. *Financial Times*. https://www.ft.com/content/76813a44-085f-11e4-9afc-00144feab7de

Howard, T. C. (2020, June 21). *Statements supporting Black Lives Matter are not enough, schools must do more*. EdSource. https://edsource.org/2020/statements-supporting-black-lives-matter-are-not-enough-schools-must-do-more/633978

Lassiter, C. (2017). *Everyday courage for school leaders*. Corwin.

Nevins, M. (2020, March 19). Leadership in the time of COVID-19. *Forbes*. https://www.forbes.com/sites/hillennevins/2020/03/19/leadership-in-the-time-of-covid-19/#28ab44f95e4e

Payne, C. (2008). *So much reform, so little change: The persistence of failure in urban schools*. Harvard Education Press.

Roegman, R., Allen, D., Leverett, L., & Hatch, T. (2020). *Equity visits: A new approach to supporting equity-focused school and district leadership*. Corwin.

Sawchuk, S., & Superville, D. R. (2020). Leaders to Learn From: About this project. *Education Week*. https://leaders.edweek.org/about/?intc=ltlfnavtop

Toastmasters International. (2020). *Public speaking tips*. https://www.toastmasters.org/resources/public-speaking-tips

Tutu, D. (2016). Foreword. In A. M. Blankstein & P. Noguera (Eds.), *Excellence through equity: Five principles of courageous leadership to guide achievement for every student* (pp. vii–ix). ASCD.

Vasel, K. (2020). *The rules of video conferencing at home*. CNN. https://www.cnn.com/2020/03/16/success/video-conference-work-from-home/index.html

Index

A SAGE Publishing Company

Helping educators make the greatest impact

CORWIN HAS ONE MISSION: to enhance education through intentional professional learning.

We build long-term relationships with our authors, educators, clients, and associations who partner with us to develop and continuously improve the best evidence-based practices that establish and support lifelong learning.